Law and Society
Recent Scholarship

Edited by Eric Rise

A Series from LFB Scholarly

Libel Law, Political Criticism, and Defamation of Public Figures
The United States, Europe, and Australia

Peter N. Amponsah

LFB Scholarly Publishing LLC
New York 2004

Library of Congress Cataloging-in-Publication Data

Amponsah, Peter Nkrumah, 1961-
    Libel law, political criticism, and defamation of public figures : the
United States, Europe, and Australia / Peter N. Amponsah.
        p. cm. -- (Law and society : recent scholarship)
    Includes bibliographical references and index.
    ISBN 1-59332-011-6 (alk. paper)
    1. Libel and slander. 2. Freedom of speech. I. Title. II. Series: Law
and society (New York, N.Y.)
    K930.A957 2004
    342.08'53--dc22

2004000663

ISBN 1-59332-011-6

Printed on acid-free 250-year-life paper.

Manufactured in the United States of America.

Table of Contents

Acknowledgments

I owe all that I am to God and I attribute my academic achievements to his Church that offered me the opportunity to advance my career and scholarship. So it is my pleasure to acknowledge my indebtedness to the Society of St. Peter the Apostle, a branch of the Office of the Propagation of the Faith in Rome, Italy, that sponsored part of my Master's Degree studies as well as awarded me a grant for my Ph.D. studies.

While I ascribe my career achievements to the Church, I am forever grateful to the following Bishops in Ghana, West Africa: Most Reverend Peter K. Sarpong (the Metropolitan Archbishop of Kumasi) for discovering my talents and being the brain behind my career in Communication Studies; Most Reverend Thomas K. Mensah (Bishop of Obuasi) for allowing me to continue my studies at the doctoral level, and Most Reverend Joseph Osei-Bonsu (Bishop of Konongo-Mampong) for being a mentor to me at each important stage of my career. Also, I thank Most Rev. Wilton D. Gregory (Bishop of Belleville, Illinois) and Most Rev. David E. Fellhauer (Bishop of Victoria, Texas) for the numerous ways they supported my stay and studies in the United States.

For the magnificent assistance received in my academic studies, special acknowledgement must be made to all my professors. Particular acknowledgment must be given to Professor Robert Spellman of Southern Illinois University at Carbondale, for his invaluable encouragement and direction during my entire doctoral studies.

A special appreciation should go to Mrs. Doreen Osei Bempah, who is more than a sister to me. She deserves credit for her irreplaceable role as well as her extraordinary support to every endeavor toward my academic achievement. Finally, I thank Mrs. Cathy Cerame, for her assistance, encouragement, and prayers.

Introduction

Around the world, there are several forms of government that allow different levels of freedom of speech as part of citizens' political participation. Freedom of speech, as a right of communication, provides citizens the means of knowing, thinking, deciding and participating in self-governance as their right of citizenship.[1] But free speech is always an area of dispute because of its conflicting characteristics. As Rodney A. Smolla put it:

> Speech may be uplifting, enlightening, and profound; but it is often degrading, redundant, and trivial ... may confirm and affirm; it may be patriotic and supportive of prevailing values and order; but it may also be challenging, threatening, and seditious, perhaps even treasonous.[2]

These conflicting tendencies of free speech confront governments, all of which regulate or even suppress speech. However, democratic countries are different from totalitarian and theocratic states in the amount of protected speech. While people in totalitarian regimes have little free speech, democratic societies either guarantee freedom of speech in written constitutions or accept it as the political norm.[3]

Amy Gutmann described two principles that democracies must support on democratic grounds, namely "nonrepression and nondiscrimination."[4] A complement of this view is Kent Greenawalt's comment that it is "an important political principle that government should not suppress the communication of ideas. Indeed, this principle is frequently regarded as a cornerstone of liberal democracy."[5] So, as a constitutional right or an accepted political principle, political expression is an essential element of democratic self-government. In this vein, political speech is vital to a democratic society because it serves citizens' interest in equality, deliberation, participation, truth-seeking, and checking official abuse of power. Nevertheless, the exercise of free political speech often comes into conflict with the societal interest of maintaining personal reputation.[6]

To protect people from injury to their reputation, societies create laws of defamation to settle issues of truth or falsehood and reputational harm that result from defamatory statements. In a two-way function, the defamation laws act as deterrent to imputations either by publication or broadcast against individuals' reputation and also give remedy to any such damaged reputations. According to Randall P. Benzanson, libel laws assume that people's reputations can be seriously harmed by defamatory statements, and that judicial decisions settle claims of falsity and reputational harm.[7] But, the liberal concept of free expression usually favors political speech. As Lord Bridge of Harwich remarked, the right to freedom of speech is one of the requisite freedoms to a free society.[8] Also, "[t]he interest in encouraging freedom of expression in a democratic society outweighs any theoretical but unproven benefit of censorship."[9] So, despite the presumable cost to personal reputation, the right to criticize freely and publicly the institutions and officials of government is important for maintaining representative democracy.

Obviously, there is an attempt to find a balance between societal interests of speech and reputation, but jurisdictions differ in their legal attempts to negotiate both rights. Previous studies in this area mostly used surveys and interviews to examine broadly defamation laws and generally compared the United States defamation law with one or two jurisdictions. This study considers the same perennial problem by examining how four jurisdictions seek a just balance between specifically encouraging free political speech while protecting the reputation of public institutions and public figures.[10] As studies suggest that solutions countries take to resolve political speech and reputational interests are diverse, this study sought to find similarities and differences among them. For instance, the United States Supreme Court held that public officials cannot claim damages for a defamatory falsehood about their official duties unless they prove with convincing clarity that the statement was made with knowledge of its falsity or with reckless disregard of whether it was false or not.[11] This rule, called the "actual malice" defense, was rejected by the Supreme Court of Canada.[12] But, similar to the United States, the Supreme Court of India held that public officials cannot recover damages for defamation in matters concerning their official duties unless they prove that the statement was made with reckless disregard of the truth or out of personal spite. In India, it is sufficient for the defendant to show that he or she took reasonable care in verifying the facts to defeat an allegation of malice.[13]

In quite a different approach, Australia protects political speech, but rejects any semblance of a public figure defense. The High Court of Australia held that a new extended qualified privilege protects the dissemination of information, opinions and arguments in relation to government and political matters that affect the people of Australia. But, this rule requires the publisher to prove reasonableness of conduct.[14]

The European Court of Human Rights takes a different approach that weighs whether an infringement on free speech is "necessary in a democratic society ... for the protection of the reputation of others."[15] In the case law of the Court, the protection of freedom of expression is generally the rule and any interference is an exception, and such interference must be proportionate to the "legitimate aim pursued."[16] Recently a strong affinity was established between this Court and the United Kingdom jurisdiction because of the Human Rights Act 1998. Whereas in the past the United Kingdom followed the common law of libel which usually favored the protection of personal reputation, the United Kingdom in October 2000 incorporated the European Convention provisions through the Human Rights Act 1998 into its domestic law. This incorporation implies a change in the legal culture of the United Kingdom because not only should the country assimilate the Convention provisions, but also the regime has to absorb the case law on those provisions as developed in the European Court of Human Rights and its Commission.[17] It also meant the United Kingdom has to abandon the traditional "interpretative frame of mind ... [and] the traditional canons of statutory interpretation" for an effective protection of human rights and promotion of democratic values under the Convention provisions.[18]

As the cases of countries cited suggest, the solutions are not uniform. The present analysis aimed at finding how four jurisprudential approaches -- those of the United States, the European Court of Human Rights (ECHR),[19] the United Kingdom and Australia -- balance free political speech and the reputation of public figures. These countries were chosen to represent the evolution of strict liability on the nature of speech in common law countries, except the ECHR, which is an example of jurisprudence based on international treaty.

The United States was chosen for the study because it is an example of a country that experienced colonial libel laws. More important, the United States' jurisprudence shows how a country can depart from the English common law of defamation to develop a constitutional protection of political speech: the First Amendment model.

The ECHR is the judicial enforcement mechanism of the European Convention for the Protection of Human Rights and Fundamental Freedoms. The Convention was ratified on September 3, 1953. As a transnational law jurisdiction, "the European Court of Human Rights can be said to have become the constitutional court for civil liberties of Western Europe."[20] This Court was important for the study because it impacts domestic law in Western Europe. As a British legal scholar put it, "In theory Parliament may be supreme, but in practice decisions of the European Commission and Court have had an undeniable impact on British law."[21]

The United Kingdom was selected because it is the progenitor of the common law of libel. Besides, it has great influence on the constitutions of British Commonwealth countries. As the original and leading common law jurisdiction, the jurisprudence of the United Kingdom offers insights into how by basing freedom of speech on a long history of court decisions a country can develop legal understandings that protect political speech in a democratic society. It also exemplifies how a transnational treaty can affect domestic laws. In particular, the United Kingdom accounts for changes in domestic law that began in October 2000 with the incorporation of European Convention provisions through the Human Rights Act 1998.

Australia was included in the study because, once a British colony and inheritor of English laws, it has combined English common law and constitutional law in its judicial practice. Australia is an example of a country that does not have a clear constitutional statement protecting free speech, and it was important to find how Australia protects freedom of political speech in its representative democracy. Australia is evolving in the area of political defamation, and has an adequate body of law on this topic for study. Its focus on political speech is moving toward the United States' position, especially in relation to speech of public concern. Further, as a Commonwealth country, Australia shares a collective legal background with other common law countries. So, the changing legal landscape in Australia is important because it can represent what might happen to the rest of the common law world. Furthermore, Australian cases have persuasive influence on common law cases in countries such as the United Kingdom, Canada, and New Zealand.

In light of the importance of the four jurisdictions chosen, a comparative analysis of their jurisprudence could show how they diverge or converge in political defamation judgments. Also, because there could "be strong impulses to learn from one another through comparative studies,"[22] this study focused on determining the commonalities and differences of the legal regimes, and so could shed more light on jurisprudential common ground for countries to take in balancing political speech and reputation of public figures. By doing so, this comparative analysis should contribute to the free speech debate.

After a historical analysis of the jurisdictions, this study evaluated authorities under these jurisdictions. It examined the prevailing position of the United States as indicated in three Supreme Court decisions and compared those decisions to political speech jurisprudence in the European Court of Human Rights, the United Kingdom and Australia. Democratic as the jurisdictions are presumed to be, the study searched for the kind of arguments each jurisdiction invokes to protect free speech within that democracy. Other determinations involved how the jurisdictions weigh political speech and reputation in their decisions and what doctrinal approaches they use in balancing the two competing interests. In this way, the study determined whether the jurisdictions coalesce or differ in protecting political speech. This plan of analyzing political speech decisions of the four judicial regimes helped identify arguments that underlie legal protections of political discussion in those regimes.

To achieve the research goals, the study set the following research questions to guide the analysis of political speech and political defamation in the four jurisprudential regimes: Are the libel laws in the United States, the ECHR, the United Kingdom and Australia converging or diverging? To what extent do rationales for protecting political speech justify restrictions on libel laws in a democratic society?

These questions assumed that freedom of speech is central to any democratically self-governing society. Because the public has an interest in the contribution of political speech to public discussion and the political process, it needs adequate protection.[23] Yet, individuals have the right to personal reputation. They are protected from intentional defamation that can injure their fundamental human dignity. However, different governments have different attitudes toward acceptable limits of political discussion and criticism relating to the reputation of politicians and other public persons. So, legal protections differ according to the system of government and the value placed on political speech. Because differences may show among democratic countries, a study of how they balance political speech against the interest of protecting the reputation of politicians and public figures can benefit emerging democratic states. By finding the common values underlying those democratic jurisdictions, the study can suggest one of the jurisdictions as the common ground for emerging democracies to follow in political defamation laws. Moreover, the comparative study can be informative for people who are interested in defamation laws as practiced in the United States, the ECHR, the United Kingdom and Australia. Also, this study can contribute to an ongoing debate over political defamation. By comparing the United States jurisdiction with legal regimes that do not have the United States' constitutional approach, the study provides insights into how the common law, constitutional law and supranational jurisprudential regimes apply the principles that justify protection of political speech in democratic societies.

To achieve the study objectives, Chapter One explores political speech and the concept of democracy. Because the public has interest under a democracy to protect both political speech and reputation, the chapter also explains common law defamation and the public interest. Chapter Two gives a theoretical and or philosophical framework on free speech. After such discussions, Chapter Three gives a concise historical analysis of political speech as related to defamation laws in the United States, the ECHR, the United Kingdom and Australia as paradigms of legal solutions to the balance between protecting speech and reputation. Chapter Four combines case law analysis and qualitative content analysis to examine cases for principles that underlie standards of political speech in the United States, the ECHR, the United Kingdom, and Australia. Here, the comparative legal analysis compares and contrasts standards of weighing political speech against reputation in the four regimes. The final chapter summarizes the findings and draws out the principles of political speech that the four regimes present. Also, it discusses whether the four legal frames of the United States, the ECHR, the United Kingdom and Australia are converging or diverging. Then, it offers some policy implications suggesting foundational values that emerging democracies ought to adopt.

Chapter One

Political Speech and the Concept of Democracy

Freedom of speech is an umbrella of several forms of expression, but at the core of democratic self-government is political speech. Using the definition of Eric Barendt, "'political speech' refers to all speech relevant to the development of public opinion on the whole range of issues which an intelligent citizen should think about."[1] Because, political speech concerns potentially public issues, Cass R. Sunstein wrote that speech is considered "political when it is both intended and received as a contribution to public deliberation about some issue."[2]

The elements of intent and receipt are requisite. The intent is present when speech is either intended as political or reasonably inferred from the issue as such. According to Sunstein, "Public deliberation can deal with social norms as well as with legal requirements ... even if it does not bear explicitly on what government should do."[3] Whatever shape it takes, the important ingredient of political speech is that the intended and received speech contributes to political deliberation. Generally, "political speech is truthful facts or statements of opinion concerning government, or expression that contributes to the governing process. In practice, ... it is speech that does not fall into less-protected categories of expression."[4] For example, criticism of parliamentary and public conduct of government, matters of civil rights, and issues of public debate on education fall within the protection of political speech.

One can say that the United States and other democracies highly value political speech because political speech concretely advances openness needed in self-government.[5] Democratic societies value openness not only for allowing citizens' participation in decision making processes, but also to unmask government operations for public scrutiny. This emphasizes the socio-political nature of speech in a democratic self-government and promotes citizens' interest in expression, deliberation, and information.

Through free political speech, citizens can actively exercise some role in self-governance and help political leaders make decisions about issues that are important to their constituents. Sharing this view, John Dewey agreed with Lippmann that the public has to "be the judge and umpire of last resort, to be able to compel submission of important issues to popular judgment, to force political governors to appear now and then on trial before their constituents to give a reckoning of their stewardship."[6]

DEMOCRATIC SOCIETY

Arguments for the preference of free political speech lie in democracy.[7] So a discussion of the underlying concepts of democracy can illuminate an understanding of the need to guarantee free political speech.

According to Thomas Christiano, "'democracy' is a generic term... vaguely ... defined as a society in which all or most of the population has the opportunity jointly to play an essential if not always very formative role in the determination of legislation and policy."[8] But, democracy as a "formal decision-making method and the notion of democracy [as] a value, a practice that has intrinsic worth, stand in uneasy tension."[9] Both notions of democracy as a method and a value aspire after the ideals of popular sovereignty, equality, and democratic discussion that prevailed in Periclean Athens, the prototype of democracy.[10] In Periclean Athens, citizens could assemble for discussion and individual orators could freely express their views to the public. Though contemporary types of democracy differ from this early model, they share important democratic principles such as open public debate, toleration of unpopular opinion, and decisions taken by voting and accepting the results.[11]

An explanation of three major philosophical notions -- the contractualist liberalism, deliberative democracy and pragmatic democracy -- can help in generating a more thorough concept of a true democracy and the inherent necessity to guarantee free speech. However, in spite of some philosophical differences that underlie these concepts, all three of these main philosophical notions justify democracy as the ideal form of government.

The Contractual Liberalism

Contractualists hold that state institutions, laws and rights develop from citizens entering into a social contract. For the contractualists, democratically justifiable institutions must guarantee freedom of speech, conscience and assembly, freedom of the press, and the right to vote and to hold political office.[12] By consent to the social contract, contractualists argue that citizens obtain political rights and liberties.[13]

Contractualists, such as Thomas Hobbes, John Locke, Jean-Jacques Rousseau, Thomas Paine, John Stuart Mill, and John Rawls provided insights into the social rules.[14] In his book *Leviathan*, Hobbes said that the life of man in the natural state was "solitary, poore [sic], nasty, brutish and short."[15] He held that, left to their own desires, people are naturally greedy. In such a society, a person is judged by his or her power such that unbridled competition may lead to self-destructive greed and social anarchy. For self-preservation, Hobbes argued, a contract is made between people and their ruler, because only absolute sovereignty safeguards against the state of nature. While the people authorize the ruler to govern, the ruler protects the natural rights of the people, acts as an arbiter in any disputes between them, and makes laws to maintain order. Of this contract, Gregory S. Kavka elaborated:

> (1) If people were rational in such-and-such circumstances, they would choose or agree to social arrangements of a certain kind; (2) Therefore, people actually living under social arrangements of that kind ought to obey the rules of these arrangements and the officials designated to enforce the rules.[16]

So, for Hobbes, the sovereign is both the agent and the master of the people.[17] Although the people give their power to political rulers, the political rulers are agents because the people give them authorization.[18]

Locke's view differed from Hobbes's. In *The Second Treatise of Civil Government*, Locke argued that people must give up some of their individual rights to the community.[19] However, he maintained that nobody should be above the law, for authority should reside in the institutions of state chosen by the majority of the people. According to Locke, the government must defend the principles of naturally given individual rights: free speech, freedom to worship, freedom to hold property.[20]

Another contractualist, Rousseau, agreed with Locke. In Rousseau's view, a social contract is the foundation of individual liberty. On the basis of the same contract, people and rulers who come together must aspire at achieving their common interests for their mutual benefit. As the social contract produces the common interests, it cultivates "the general will" which in turn requires the people to abdicate some of their natural liberty in order to create "civil liberty." In this sense, Rousseau believed, an individual puts the will of the community above his or her will.[21]

Similarly, Paine argued that under the social contract, an individual should have the freedom to pursue his or her own happiness and interests provided that, in doing so, one does not harm others. Because Paine believed that the rights of people are absolute and inalienable, he maintained that people have rights that no one can either deny them or grant to them.[22] Related to this view, Mill argued in *On Liberty* that, under the social contract, a majority should not interfere with a minority in the exercise of its rights unless what the minority does directly impairs the majority's interests. As a result, the majority should not inhibit the free speech of a person even if the majority perceives the person's expression as erroneous. According to Mill, this is less threatening than censorship by an authority that can suppress liberty for all.[23]

Rawls' *Theory of Justice* presented a modern perspective of the social contract. He suggested a hypothetical situation in which a number of people come together to decide rules to govern their lives. The condition is such that they forget who they are, ignorant about their age, color, wealth and social position. So, without an allegiance to any special interest, they determine their expectations from society. In this situation of fairness, Rawls held, justice is based on two principles: (1) that each person has an equal right to the maximum amount of liberty that is compatible with allowing liberty for all, and (2) inequalities are only allowed if there is reason to think that such inequalities will benefit the least well-off in society.[24] For Rawls, liberty has priority over social equality, and he argued that social institutions, including laws, are created artificially and imposed on society to preserve the social contract. So he said:

It is reasonable to assume that even in a well-ordered society the coercive powers of government are to some degree necessary for the stability of social cooperation ... the existence of effective penal machinery serves as men's security to one another. This proposition and the reasoning behind it we may think as Hobbes thesis.[25]

The contractualists' arguments offer political and moral reasons for rights and liberties in democracy. They try to establish a balance between the rights of an individual and the needs of society. So they argue that individuals have rights and must have a task in the process of government. Critics, however, argue that the contractualists use "instrumental assessment of institutional arrangements for recognizing political rights and liberties."[26] Because the institutional "possibilities are to be assessed by their effectiveness at promoting ends of which contracting parties would approve," critics say that "appeal to institutional effectiveness fails to capture the reasons political equality is justified."[27]

Deliberative Democracy

The failure of the social contract to justify political equality has led some to accept deliberative democracy as an alternative model. The key idea of this paradigm is an ideal of democratic deliberation in which citizens are free and equal. Proponents of this notion do not justify political institutions because they can effectively help achieving "morally required ends;" instead they defend the institutions because they work to promote freedom and equality, and political values that are built on the democratic ideal.[28]

For proponents of deliberative democracy, political participation is the lifeblood of the democratic society. As Sunstein explained, political participation does not require that all decisions be made by town meeting. But he said that citizens' political participation must not be treated as simply another "taste" that people have or can forgo in a well-functioning democracy.[29] According to him, deliberative democracy "seeks to ensure that political outcomes benefit from widespread participation by the citizenry. A system in which sure participation is lacking is to that extent a failure."[30]   This form of democracy is understood not in the Locke's theory of government by consent,[31] but as a process of government by discussion.[32] Discussion and enlightenment interconnectedly support democracy. So openness, exchange of opinions and discussion are realized as important parts of the family of knowledge.[33]

For the operation of deliberative democratic political institutions, Cohen argued that three characteristics are necessary. First, deliberation and debate about legislation and policy should help determine what policy best advances the common good or public interest.[34] Democratic politics should not become competition among special interest groups that promote legislation based on economic, social and sectional interests.[35] Second, "Political opportunities and powers must be independent of economic or social position -- the political liberties must have fair value -- and the fact that they are independent must be more or less evident to citizens."[36]   Third, democratic politics should shape the self-understanding of citizens so that they can consider themselves politically equal, competent and free.[37] Besides, democratic politics should help the citizenry develop a sense of their own legitimate interests as well as help them arrive at what is best for the common good.[38]

Put briefly, in the operation of political power, deliberative democracy requires both openness and citizens' effective participation in the social debate and in decision making which concerns them. So the judicial system must ensure freedom of discussion among citizenry.[39]

Pragmatic Democracy

The pragmatist model of democracy is inspired by John Dewey's ethics and self-realization. According to Dewey, society can survive only through "the constant reweaving of the social fabric by communicating its ideals, hopes, standards, and beliefs from one generation to the next."[40] And "to learn to be human is to develop through the give-and-take of communication the effective sense of being individually a distinctive member of a community."[41] In this way, Dewey recognized that only through communication can a common understanding be reached. It is not intended that communities become "homogenous and intolerant of difference," but that communities thrive on the ideal of sharing common ends that shape their activities.[42]

Pragmatists see the political form of democracy "as a form of association especially appropriate for persons who are constituted by the multiple relations through which consciousness evolves and values develop."[43] In this notion of democracy, people "cooperate with others in that continual transformation of varied and interactive forms of life toward those better ends that pragmatism seeks."[44] As Charlene Seigfried understood Dewey's viewpoint, "it is not the numerical triumph of the majority rule that constitutes the spirit of democracy but the principled inclusion of all people in decision making because all are valued for their unique contributions."[45]

Another advocate of pragmatic democracy is Hilary Putman. He defended democracy on what he called Deweyan social and epistemological justifications of democracy.[46] He argued that democracy is primarily justified on social grounds because it concerns a community and its values. As Putman put it, democracy is "addressed to us as opposed to being addressed to each me."[47] And, its goal is to give "reason to people already disposed to hear it, to help in continually creating a community held together by that same disposition."[48]

Adding to the social argument is what Putman described as Dewey's "epistemological justification of democracy."[49] It is the pragmatist idea that knowledge is based on a community that indulges itself in inquiry; so Putman said, "epistemology is hypothesis."[50] He maintained that knowledge is best acquired through "intelligently conducted inquiry,"[51] which involves the scientific method of finding answers to problems through formulation of hypotheses and testing them in experimentation, reflection and discussion.[52]

Because the community of intelligent people exchange their different views and results, "[t]he need for such fundamental democratic institutions as freedom of thought and speech follows ... from requirements of scientific procedure in general: the unimpeded flow of information and the freedom to offer and to criticize hypotheses."[53] In Richard Shusterman's assessment of this pragmatist view, this Deweyan line of thought suggests positive freedom as citizens reflect and discuss their democratic self-government.[54] Thus, democracy involves active participation by all; government is not the sole right of experts or politicians.

Pragmatic democracy holds that experts do not possess the fullest intelligence to direct society. So despite the professional knowledge of experts, good government requires that the knowledge citizens acquire from their diverse situations and contexts be shared. Putman believed that "[t]here is no one field of experience from which all the considerations relevant to the evaluation of democracy come."[55] Therefore, to encourage open discussion and uninhibited criticism, Putman added:

> We do not know what our interests and needs are or what we are capable of until we actually engage in politics. A corollary of this view is that there can be no final answer to the question of how we should live, and therefore we should always leave it open to further discussion and experimentation. This is precisely why we need democracy.[56]

Another defender of pragmatic democracy was Stanley Cavell. Like Dewey and Putman, he devoted his inquiry to the "essential integration of democracy and self-realization."[57] In particular, he was inspired by Dewey's democratic ethics of the self and Emerson's perfectionism.[58] Cavell thought that perfectionism is "essential to the criticism of democracy," and that self-improvement can form the "character to keep the democratic hope alive in the face of disappointment with it."[59] So he recommended that individuals try to better themselves and, through this, improve society.[60]

Cavell argued that the cultivation of self-perfection recognizes the value of others and serves democracy by providing a more democratic society.[61] This mode of perfection means being "open to the further self, in oneself and in others."[62] It involves:

> [H]olding in knowledge of the need for change; ... which in turn means expecting oneself to be, making oneself, intelligible as an inhabitant now also of a further realm ..., call this the realm of the human -- and to show oneself prepared to recognize others as belonging there.[63]

Taken together, free political speech embodies values that are argued in the different models of democracy. The values defended as "intrinsically worthwhile properties" of the democratic ideal are equality,[64] political and social deliberation, free expression regarding matters of public opinion, citizens' consent and participation in self-government as self-realization. So citizens have a right of political speech because the right manifests the liberty and equality of citizens.[65]

The democratic arguments for political speech can serve citizens' interest in participation, truth seeking and checking of official abuse of power. However, political speech can clash with the personal right of reputation. As Robert Trager and Donna Dickerson put it: "As humans, we treasure our self-worth above all else. When our reputation is sullied or tarnished with false accusations or damaging innuendoes, there is a natural urgency to set things right and correct misimpressions before they become accepted."[66]

One can conclude that a libel action is a means to redress damaged reputation. Thus, the law of defamation is not a form of prior censorship but deterrence, a form of subsequent punishment for harming an individual's reputation.[67] This is codified in the operation of common law of defamation.

COMMON LAW OF DEFAMATION

Laws against libel or slander are intended to protect the right of reputation, and this has "historically much more venerable ancestry" than the right of speech.[68] For instance, the Athenians had laws that barred "speaking evil" of the dead and slandering fellow citizens with "actionable words," including false charges of heinous crime. Also, the Roman law principle of *iniuria* punished a variety of wrongs, such as injury to reputation.[69]

English common law of defamation "is not the deliberate product of any period. It is a mass which has grown by aggregation, with very little intervention from legislation, and special and peculiar circumstances have from time to time shaped its varying course."[70] The early Middle Ages and Church law understood defamation as making a person suffer "that evil reputation which is sufficiently notorious to put a man on his trial."[71]

According to common law, libel is a harm to a person's reputation and good name.[72] Defamation consists in the publication of a false, defamatory and unprivileged statement to a third person or persons.[73] Defamatory statements can be either libel *per se* (libelous within themselves) or libel *per quod* (libelous because of the context in which they are spoken).

Libel *per se* applies to statements that accuse a person of a crime; or impute that that person has a contagious or heinous disease; or injure a person's reputation in his or her business, trade, profession, or vocation; or charge a person with sexual immorality.[74] However, "Where the defamatory nature of the writing does not appear upon the face of the writing, but rather appears only when all of the circumstances are known, it is said to be libelous *per quod*, as distinguished from libel *per se* ...."[75] In all of this, liability is attached to the publication, for it exposes the person to hatred, contempt or ridicule, or lowers the person in the estimation of ordinary members of society, or causes the person to be shunned and avoided by others, or tends to injure the person in his or her occupation.[76]

Traditionally, for a defamation case to be actionable it must meet basic conditions.[77] First, defamation must occur, i.e., the statement should be seen as insulting or harmful among "right-thinking persons." Second, the statement must be published, i.e., the message must be communicated to a third party, whether by voice, print, or some other means. Third, the plaintiff must be identified as the person defamed. Besides the three conditions, the United States' Supreme Court added "fault" as another basic requirement.[78] Fault requires that a plaintiff must prove that the defamation was deliberate or reckless, or at the least negligent falsehood.[79] Another First Amendment requirement is falsity. However, under common law falsity is presumed from the fact of publication of defamatory statements and the plaintiff does not have to prove that the words are true or false,[80] the United States Supreme Court held that the Constitution requires the plaintiff to prove that such statements on matters of public concern are false before there can be liability.[81] The sixth essential condition is about damages. Damages are legal means of remedying any unlawful injury to a person defamed. Under common law, damages are presumed when the defamatory publication constitutes libel *per se*.[82] However, generally, "it is necessary to prove a specific loss to have been sustained, by the evidence of which a jury is to be guided in assessing pecuniary damages."[83] The pecuniary damages serve "as a vindication of the plaintiff to the public and as consolation to him for a wrong done. Compensation is here a solatium rather than a monetary recompense for harm measurable in money."[84] The pecuniary damages are of three types: special or actual, general, and punitive. While special damages are those based on quite precise calculation of the damage to reputation or loss because of the defamatory falsehood, general damages "reflect the jury's subjective opinion of the seriousness of the harm inflicted by the defamatory statement."[85] Awards of punitive damages are intended to punish the publisher of defamatory falsehood because of the seriousness of the injury to reputation. Often the punitive damages awarded are larger than special and general damages.[86]

The common law defenses of a defamation action are mainly justification, fair reportage,[87] qualified privilege, and fair comment. Justification requires that the defendant prove the truth of the statement "in substance and in fact."[88] The common law libel defense of fair reportage concerns fair and accurate reports of public proceedings or of meetings open to the public about a matter of public concern.[89] Privilege allows news media to publish fair and accurate accounts of public proceedings even if the reports contain defamatory matter.[90] The publisher is protected from liability because accuracy is judged in terms of information available in the public record, not by what actually occurred before the proceeding.[91]

Qualified privilege as a common law defense protects the publication of defamatory matter where the publisher had a duty to publish the material and the recipient had a reciprocal interest in receiving it, or where the material was published according to a common interest between the publisher and the recipient.[92] It can also apply in a situation where the publisher was not motivated by malice, i.e., ill will toward the plaintiff, a lack of honest belief in the truth of the material published or some other improper motive.[93]

Fair comment as a common law libel defense invokes public interest as its criterion.[94] The fair comment privilege assumes that matters of public concern are the legitimate subject of fair and honest criticism, and not published only to harm the defamed.[95] In English law, fair comment is privileged for the "common convenience and welfare of society."[96] As Justice Pearson defended it: "Could there be a plea of 'fair information on a matter of public interest' which would be coordinate with the familiar plea of 'fair comment on a matter of public interest?'... In my view there not only ought to be, but there is such privilege."[97] However, the comment must be objectively fair, based on ascertainable facts or factual grounds.[98]

PUBLIC INTEREST

Public interest occurs both as a defense to defamation action (fair comment) and as an argument for free speech in a democratic society. But the history of the question of public interest is associated with two main philosophical or political traditions, namely of Bentham and Rousseau.[99] The Benthamite view stands for "a distributive conception of public interest."[100] It claims that the public interest is "the sum of the interests of the several members who compose [the community],"[101] and public policy is in the public interest when it satisfies individual interest of the requisite number of the public.[102] Bentham argued from an utilitarian point of view that an interest of government expresses the public interest "when the tendency it has to augment the happiness of the community is greater than any it has to diminish it."[103] This account of Bentham suggests that acts and policies which are in the public interest are those "in the interest of each member of the public and that then apply some sum-function to these interests."[104]

For Rousseau the public interest consists of commonly held private interests.[105] He thought that an act or policy is in the public interest if it is the will of the general public.[106] This collective notion considers something as in the public interest neither because it is in the interest of particular individuals nor because it is in the general interest of every citizen.[107] But, it is in the public interest "because it promotes an interest of the public, i.e., an interest of anyone who is a member of the public."[108]

Underlying the two principles of public interest are the values of the basic equality of people, who make up the democratic society and safeguard its interests. In the words of Eric Barendt:

> Restrictions on the free flow of political information are suspect because they invade the audience's interests in having enough material before it to make informed choices and to participate fully in the democratic process ... The argument from democracy could indeed be framed either in terms of the right of individuals to receive information and views pertinent to their political choices or in relation to the general public interest in the disclosure of such information.[109]

Obviously, government policies and official conduct are of public interest. Other affairs that are subject to public interest include issues concerning basic and survival needs, health, sanitation, education, and improvement of citizens' welfare and well-being.[110] And, citizens have a legitimate right to know and freely discuss such matters of public interest.

In legal terms, public interest is not taken literally but "has become shorthand for a judicial appraisal of public importance" rather than substantive interest of recipients.[111] In common law courts' attempt to balance public interest and private injury, courts focus on the content at issue in terms of "legitimate" public interest.[112]

To summarize, one can say that the principle of democracy supports arguments for the preference of political speech. Because political speech can clash with a person's right of reputation, the law of defamation is designed to redress harm to an individual's reputation. In defamation cases, both constitutional and common law jurisdictions require plaintiffs to satisfy some conditions in order to claim damages. Defamation laws also allow defendants the use of defenses to protect publication of alleged defamatory materials. Public interest is one of such defenses under "fair comment." However, public interest can be an argument from democracy that seeks the equality of people who form the democratic society. It represents what is considered to be of public importance, the safeguard of citizens' concerns and distributive benefit from the society's resources. In addition, public interest serves as ways of bettering the people's capacity to make informed choices and participate in the democratic process.

Chapter Two

Philosophy of Freedom of Speech

To understand whether the protection of political speech is sound, one must examine the justifications for it. This task involves showing the importance of preserving freedom of speech in a democratic society. Thus, an overview of the different rationales and theories of free speech provides grounding for heightened protection of political speech that lies at the core of the debate about freedom of expression. Also, it explains the theoretical framework in support of the claim of a necessary protection for political speech in a democratic society and the courts' attempt to strike the balance between the reputation of politicians on one hand and the freedom of expression on the other.[1]

Political participation in a democratic dispensation is not limited to the exercise of voting franchise nor demonstrations as well as protests. But, political speech is an indispensable value to democratically informed public and the principal means of protecting democracy itself. While it ensures public discourse in such free expression as political deliberation and criticism of matters of public concern, political speech subsists for the integral operation of democratic institutions that should promote the governance and the political well-being of the citizenry. The literature on free speech theory gives three key justifications – "marketplace of ideas," "human liberty and self-fulfillment," and "democratic self-governance."

MARKETPLACE OF IDEAS RATIONALE

The "marketplace" metaphor considers the democratic society as an open market where people enlighten each other through a process of free interchange and competition of ideas.[2] Milton, Mill, Holmes and Brandeis were the best known exponents of this form of free speech justification.

John Milton in 1640 wrote about the human enlightenment process as a constant struggle between truth and falsehood. He believed that freedom of speech is the best way of assuring the discovery of truth. In *Aeropagitica*, Milton argued that truth would ultimately triumph, saying:

> [T]hough all the winds of doctrine were let loose to play upon the earth, so Truth be in the field, we do injuriously, by licensing and prohibiting, to misdoubt her strength. Let her and Falsehood grapple; who ever knew Truth put to the worse, in a free and open encounter?[3]

A similar idea was developed by John Stuart Mill in his famous essay *On Liberty*. For Mill, it is always dangerous to suppress the expression of opinion, even when it is considered wrong by the majority:

> [T]he opinion which it is attempted to suppress by authority may possibly be true. Those who desire to suppress it, of course deny its truth; but they are not infallible. They have no authority to decide the question for all mankind, and exclude every other person from the means of judging. To refuse a hearing to an opinion, because they are sure that it is false, is to assume that *their* certainty is the same as *absolute* certainty ... Complete liberty of contradicting and disproving our opinion is the very condition which justifies us in assuming its truth for purposes of action; and on no other terms can a being with human faculties have any rational assurance of being right.[4]

Most broadly, Milton and Mill thought that free speech involves uninhibited competition and testing of opinions and ideas. They believed this was the best way to ensure the discovery of truth and increase knowledge.

Justice Oliver Wendell Holmes, Jr.'s depiction of the "marketplace of ideas" captured the free speech tradition of Milton and Mill. In his dissenting opinion in *Abrams v United States*,[5] Holmes wrote:

> [T]he best test of truth is the power of thought to get itself accepted in the competition of the market, and that truth is the only ground upon which their wishes can be carried out. That

at any rate is the theory of our Constitution ... I think that we should be eternally vigilant against attempts to check the expression of opinions that we loathe and believe to be fraught with death, unless they so imminently threaten immediate interference with the lawful and pressing purposes of the law that an immediate check is required to save the country.[6]

Later, Justice Louis Brandeis approved Holmes' opinion in *Whitney v California.*[7] According to Brandeis, the American founders appreciated liberty as both an end and a means, and he believed "in the power of reason as applied through public discussion [so] they eschewed silence coerced by law."[8] He also said that "[f]reedom to think as you will and to speak as you think are means indispensable of the discovery and spread of political truth."[9]

Zechariah Chafee, Jr., a law professor, favored the marketplace idea, and argued for "public discussion of all public questions" in a democratic society.[10] He said: "One of the most important purposes of society and government is the discovery and spread of truth on subjects of general concern. This is possible only through absolutely unlimited discussion."[11] Nevertheless, Chafee did not argue for an absolute right to free speech. He mentioned that "other purposes of government" have to be balanced against societal interests, but he thought that free expression "ought to weigh very heavily in the scale."[12] He explained that every reasonable attempt should be made to maintain interests in public safety and the search for truth unhindered.[13]

The Self-righting Principle and Notion of Rationalism

By claiming that search for truth must be unhindered, the marketplace theory supposes that human beings are rational and are capable of identifying truth. The principle suggests that people know systems that promote the discovery of truth and can discern truth from falsehood in the marketplace. As law professor Kent Greenawalt explained, people can assess scientific claims, have a high degree of confidence in the accuracy of scientific truths, and learn from personal experience and communications of the experiences of others.[14] Though people can evaluate facts and be enlightened by experience, "people are notoriously incapable of assessing much of their own experience objectively."[15] Also, the human capacity to discover the truth is limited because "people are persuaded to believe what is already dominant and what fits their irrational needs."[16] So one can say that the discovery of truth does not mean any claim for absolute certainty and objectivity, but must represent an enlightenment function of citizens in a democratic regime.

Marketplace Metaphor and Search for Truth

The marketplace of ideas is criticized because, as the metaphor suggests, it is based on laissez-faire economic theory.[17] In the actual marketplace, the function of a free market differs from what the theory suggests because in real economic operations the wealthy and powerful usually dominate market forces. Governments often use some market controls to check excesses, reform imperfections and regulate inequities. Thus, if the free marketplace of ideas metaphor can favor those with the resources, then one can infer that governmental control is as well acceptable for checking shortcomings in the real world of speech.[18]

If the marketplace rationale should guarantee ultimate victory of truth over falsehood, the basic argument of the metaphor would be inaccurate. In everyday experience, it appears that truth does not win all the time, and humans do not achieve absolute truth. So Edwin Baker said that the marketplace of ideas justification should be rejected. According to him, "truth is not objective," for "people's perspectives and understanding are chosen or created rather than 'discovered.'"[19] Because individuals and groups have different true interests, he concluded:

> [I]f groups have divergent interests concerning the choice of perspectives, one can presume that the marketplace of ideas ... leads to the 'best' or 'proper' or 'progressive' understanding only if the marketplace favors those groups who should be favored or 'properly' distributes influence among various people or groups such that optimal compromises are reached. For example, Herbert Marcuse concluded that in the present historical circumstances the marketplace of ideas would work properly only if the rich and powerful were completely excluded and access were limited to progressive, leftist elements ....[20]

From those observations, Baker suggested that the democratic society can achieve the discovery of truth only if citizens have all the appropriate tools for the search, such as education, access to information, and unhindered fora for open debate. As Cass Sunstein put it, the search for truth needs an open process of discussion that can take place in political equality, and not manipulated by power, authority, and money.[21]

Marketplace As a Process of Open Discussion

While the marketplace of ideas may be imperfect, its deficiencies as a guarantor of the final conquest of truth can be overcome by seeing the discovery of truth as a process. As a process, truth in the marketplace metaphor would not mean certainty. As John Locke wrote in *A Letter Concerning Toleration*:

> [T]ruth is not taught by laws, nor has she any need of force to procure her entrance into the minds of men. Errors indeed prevail by the assistance of foreign and borrowed succors. But if truth makes not her way into the understanding by her own light, she will be the weaker for any borrowed force violence can add to her.[22]

Also, as Holmes explained the notion of the marketplace metaphor, truth is always conditional and it is subject to modifications. For him, "Such matters really are battlegrounds where the means do not exist for determinations that shall be good for all time, and where the decision can do no more than embody the preference of a given body in a given time and place."[23]

Besides, the marketplace of ideas is defended because the metaphor expresses the need for open minds in a democratic society. Entrepreneurship in the open marketplace involves risks, but as Justice Robert Jackson said: "It is not the function of our Government to keep the citizen from falling into error; it is the function of the citizen to keep the Government from falling into error."[24] Though the open marketplace of ideas can be challenging as long as occasionally certain disorder occurs in an open market, the metaphor is still a better way of ensuring "the best test of truth" than a closed society with a regulated marketplace.[25] Tolerance in the changing and competitive marketplace is necessary because "a certain amount of expressive disorder not only is inevitable in a society committed to individual freedom, but must itself be protected if that freedom would survive."[26] In this way, the marketplace of ideas expresses an ongoing search for truth.

Here, again, enlightenment of citizens through encouraging open interchange of ideas assumes that people in the market have open minds. While one can find some intellectuals who feel uncomfortable with free discussion, it is possible and fruitful to have intellectuals who are open and flexible to other ideas.[27]

All in all, the marketplace of ideas theory justifies special protection of political speech. It defends free speech as a means to an end. Speech is considered valuable, because public debate is a useful instrument for achieving other public objectives. Though the marketplace metaphor is imperfect, it has merits that express the value of individuals developing open minds, and the importance society places on an open process of discussion.

HUMAN DIGNITY AND SELF-FULFILLMENT RATIONALE

Some scholars and jurists, such as Professor Thomas Irwin Emerson and Justice John Marshall Harlan, argued that freedom of speech encourages the self-fulfillment of individuals in society. Proponents of this justification of free speech argue that the toleration of a wide range of ideas is helpful in a democratic society because it fosters the development of the personality of those who express the ideas and of those who receive them.

Thomas Irwin Emerson, in his book, *The System of Freedom of Expression*, used the phrase "the achievement of self-realization" to capture the idea of self-fulfillment to justify free speech. He defended free speech on four fundamental values: (1) individual self-fulfillment through expression; (2) the advancement of knowledge and truth; (3) the participation by all members of society in the decision-making process, and (4) the achievement of a stable community through consensus.[28] Emerson considered these as distinct values; yet, he held that "[e]ach is necessary, but not in itself sufficient, for the four of them are interdependent."[29]

One can identify two weaknesses in Emerson's theory. First, he admitted that his theory was tentative, though he wanted a theory that could guide the development and interpretation of an ever-changing society that is truly democratic. As a result, his theory would not adequately answer questions in a changing society such as a shift from the liberal laissez-faire to the mass technological society.[30] Another weakness in Emerson's approach is that the goals of self-fulfillment, discovering truth and participating in decision-making are not always compatible; they can be conflicting values. Since conflicting values cannot be consistently followed to resolve cases, one must balance the conflicting values and decide each time which value should be given greater weight in a particular case.[31]

In addition, the idea of self-fulfillment gives the impression that this theory is concerned only about individual interests and not those of society. On the contrary, self-fulfillment can be viewed as complementing other interests. Seeing this from Justice Harlan's words:

> [P]utting the decision as to what views shall be voiced largely into the hands of each of us, in the hope that use of such freedom will ultimately produce *a more capable citizenry* and *more perfect polity* and in the belief that no other approach would comport with the premise of *individual dignity* and choice upon which our political system rests.[32]

As Justice Harlan's speech moved from the collective interests of speech to individual values, so both interests can be seen as compatible under the self-fulfillment rationale.

Scanlon argued that free expression is an important element of individual autonomy.[33] According to him, if autonomy is at the root of self-government, the right to receive and give information is a core ingredient of citizens' freedom of expression. In this vein, Scanlon believed that one's ability to be challenged, provoked or encouraged by the ideas of others is essential to the development of personal beliefs which are fundamental to the human capacity for self-realization.[34]

Advocates of human dignity and self-fulfillment consider free speech as an end in itself. So that people can fully develop their personalities in society, they need freedom to express their feelings and opinions. For the fulfillment of those human desires, Justice Thurgood Marshall wrote, "The First Amendment serves not only the needs of the polity but also those of the human spirit -- a spirit that demands self-expression."[35] Putting it this way, the argument for free speech would depend neither on the collective search for truth nor participation in self-government, but that "[t]he First Amendment presupposes that the freedom to speak one's mind is ... an aspect of individual liberty -- and thus a good unto itself."[36]

Adding to it, scholars like Frederick Schauer and Robert Bork criticized the self-fulfillment rationale for justifying free speech because the free expression it defends is not clearly distinguished from other forms of self-gratification.[37] However, Rodney A. Smolla gave two notable responses to this criticism. The first is grounded in classic libertarianism and, the other, in the relationship between speech and thought -- a linkage that defines freedom of speech as central to human self-definition.[38]

Pursuit of Pleasure and the Harm Principle

While critics consider the self-fulfillment notion of free expression as a form of self-indulgence that must be reasonably restrained with majority approval, libertarians contend that speech is different from other pursuits of pleasure that the government is permitted to regulate. According to the libertarians, unless the government finds actual danger in a form of human pursuit of pleasure, the government should not interfere in it just because it is offensive to the majority of people.[39]

Relation of Speech and Thought

Another argument that distinguishes self-realization from other forms of pleasure seeking is the distinction between expression and thought. Speech is different from other forms of self-gratification because it is associated with human thought. As Professor Vincent Blasi said:

> The most important beneficial consequence of unregulated expression is simply the stimulation individuals receive from a diverse reading and listening fare; this stimulation may contribute to human happiness directly, and hence be thought to have value quite apart from its relationship to search for the truth.[40]

Professor Edwin Baker elaborated that people must freely express themselves without restraint in order to actualize their human potential. He said:

Speech is protected not as a means of a collective good but because of the value of speech conduct to the individual. The liberty theory justifies protection because of the way the protected conduct fosters individual self-realization and self-determination without improperly interfering with the legitimate claims of others.[41]

Thus argued, speech deserves special protection because it is not only related to thought, but also it is about one's self-expression and one's relationship with others and government. Australian journalist Robert Pullan said:

Speech expresses the self and like the self is free ... Words are our ... connection to each other and to all that has gone before. Our speech is inherently free because violating this connection violates our humanity. When we are censored we are diminished ... Free speech seems part of our human programming whatever the culture.[42]

So central to the self-fulfillment theory is the notion that speech is linked to thought and consequently human capacity to reason and communicate in society. In light of this, speech is different from other forms of gratification and any interference requires special care on the part of government. As David M. Rabban noted about Dewey's postwar writings, free speech "is the central right in a democracy because the essential democratic principle is persuasion rather than coercion."[43]

DEMOCRATIC SELF-GOVERNANCE RATIONALE

Advocates of the self-governance position assert that free speech facilitates the political process. While political speech is necessary for the maintenance of self-governance, it gives corrupt and incompetent governments much discomfort.[44] John Locke wrote that freedom of speech can be a vehicle for expressing dissent and, hence, restraining government tyranny, corruption, and incompetence.[45]

Also, free speech is justified because it helps the proper functioning of a representative democracy. In the words of James Madison, "A popular Government, without popular information, or the means of acquiring it, is but a Prologue to a Farce or a Tragedy; or perhaps both ... And a people who mean to be their own Governers, must arm themselves with the power which knowledge gives."[46] Much the same, Alexis de Tocqueville complimented the relationship between democracy and free political discussion. He wrote, "When the right of every citizen to a share in the government of society is acknowledged, everyone must be presumed to be able to choose between the various opinions of his contemporaries and to appreciate the different facts from which inferences may be drawn."[47]

Similarly, Judge Thomas Cooley's treatise on constitutional law supported the values of an informed citizenry. For him, democratic self-governance should prevent "any action of the government by means of which it might prevent such free and general discussion of public matters as seems absolutely essential to prepare the people for an intelligent exercise of their rights as citizens."[48]

According to the legal philosopher Alexander Meiklejohn, democratic self-government operates on the ability of citizens to choose representatives who know the concerns of their constituents and effectively represent the beliefs and interests of those constituents. He believed that full discussion of issues could generate effective results in representative democracy.[49] So he argued that free speech is a requisite tool in democratic self-government.[50] Meiklejohn stressed this position by saying that genuine self-governance has no distinction between the governors and the governed: "And the crux of the difficulty lies in the fact that, in such a society, the governors and the governed are not two distinct groups of persons. There is only one group -- the self-governing people. Rulers and the ruled are the same individuals."[51] By this, Meiklejohn meant that the citizens are themselves the sovereign in a democracy.

Meiklejohn further commented that free speech gives citizens access to all the information necessary for performing their political duties. So he wrote: "What is essential is not that every one shall speak, but that everything worth saying shall be said ... no suggestion of policy shall be denied a hearing."[52] Meiklejohn used a "town meeting metaphor" to explain the nature of free speech in relation to self-governance. He believed that this metaphor better expresses the objectives of public discussion in self-governance and rationale for the protection of freedom of speech than the marketplace metaphor.[53]

Because Meiklejohn viewed freedom of speech in the light of the ideal of democratic self-government, he thought political speech must have absolute protection.[54] He explained that absolute protection for free speech should cover only speech that concerns self-governance, because only political speech concretely expresses the public weal. Unlike political speech, which is for the communal good, speech that works for private gain is merely for individual good and does not deserve the absolute protection under the First Amendment.[55] Meiklejohn's view influenced the legal thought of Justice William Brennan. In his position on First Amendment jurisprudence, Brennan wrote: "[T]he First Amendment embodies more than a commitment to free expression and communicative interchange for their own sakes; it has a *structural* role to play in securing and fostering our republican system of self-government."[56]

Self-governance Principle and Promotion of Citizenship

Robert Bork agreed with Meiklejohn's argument that free speech promotes political discourse and effective participation of people in the governing process, but Bork accepted promotion of citizenship as the only justification for protecting political speech. He argued that only speech that promotes citizenship and the communal good should be highly protected. He favored the self-governance theory as the only justification for heightened protection for speech, and limited such protection to political affairs. For him, "radical individualism" and too much personal freedom works against individual responsibility and the social good.[57]

Law professor Paul Chevigny shared Bork's idea of free speech and the common good. Chevigny defended protection of free speech primarily because it is good for society, rather than being an important individual right. In his view, society needs open discussion so that governors and the governed can reason through public discussion because government policy decisions cannot be intelligently made without discussion and criticism.[58]

Toleration As a Value for Stability

Some liberal theorists, including Frederick Schauer[59] and Lee Bollinger,[60] consider toleration as the main justification for free political speech. They believe that free speech promotes tolerance while tolerance encourages stability in self-governance. They asserted that free speech receives special protection in contrast to other activities because the state has the inclination to be intolerant. Schauer said that the state has a self-serving tendency to suppress speech critical of state policies. He believed that the protection of free speech opposes the harm of intolerance and the state's tendency to interpret criticism as sedition. So, for Schauer, principles of free speech create more political good by combating state power and checking the state's tendency of intolerance.[61]

Bollinger agreed with Schauer's argument that the state can cause harm if free speech is not protected. According to Bollinger, the protection of free speech outweighs any political evils of government intolerance, because the state's judgments about the harmfulness of speech may be mistaken or such judgments may inflict the harm of intolerance.[62]

The free speech principles of Schauer and Bollinger do not spell out the scope of legitimate interests that qualify for protection by free speech. For example, individuals can manipulate easily the principle of tolerance to defend harmful speech, such as advocacy of racial genocide.

The Conservative Stance against Tolerance

Social conservatives reacted against the civil libertarian view of toleration and absolutist tendencies about free speech. For instance, James Fitzjames Stephen criticized liberal theorists, and said that Mill's utilitarian argument for free discussion neither proved that free speech maximized scientific truth nor that maximizing people's knowledge of the truth always increases satisfaction.[63]

The Marxist view of Herbert Marcuse was similar to the social conservative argument. In his essay, *A Critique of Pure Tolerance*, Marcuse thought that the liberal stance of free speech was defective. He said:

> Tolerance cannot be indiscriminate and equal with respect to the content of expression ... it cannot protect false words and wrong deeds which demonstrate that they contradict the

possibility of liberation ... Certain things cannot be said, certain ideas cannot be expressed, certain policies cannot be proposed.[64]

Just as the liberal theorists claimed a right of free speech against intolerance of religious and political dissent, Marcuse argued, free speech should not override other rights and freedoms of citizens.[65]

Few liberals would join social conservatives who support censorship in relation to matters of national security and what they consider immoral and indecent speech. However, for the social conservatives, it would be justifiable for the state to control the sale of pornography and obscene expression in the media and on the Internet just as the state restricts the possession of illicit drugs.[66] Beyond censoring of pornography, Thomas Storch argued that government should prohibit "expressions of erroneous ideas."[67] He elaborated:

Ideas lead to actions, and bad ideas often lead to bad acts, bringing harm to individuals and possible ruin to societies. Just as the state has the right to restrict and direct a person's actions when he is a physical threat to the community, so also in the matter of intellectual or cultural threats, the authorities have duties to protect the community.[68]

Such conservative views about free speech oppose the liberal claims of toleration. But, the conservative position against harmful speech must reconcile with liberal toleration.[69] A pragmatic compromise, as David Heyd suggested, "implies that the reasons for disapproval and those for restraint are *balanced* against each other by some sort of a weighting procedure."[70]

Bias of Exclusive Protection for Political Speech

The relationship of free speech to self-governance indisputably justifies special protection for political expression.[71] However, advocates of the self-governance position fail to establish that protection of free speech includes values other than the functioning of the representative democracy.

As Rodney Smolla argued, the self-governance justification should not be an exclusive rationale but "*one of many* arguments that, in combination, provide an overwhelmingly compelling case for heightened constitutional protection for freedom of speech."[72] Smolla considered the special protection of political speech as irrefutably important in a democratic society, but he attacked the notion of its exclusivity. He explained:

> There is no logic *internal* to the self-governance theory that demands exclusivity. Nothing in the self-governance rationale "knocks out" the marketplace of ideas rationale or the self-fulfillment rationale. Nothing in those theories is limited to politics. The collective search for truth and the individual quest for intellectual fulfillment embrace the full life of the mind. Indeed, the argument that the self-governance theory is alone a sufficient justification for heightened protection for speech is linked to an exceedingly narrow view of the self-governance theory itself ... There is, in sum, nothing *inside* the self-governance theory that disqualifies the marketplace or fulfillment theories, and nothing *outside* those two theories that limits them to self-governance issues.[73]

For Smolla, it is difficult to separate political from nonpolitical speech. He argued that understandings gained in the areas such as health, art, religion, education, and professional and social relations are also important in making life fulfilling. In his view, therefore, limiting freedom of speech to matters relating to political affairs is a form of bias.[74] Besides, as the United States Supreme Court maintained, the "guarantees of speech and press are not the preserve of political expression or comment on public affairs, essential as those are to healthy government."[75]

FINDING A COMMON GROUND

To bridge what he believed were the dangers in both tolerance and intolerance, professor Amitai Etzioni, the communitarian proponent, sought a common ground between freedom and control, order and autonomy, and rights of individuals and their social responsibilities. He did not ask for government intervention in harmful speech, but that citizens advance community spirit in discussing and addressing their concerns and interests. Etzioni argued that the common ground demands the readiness to forfeit some individual rights for the common good instead of creating more rights.[76] A related attempt at finding a common ground stance of free speech is found in Joshua Cohen's three considerations for protected speech.[77] Cohen suggested that speech that serves "expressive," "deliberative" and "informational" interests must be strictly protected as the common ground.[78] The expressive interests involve expression of thoughts, attitudes, and feelings on personal and general human concerns, such as matters about political justice and quality of human life.[79] He considered the expressive interests important because they can influence the thought and conduct of others. His idea of deliberative interests deals with human reflection on matters of concern, which often cannot be pursued solely by an individual. The deliberative interest engenders enlightenment and discussion and opens people to alternatives.[80] The third basic interest concerns acquisition of relevant information about the conditions necessary for pursuing one's aims and aspirations.[81] Cohen believed that the expressive, deliberative, and informational interests promote democratic values that political speech achieves, and so must be protected at all cost.[82] Cohen said that speech can be costly because:

> It is sometimes offensive, disgusting, or outrageous; it produces reputational injury and emotional distress...the presence of such costs does not as a general matter suffice to remove protection from expression. Neither offense ... nor reputational injury, nor emotional distress, for example, suffice by themselves to deprive expression of protection.[83]

According to Cohen, this idea of strict protections is "driven principally by the substantive value of expression and the possibilities of using speech to combat the harms of speech; such protections are only secondarily remedial, only secondarily driven by fear and mistrust underwritten by our tendency -- or the tendency of government -- to undervalue or suppress expression."[84] For instance, speech may harm people in a way that libels a group or public figures, but such speech should receive more stringent protection than individual libels because it is usually a form of political speech.[85] However, for Cohen, hateful fighting words should not be protected because they are intended to insult and they lie at the periphery of the basic expressive and deliberative interests. Also, "Because of the requirement of immediate provocation and injury associated with fighting words, some of the costs are direct and there is no deflecting them with 'more speech.'"[86]

MULTIPLE RATIONALES

The issue of overemphasizing free speech engaged the attention of some theorists. For example, law professor Harry Kalven, Jr., warned against theories of free speech constructing guidelines for interpretation and setting limits of protection for free expression.[87] For him, the issue of free speech is a matter that involves the content of speech and interests of equal protection.[88] Kalven's comment can be a description of the different concerns of free speech theories.

Sometimes the marketplace of ideas, self-fulfillment, and democratic self-governance rationales are presented as mutually exclusive arguments for protecting freedom of speech. However, a more compelling argument for free speech rests on synthesizing them. As Professor Steven Shiffrin noted, multiple values combine in support of free speech, including "individual self-expression, social communion, political participation, the search for truth and for informed choice, social catharsis, the social affirmation of the rights of equality, dignity, and respect, and the freedom from arbitrary, official aggrandizing or excessively intrusive government regulation."[89] So put, "There is no single correct way of presenting the justifications that matter for a principle of freedom of speech."[90] Argued most briefly, an adequate justification of free speech must "draw upon several strands of theory in order to protect a rich variety of expressional modes."[91] In support of this view, Smolla said, there "is no logical reason why the preferred position of freedom of speech might not be buttressed by multiple rationales."[92]

To summarize, the theoretical framework of free speech suggests multiple values that are justified by various rationales for protecting free speech. The rationales combine to offer a stringent protection for political expression. The search for truth and for informed citizenry, individual self-expression and self-fulfillment, political participation, and open discussion and criticism of public affairs are informational, expressive and deliberative features of free speech. They are not conflicting values, but rather, they are mutually sustaining and interrelated. Together they form a rich congruity of democratic values, and give the quintessential justification for heightened protection of political speech. What is more, political speech is worth stringent protection because it is grounded in what Cohen called "the fact of reasonableness," respecting the citizen's freedom to receive, share, hold, modify or express opinions.[93] These values are democratic goals and free political speech, above all, promotes them concretely.

The next chapter involves a historical analysis which leads to case-law analysis. Case-law analysis, as a strategy, employs analogical analysis and qualitative content analysis. Because the conceptual focus of this study was on political speech and defamation, jurisprudential activity recorded in legal artifacts (court decisions of political libel cases) formed the sampling unit of investigation.[94] For a case-law analysis, this study did not randomly select sample cases within a uniform time frame. Instead, it purposefully chose landmark decisions and important cases that followed to reflect the prevailing jurisprudence. The study examined prevailing jurisprudence about political defamation, and used critical case sampling strategy. Critical case sampling in qualitative research is a method of selecting cases that exemplify the theoretical problem.[95] This "[p]ermits logical generalization" of the legal position of each regime and allows "maximum application of information to other cases."[96] The criteria for selecting political defamation cases consisted of court decisions that manifest some theoretical considerations.

Chapter Three

Historical Analysis of the Four Jurisdictions

To develop an analytical framework, this chapter considers the historical development of defamation law in the United Kingdom, the United States, the ECHR and Australia. While the chapter examines the growth and complexity of the law of defamation in those jurisdictions, it seeks the common thread and divergent lines of protecting political speech. The historical study establishes the background to sanctions against defamation of public officials leading to First Amendment protections in the United States, libel reforms in the United Kingdom, the influence of the European Court on the domestic law of the United Kingdom, recent changes in Australian defamation law and consistency in the judicial interpretations of the regimes.

EARLY LAWS OF LIBEL FOR RESTRICTING POLITICAL DISCUSSION

The United States and Australia share the background of common law of defamation with England. Social and political conditions combined to affect the common law of defamation. Until the eighteenth century, libel prosecutions brought by public officials against their critics were mostly called seditious or criminal libel. So the two terms were interchangeably used to describe parliamentary and judicial restrictions that burdened political discussion and criticism of public officials.[1] One would say that a modern form of seditious libel involves government use of restrictions such as official secrecy and national security to silence public discussion of information the authorities consider classified.[2]

Defamation laws were created at a time when Great Britain was under a monarchical rule. Women were not enfranchised. Neither were most ordinary men. Government was accountable to the monarchy and parliament rather than the citizenry. So the monarchy did not guarantee free speech of the citizenry. Given the monarchical political system, the common law offense of libel called *De Scandalis Magnatum* (slander of the magnates) was created by a 1275 statute. The statute provided that:

> Whereas much as there have been aforetimes found in the country devisers of tales -- whereby discord or occasion of discord hath arisen between the king and his people or great men of this realm -- it is commanded that none be so hardy as to tell or publish any false news or tales whereby discord or occasion of discord or slander may grow between the king and his people or the great men of the realm; he that doth so shall be taken and kept in prison until he hath brought into the court which was first author of the tale.[3]

The law was made to protect governmental officials and nobles from embarrassing stories that could become public and might stir the people against them,[4] and so the law of libel aimed at preventing breach of the peace.[5] This statutory offense of defamation condemned and punished falsehoods. Truth was not a defense because criticisms based on truth were considered a greater threat as they were more likely to cause breach of the peace.[6] This rule governing the English law of seditious libel gave rise to the maxim "The greater the truth, the greater the libel."[7] It did not distinguish between spoken and written false news or tales. However, with the coming of printing, seditious libel became a controlling mechanism against printed criticism of government, officials or legislation.[8]

Afraid that the public would lose confidence in the government, the institutional monarchy used defamation laws and did not guarantee political participation of citizens as a civil right. In light of this, in 1606, Attorney General Edward Coke brought Lewis Pickeringe to trial for violation of the law called libel of magistrates, a remedy for written defamations against "magistrates" or officials.[9] Pickeringe wrote and gave to a friend a defamatory rhyme about the dead Archbishop Whitgift and the then living Archbishop of Canterbury. Though the deceased Archbishop Whitgift could not suffer Pickeringe's libel, the government considered it an attack on its late servant. Pinkeringe was punished not only for breach of the peace, but also for committing a greater offense of libel of magistrates that was also a scandal upon the government. In his report of the case, Coke separated a libel "against a private man" from one "against a magistrate or public person."[10] In essence, Coke punished defamations of individual officials rather than criticisms of institutions, such as the government in general.[11]

Similarly, the libel of magistrates was applied in the American colony in a 1635 case involving Roger Williams, the founder of Rhode Island. He wrote letters that asked Puritan churches in Massachusetts to censure the General Court for oppression. According to the court, Williams sent "letters of defamation, both of the magistrates and churches" and of spreading "new and dangerous opinions, against the authority of magistrates."[12] When Williams rejected the court's instruction to withdraw his defamatory statements, the court banished him from Massachusetts.

The Law of Seditious Libel

After the abolition of the Star Chamber in 1641, seditious libel became the Crown's chief means of prosecuting written and political defamation, and it was followed until the late eighteenth century in England and the American colonies. Three main allegations formed elements of the offense of seditious libel and the requirements for establishing those elements.[13]

First, the content of the writing had to defame an individual[14] and clearly identify its victim.[15] Second, proof of publication or the defendant's intent to publish the defamatory writing to a third party was essential in prosecutions for libels of public persons as it was in libel actions of private persons. As Chief Justice Hyde instructed a jury in 1663, "Printing alone is not enough; for if a man print a book to make a fire on, that is no offense, it is the publishing of it which is a crime."[16]

Third, allegations about the defendant's state of mind were sometimes considered in defamation cases. Though precedents concerning this element were not as clear as the defamatory content and the publication, the defamatory content of the writing suggested defendants' knowledge and malice. However, where the judge or the defense called into doubt the issues of knowledge and malice, the court required the jury to consider them. For example, Sir Samuel Barnardiston wrote alleged libelous letters that questioned a publicized popish plot, and criticized members of the government and the bench.[17]

During his trial, Chief Justice Jeffreys repeatedly asked the defense to show evidence of lack of malice:

> You would have the jury find, I warrant, that he did it piously, and with a good intent ... You would have the jury find he had no ill design in it ... Do you think he did it to serve the Crown? If the jury will take it upon their oaths, that Sir Samuel Barnardiston wrote these Letters to serve the Crown, you say something. Pray ask them that question. Try if you can make them believe that, Mr. Williams.[18]

So, acknowledging that juries could consider proof of good intentions, Jeffreys summarized for the jury: "Gentlemen, the question before you is, Whether the Defendant be guilty of writing these malicious, seditious Letters; for that they are malicious and factious, no honest man can doubt in the least; and I do not find that the defendant do offer to say any thing in defense of the Letters."[19]   While Barnardiston's counsel argued with Jeffreys over the proper requirements for proof of malice, he failed to offer the jury proof of Barnardiston's intentions. As a result, the issue of whether he acted with malice did not arise, and the Crown prevailed in the libel action.

More important, political and ideological interests in the trial of the Seven Bishops in 1688 affected the libel law. King James II issued the *Declaration of Indulgence* that suspended laws that called for imprisonment of religious nonconformists, and ordered the Bishops to read the declaration in their churches. The Bishops petitioned the king that they could not "in prudence, honor or conscience" publish the declaration because James had no authority to override statutory religious restrictions.[20]   The king brought them to trial. The four justices and lawyers were divided as to the type of writing that established a libel.[21]   The justices left the actual decision of that question to the jury. The jury acquitted the Bishops.

The acquittal of the Seven Bishops was politically and ideologically significant because it contributed to the fall of James, and it reflected a Protestant victory against James' sympathy for Catholics. The case also showed that the law of seditious libel in the seventeenth century punished only defamations of individuals in government, and the word "libel" was becoming exclusively used for prosecutions for written defamations.

At this time, the British monarchy allowed freedom of speech as a specific privilege of the Lords and Commons to conduct their debates independently and against challenge of the Crown, judges and citizens.[22] The parliamentary privilege became entrenched by Article 9 of the Bill of Rights 1689. It provided: "The freedom of speech and debates in Parliament ought not be impeached or questioned in any court or place out of Parliament." As a result, colonies of England also gained the absolute privilege for parliamentary proceedings.

Shifts in Libel Prosecutions in the Eighteenth Century

The law of seditious libel in the seventeenth century prosecuted written defamatory statements against government officials and important personalities of the society. At the close of the century, parliamentary privilege was created to ensure free debate in public proceedings. In the eighteenth century, public displeasure with the libel law, as inherited from Coke, led the courts to modify seditious libel law as the government's chief means of prosecuting the printed press. Libertarianism in Britain, at this point, augured a movement that called for greater expression of thought and opinion.[23]

While England remained conservative in protecting the reputation of public persons, the colonial America started creating a more liberal doctrine toward the press.[24] For example, John Tutchin was prosecuted for "falsely, seditiously and scandalously" publishing in his semiweekly newspaper that the navy was being mismanaged, and that English officials were being bribed with French gold.[25] In Tutchin's trial in 1704, Chief Justice John Holt considered it a criminal offense to defame the government or particular persons within it. In contrast, Tutchin's counsel based his arguments on the traditional law of defamation and insisted that libels must reflect on individuals, for "nothing is a libel but what reflects upon some particular person."[26] Holt, however, ignored defamation precedents and said that criticism of the government was criminal. From seemingly political considerations Holt argued:

> But this is a very strange doctrine, to say, it is not a libel, reflecting on the Government ... If men should not be called to account for possessing the people with an ill opinion of the Government, no Government can subsist; for it is very necessary for every Government, that the people should have a

good opinion of it. And nothing can be worse to any Government, than to endeavor to procure animosities as to the management of it. This has been always look'd upon as a crime, and no Government can be safe unless it be punished.[27]

Tutchin was not convicted because of an error in a writ.[28] Probably due to Whig sympathy for free discussion of politics, Queen Anne's Whig administration of 1708-1710 suspended seditious libel prosecutions. Still, the prosecutions resumed when the Tory ministry came into power in 1710. The traditional, conservative Tory party did not tolerate the idea of vigorous criticism of authority and public discussion of political issues.[29] But when, the Whigs regained office in 1714, they also prosecuted the printed press for seditious libel because of political criticism, though the political environment was becoming more moderate.[30]

As James Fitzjames Stephen wrote, the prevailing view was that "the ruler is regarded as the superior of the subject ... [and] it must necessarily follow that it is wrong to censure him openly...."[31] So, in the seventeenth century and a large part of the eighteenth century, governments thought of themselves as unequals of the ordinary people, and their libel laws evidenced their unfriendly attitudes and policies toward political speech. Colonial American courts, on the other hand, became reluctant to prosecute critics for political discussion. Typically, in the 1723 case of James Franklin, a grand jury opposed the Massachusetts Council and House's effort to indict Franklin, publisher of the *New England Courant*, for his satirical criticism of ministers' hypocritical prayers about public officials.[32] Then, with the unsuccessful trial to convict John Peter Zenger in 1735, "seditious libel ended as a serious threat" to free political speech and press freedom.[33]

Zenger was prosecuted for printing allegedly seditious attacks upon New York Governor William Cosby. Andrew Hamilton, in Zenger's defense, conceded that Zenger had printed material critical of Cosby. The Attorney General took Hamilton's statement as a confession and inferred that Zenger was guilty. When Hamilton argued for justification as a defense, the Chief Justice James DeLancey refused to allow any evidence of truth to go before the jury. Nevertheless, in a rebuttal, Hamilton addressed the jury and argued that all free citizens had the natural right to complain about bad administration of government as far as truth backed their complaints.[34] In the end, the jury ignored DeLancey's instructions and found Zenger not guilty of libel.

The acquittal of Zenger was a symbolic victory on behalf of the press. It allowed truth as a defense and demonstrated a checking of governmental interference with political criticism. Justice William O. Douglas characterized it as "the milestone in the fight for the right to criticize the government."[35] Liberal views about citizens' liberties, especially about free political communication, were gaining grounds and colonial courts were becoming more suspicious of seditious libel prosecutions.

Political Communication from 1750-1800

The enlightenment promoted liberal views that brought freedom of speech into the political arena and affected public attitudes toward seditious libel. Particularly in the 1760s, relentless printed criticism of colonial and British political leaders became a part of the political culture.

In colonial America, getting juries to convict political critics of seditious libel became difficult. Between 1767 and 1771, Governor Sir Francis Bernard and Lieutenant Governor Thomas Hutchinson of Massachusetts several times sought unsuccessfully seditious libel prosecutions against their political opponents. In one of his instructions to grand jurors, Hutchinson said, "Every man who prints, prints at his peril," for to allow "the licentious Abuse of Government is the most likely Way to destroy its Freedom."[36] Though his comment was to silence political criticism in the *Boston Gazette* and the *Boston Evening Post*, he did not excuse legitimate criticism of corrupt officials either. When he failed to get grand jurors and legislators to indict political critics and printers on grounds of Blackstone's libel doctrines,[37] Hutchinson told a grand jury:

> I do not mention the Matter of Libels to you, Gentlemen -- I am discouraged -- My repeated Charges to Grand Juries … being so entirely neglected … [B]ut I have discharged my own Conscience … from finding that they multiply so fast, are become so common, so scandalous, so entirely false and incredible, that no Body will mind them; and that all Ranks among us will treat them with Neglect.[38]

Political critics and journalists in colonial America succeeded in enfeebling the seditious libel law and made it nearly impossible for officials to obtain libel convictions. Meanwhile, advocates of free political speech in England still suffered prosecutions and often were convicted of seditious libel. Key to the legal battle against traditional British controls of political criticism was John Wilkes's case in 1763.[39] Wilkes was a sitting member of British Parliament when he was arrested for anti-government statements published in his popular radical newspaper, the *North Briton*. After his release, a week later, from the Tower of London because of parliamentary privilege, he fled from prosecution for seditious libel and was convicted *in absentia*. He returned in 1768 and was imprisoned for 22 months.[40] Riots and protests during his imprisonment contributed to his release. In 1778, Wilkes was permitted to take his seat in the House of Commons.[41] As part of the political and ideological conflicts of the time, the Wilkes riots discouraged Parliament from prosecuting printers of parliamentary debates and such prosecutions lessened.[42] The Wilkes' episode also contributed to the passage of the Fox Libel Act of 1792 which gave the jury the authority to give "a general verdict of guilty or not guilty upon the whole matter put in issue ..."[43] Though the Fox Act was intended to make the burden of proving seditious libel more difficult,[44] it did not reduce libel convictions.[45]

Though the United States and England shared a common political and legal culture, the American colonies began major changes when they declared independence from England in 1776. Political libel suits were rare in the 1980s. One of the exceptional cases was in 1782, when Pennsylvania's Chief Justice Thomas McKean tried to prosecute Eleazer Oswald for criticizing him (McKean) in the *Independent Gazetteer*.[46] While he awaited appearance before the grand jury, Oswald and his supporters attacked McKean in the newspaper's columns and argued against the use of seditious libel law in the United States. Oswald's pseudonymous supporters like "Wilkes" wrote that, by criticizing public persons and policies, the free press "exposes and defeats the end and objects of tyranny and misrule."[47] Another writer called "Junius Wilkes" also said that public officials were "merely public servants and stewards, and, as such, accountable at all times to the people," and that the Pennsylvania Constitution of 1776 justified "publications which respect the conduct of public servants; and, when they even appear false and groundless, it is rather an inconvenience."[48] The writings of the *Gazetteer*'s supporters helped Oswald because they reflected on the Constitution. So the Grand Jury voted against indicting Oswald.

In 1789, the United States Constitution was ratified and its Bill of Rights went into effect in 1791. After independence, the United States did not have rules in place on political libel, and did not immediately break away from the English common law of libel. So prosecutions of political criticism in the United States continued into the nineteenth century. Typifying the situation was ideological conflict that led to the passage of the Sedition Act of 1798.[49]

Though it could have used political libel prosecutions under common law, the Federalist majority passed the Sedition Act to protect the Federalist party and its views from criticism.[50] The act made it a crime to "write, print, utter or publish ... any false, scandalous and malicious" comments about the government, members of Congress, or the President "with intent to defame ... or bring them ... into contempt or disrepute, or to excite against them ... the hatred of the good people of the United States ..."[51] Federalists believed that effective libel laws would control publication of falsehoods by the press, protect the reputation of public officials and ensure an enlightened public opinion.[52] So the act was passed to control political debate. The act allowed truth as a defense as it stated that a defendant could "give in his defense, the truth of the matter contained in the publication of a libel."[53] However, the defense of truth was not applied to Jeffersonians in practice. At least eighteen people were prosecuted under the act.[54]

Partisan conduct of Federalists in the judiciary awakened popular condemnation of the act.[55] According to Leonard W. Levy, "broad libertarian theory of freedom of speech and press did not emerge in the United States until the Jeffersonians ... were forced to defend themselves against the Federalist Sedition Act of 1798."[56] Though Jeffersonians recognized that the reputation of political figures had some value in the marketplace of ideas, they considered the Sedition Act unconstitutional and advocated an end to political libel prosecutions.[57]

Some provisions in the American Bill of Rights helped the United States' gradual shift from the common law libel to establish a legal system different in some respects from the English common law model. More important, the First Amendment provision that guaranteed freedom of speech and of the press motivated a gradual discontinuity with England.[58] The different political attitudes of the Tory and Whig governments in Great Britain and those of the Federalists and Jeffersonians in the United States toward political libel demonstrated that ensuring free political speech was sometimes beset by government measures such as sedition laws to muzzle criticism of political opponents.

Prosecution of Political Criticism in the Nineteenth Century

Criminal defamation prosecutions were common in the nineteenth century. Yet, at common law, the defendant could not use truth as a defense to a prosecution of criminal libel.[59] The years between 1800 and the 1830s represented a transitional period in America when some states modified provisions that subjected defamatory attacks against the reputations of public officials to criminal libel prosecutions. However, as several American states made revisions in their libel doctrines,[60] criminal libel prosecutions began drifting away from the English law of libel. So prosecutions for libeling public officials abated because of the statutory revisions made in the common law.[61] Then, in the United States, political conflict and increasingly popular outcry surrounding criminal libel prosecutions made public officials use more civil than criminal libel as their legal redress.[62] In *United States v Hudson and Goodwin*,[63] the Supreme Court excluded federal courts from criminal libel prosecutions. This shift was important because the judiciary began weighing political criticisms and reputations of public officials. While the legal system maintained that the press should exercise self-censorship, it sought a privilege for defamatory falsehoods honestly made in the course of political criticism.[64]

From the mid-nineteenth century, development into mass society and the principle of democratic government encouraged debating freedom of expression and libel laws in courtrooms. As an anonymous reviewer for the *American Law Magazine* wrote, the prevailing nineteenth century democratic political culture condemned English defamation laws as outdated and interfering with free political speech. So the reviewer said that people who could not bear "the ordeal of the most searching scrutiny ought not in these days of the supremacy of public opinion, to solicit the suffrages of that opinion, either with a view to fortune, fame, or station."[65]

Advocacy of liberal libel rules brought some legal changes in the United States. For example, a Connecticut law of 1855 favorably considered the legal current in a statute that provided: "[I]n every action for an alleged libel the defendant may give proof of intention, and unless the plaintiff shall prove malice in fact he shall recover nothing but his actual damage proved and specially alleged in the declaration."[66] In 1862, the Connecticut Supreme Court upheld this law making it difficult for public officials to recover "punitive damages for ... proper and just criticisms upon public men, public measures or candidates for office, or other matters of public interest," unless plaintiffs showed that the newspaper published libelous falsehoods from "improper and unjustifiable motives."[67] Similarly, in Maryland Supreme Court, Justice John Mitchell Robinson considered the right "to discuss and criticize boldly the official conduct" of public officials "as a right which, in *every* free country belongs to the citizen, and the exercise of it, within lawful and proper limits, affords some protection at least against official abuse and corruption."[68]

As criminal libel prosecutions declined in the United States, so Britain began modifying traditional doctrines by the mid-nineteenth century. Britain enacted the Libel Act 1843, which established that, besides the truth of the defamatory matter, the accused must also show that the publication was for the public benefit.[69] However, although the defendant bore the burden of proof, it dissolved the element of breach of the peace. Although breach of the peace suggested that criminal libel was a public order offense, the prosecution did not need to prove the likelihood of public disorder.[70] The law extended to defamation of the dead and group libel.[71] Apart from an approval of a High Court judge that proceedings required it, there was no restriction on prosecutions against the proprietor or editor of a newspaper. Conviction carried a maximum penalty of twelve months' imprisonment. In cases where the defendant published with knowledge of the falsity of the defamatory matter, he or she faced two years' imprisonment.[72]

By the end of the nineteenth century, liberal libel rules were changing the pattern of criminal libel prosecutions in the United States. Several states made revisions that started a drift away from the English libel law. Great Britain also made some progress toward liberalization by enacting the Libel Act 1843 that allowed justification and fair comment defenses and thus helped a decline in criminal libel prosecutions.

TWENTIETH CENTURY POLITICAL LIBEL LAW

Since the promulgation of the Bill of Rights, social and political conditions stimulated ongoing debates about the meaning of the First Amendment in the United States. In the early twentieth century, the Sedition Act of 1918, for a while hindered the United States' libertarian effort toward abandoning old English libel laws.

Though national security motivated the 1918 act, the act called it a crime to utter, write, print, or publish "any disloyal, profane, scurrilous or abusive language intended to cause contempt, scorn, contumely or disrepute as regards the form of government of the United States, or the Constitution, or the flag ..."[73] Limits of protected speech were set by distinguishing the nature of the speech and the circumstances of its utterance. For example, Justice Oliver Wendell Holmes, Jr., did not accept any legal protection of political speech for words that "are used in such circumstances and are of such a nature as to create a clear and present danger that they will bring about the substantive evils that Congress has a right to prevent."[74] However, Justice Holmes believed that protection against prior restraint was one of the First Amendment's central purposes and declared: "I wholly disagree with the argument of the Government that the First Amendment left the common law as to seditious libel in force. History seems to me against the notion."[75]

The act and other regulations on the state level were inclined toward prior restraint and suppression of the press. In defense of the proper role of the press, the United States Supreme Court in *Gitlow v New York* said that freedom of speech and press "are among the fundamental personal rights and liberties protected by the due process clause of the Fourteenth Amendment from impairment by the States."[76] However, the Minnesota Supreme Court upheld a Minnesota law that gave officials the power to prevent *The Saturday Press* from publishing "malicious, scandalous, and defamatory" material. Because the case was tied to political libel, the United States Supreme Court reversed the decision of the state courts and made it unconstitutional for government to exercise prior restraint of scandalous and defamatory publication.[77] This decision was to give more latitude to political speech. Important as political speech is, the Supreme Court later explained: "The guarantees for speech and press are not the preserve of political expression or comment upon public affairs, essential as those are to healthy government."[78] Thus, in the United States, free speech included other forms of speech such as artistic speech.

After *Gitlow*, criminal libel prosecution declined sharply until it was considered unconstitutional by the United States Supreme Court in

Garrison v Louisiana,[79] unless "actual malice" is proved in addition to the criminal law standard of "beyond a reasonable doubt."[80] In his concurring opinion, Justice Black wrote:

> Fining men or sending them to jail for criticizing public officials not only jeopardized the free, open public discussion which our Constitution guarantees, but can wholly stifle it. I would hold now and not wait to hold later ... that under our Constitution there is absolutely no place in the country for the old, discredited English Star Chamber law of seditious criminal libel.[81]

However, criminal libel was not to be construed as abolished. At the time of the adoption of the Constitution, according to the United States Supreme Court, "nowhere was there any suggestion that the crime of libel be abolished."[82]

Like the United States, seditious criminal libel prosecutions declined over the years in England, but the law is not yet abolished. According to the estimates of John R. Spencer,[83] there were at least 24 trials a year before early 1890s. From 1893 to 1914, there were 22 trials a year on average; from 1915 to 1930, 15 cases; and from 1931 to 1938, 19 cases. He found that the number of trials has dropped since 1940. As a common law offense, criminal libel was wider in its scope than the tort. This was because the Defamation Act 1952 broadened the scope of defenses in civil actions and did not apply to criminal libel. For example, the criminal libel defendant could not apply the defenses of unintentional defamation, justification, fair comment, and qualified privilege about certain reports and matters.[84]

In summary, the twentieth century marked a period when libertarian efforts under favorable social and political circumstances generated ongoing debates for changing old libel laws. Because the Sedition Act of 1918 became a means of muzzling political criticism, it drew some opposition. As a result, the United States Supreme Court objected to prior restraint as unconstitutional and gave more breath for political speech.[85]

United States' Departure from the Common Law

In the United States, the final clash between the traditional law of defamation and the First Amendment occurred in *New York Times v Sullivan*.[86] Political and social conditions surrounding the *New York Times* case prompted the United States Supreme Court departure from the common law of defamation.[87]

The case involved twentieth century segregationists who wanted to use Alabama state libel laws to muzzle criticism and discussion of segregationists' opposition to racial integration. The United States Supreme Court held that the First Amendment "prohibits a public official from recovering damages for a defamatory falsehood relating to his official conduct unless he proves that the statement was made with 'actual malice' -- that is, with knowledge that it was false or with reckless disregard of whether it was false or not."[88] Justice William N. Brennan suggested that the payment of huge damages would chill speech just as much as going to jail for criminal libel. Anthony Lewis, a free speech journalist, wrote that the actual malice rule is considered "rooted in our [the United States] historical antipathy to seditious libel."[89] The United States Supreme Court in *New York Times* found the common law of defamation as it was applied then was comparable to seditious libel. The Court accepted that one could not neatly distinguish criminal or seditious libel laws from their civil law counterparts when political information was in issue. As Justice Brennan put it, "Although the Sedition Act was never tested in this Court, the attack upon its validity has carried the day in the court of history."[90]

Because the First Amendment rule in *New York Times* required that the plaintiff prove actual malice "with convincing clarity,"[91] it entailed "sufficient evidence to permit the conclusion that the defendant in fact entertained serious doubts as the truth of his publication."[92] Thus, the *New York Times* ruling departed from the common law principle of strict liability in political defamation cases. The Court extended the "actual malice" standard in *Curtis Publishing Co. v Butts* and its companion case, *Associated Press v Walker* to cover "public figures."[93] Applying the "actual malice" standard to false statements by the press, the Court in *Gertz v Robert Welch, Inc.*[94] held that private libel plaintiffs would have to show at least negligence to recover "actual injuries." But, to collect presumed and punitive damages, the Court held that the First Amendment prohibits states from imposing such liability without a finding of actual malice.[95]

The liberal thought in the United States and changing attitude for equality engineered a break from the old common law of libel to allow more political speech. It was a change that came ahead of Great Britain in prohibiting strict liability in political defamation cases.

England and New Understandings of Criminal Defamation Law

From 1940, the number of criminal libel trials in Britain declined sharply.[96] The House of Lords criticized the scope of criminal libel in *Gleaves v Deakin;*[97] Lord Diplock condemned it as contrary to the European Convention on Human Rights.[98] Thus put, the criminal defamation law was defective. According to the 1985 British Law Commission Report on criminal libel, the grounds for criminal defamation and its civil counterpart overlapped, so that the plaintiff could seek punitive damages in a civil action while the defendant faced prosecution in the criminal courts; yet the defendant in criminal libel was less favorably placed than one in a civil defamation in proving the truth of allegations.[99] Besides, the relevance of a plaintiff's bad character was not admitted as evidence in criminal proceedings.[100] Because of such anomalies in the common law offense of criminal libel, the Law Commission of Great Britain recommended its abolition,[101] or its replacement with a new offense of criminal defamation.[102] The new offense would penalize "anyone who communicates to any person false information seriously defamatory of another knowing or believing that it is seriously defamatory of that other person and that the information is false."[103] The offense would be triable only on indictment, and it would give a maximum penalty of two years' imprisonment and a fine.[104]

Other recommended changes to the traditional criminal offense included the Commission's definition of statements that are "defamatory." According to the Commission, the new offense of criminal defamation would consist of a "[m]atter which in all circumstances would be likely to cause serious damage to the reputation of the person in question in the estimation of reasonable people generally."[105] Though not wide enough to decide the criteria by which statements can damage the victim's reputation in the estimation of reasonable people generally, "the assumptions of this test did not differ from those of the civil law."[106]

According to the recommendations of the Commission, the new offense of criminal defamation would require the prosecution to bear the legal burden of proving that the defendant knew or believed the information at issue to be both false and seriously defamatory.[107] Also, the procedural provisions would permit the defendant to use the defenses of absolute privilege[108] and qualified privilege[109] just as a defendant could in civil defamation. If the proceedings in the new criminal offense are similar to those in civil libel of Great Britain, the offense that the criminal defamation law addresses could also be prosecuted in the civil court. In this vein, criminal libel would lose its central meaning in Britain where democratic self-government no longer rests on the institutional monarchy but derives its governmental legitimacy from the consent of the public who should enjoy active political participation as their civil right.[110] So, free political speech demands that citizens who unintentionally err in exercising their civil right must be subject to a civil prosecution, not a criminal one.

The proposed common law offense of criminal defamation was protective of individual reputation to the detriment of free political speech. It could punish an honest error.[111] However, the new offense of criminal defamation law sought a remedy for factual error and intentional defamation. It was a move to protect public interest in criticism of governmental behavior and political activities. So, the new criminal offense shifted the burden of proof from the defendant as in the *New York Times* rule of actual malice. Also, the new criminal offense narrowed the libel law as it restricted the offense to falsity of the statements and serious damage to the victim's reputation.[112] However, it did not bear the *New York Times* implication for abolishing strict liability in legitimate political speech.

The United Kingdom and 1990s Inroads at Convergence

In the 1990s, the United Kingdom judicial interpretation of a qualified privilege test in cases involving political defamation at the Appeal Court and the House of Lords suggested some liberal developments in the common law privilege. The House of Lords in the *Derbyshire* case[113] recognized the importance of public interest in free political speech in situations where the defamatory statements were published in good faith.

Derbyshire local authority alleged that the Sunday Times Newspaper's article about the corporation's investment and control of its pension fund defamed the corporation. The House of Lords decided whether a local authority, as an organ of government, could sue for libel.[114] Lord Keith argued that it would be against the public interest, and would place an undesirable burden on freedom of speech to allow governmental organs to sue.[115] Also, "It is of the highest public importance that a democratically elected governmental body, or indeed any governmental body, should be open to uninhibited public criticism."[116]

The United States' jurisprudence influenced the *Derbyshire* decision by stating that governmental institutions cannot sue and that the common law requirement that defendants prove the truth of allegations of libel exercised an undesirable "chilling effect" on free speech. This was demonstrated in the House of Lords' reference to the cases of *New York Times* and *City of Chicago v Tribune Co.*[117] However, the law lords refused to consider the appropriateness of the actual malice defense. Neither did the lords approve incorporating the cases into the law of the United Kingdom. According to the reasoning of Lord Keith, "While these decisions were related most directly to the provisions of the American Constitution concerned with securing freedom of speech, the public interest considerations which underlaid them are no less valid in this country."[118] In any case, *Derbyshire* was a landmark decision because, until then, the courts of the United Kingdom had not adopted the United States' rules that restrict the circumstances in which government agencies could succeed in a defamation action.[119]

The *Derbyshire* decision was reflected in *Reynolds v Times Newspapers*.[120] In *Reynolds*, the plaintiff, an elected politician brought an action of defamation against Times Newspapers and others for defamatory words relating to his public role rather than his private or personal life. The plaintiff lost the trial and appealed for a retrial at the Court of Appeal, and the defendants cross-appealed. However, the defendants lost the cross-appeal that contended that qualified privilege protected a publication to the public at large. They lost because they failed in one of the three tests that Lord Bingham of Cornhill, Chief Justice, outlined as the criteria by which the news media can succeed in claiming qualified privilege:

(1) whether the publisher was under a legal, moral or social duty to those to whom the material was published [the duty

test]; (2) whether those to whom the material was published had an interest to receive the material [the interest test]; (3) whether the nature, status and source of the material, and the circumstances of the publication, were such that the publication should in the public interest be protected in the absence of proof of express malice [the circumstantial test]. [121]

Applying the principles to *Reynolds*, the Appeal Court decided that Times Newspapers had a duty to inform the public, and so it satisfied the duty test.   The Court argued that the publications of the circumstances in which the government of Reynolds, a former Irish Prime Minister, had fallen from power were matters of public interest in Great Britain. [122]   For an occasion to merit qualified privilege in Great Britain, the disseminator of a libel must have a legal, social or moral duty to publish the information to an audience that has a corresponding duty to receive it. [123]   This duty principle indicates that political speech is protected because a representative government involves open discussion and debate of political affairs.   However, the defense recognizes that political communication must be a reciprocal duty.   In addition, the principle gives protection, though limited, to political defamation because of the public interest in the stewardship role of public figures.   In this vein, the defense is not far from the Meiklejohn's idea of "informed consent."   Meiklejohn argued that the legitimacy of government in a representative democracy requires that the electorate exercise "informed consent" when casting their votes or evaluating the appropriateness of politicians' behavior. [124]

The interest test was also met since the public had a corresponding interest to receive the information. [125]   In a similar vein, the public interest test has been used also in the United States Supreme Court for *Dun & Bradstreet, Inc. v Greenmoss Builders, Inc.* [126]   The Supreme Court of the United States ruled that Dun & Bradstreet, a credit reporting agency, which falsely reported and grossly misrepresented Greenmoss Builders' assets and liabilities, had to pay damages.   The Supreme Court held that the agency's false and defamatory credit reporting was an individual interest involving no public issue or concern.   Therefore, the Court decided that "permitting recovery of presumed and punitive damages in defamation cases absent a showing of 'actual malice' does not violate the First Amendment when defamatory statements do not involve matters of public concern." [127]

About the circumstantial test in *Reynolds*, the British Appeal Court held that Times Newspapers' publication failed the test, given "the nature, status and source"[128] of Times Newspapers' information, and all the circumstances of the publication. This test is close to the reckless disregard for the truth in the *New York Times* test. For example, the United States Supreme Court in *Curtis Publishing Co. v Butts*[129] decided for Butts, because the Saturday Evening Post published an article that involved a severe departure from accepted journalistic standards.[130]

Similarly, in the opinion of the Appeal Court in *Reynolds*, the Times Newspapers were negligent in the source attribution and in checking credibility of the source. The court considered it irresponsible for Times Newspapers to judge the statement of a political opponent as an authoritative source for a serious factual allegation.[131] Other reasons of Times Newspapers' negligence included that: they had reasonable time to investigate allegations, but failed to do so; they failed to record Reynolds' own account of his conduct in their report; they did not alert Reynolds to their highly damaging allegations, and knowingly misled the Irish Parliament to get information; they failed to resolve whether Reynolds was a victim of circumstance, as conveyed to Irish readers in one article, or a devious liar, as conveyed in another article to readers in the British mainland.[132] The court believed that Reynolds could not be both.[133] For these reasons, the court ordered a retrial of the case.

On the one hand, the United States Supreme Court decision in the *New York Times* used First Amendment considerations about the plaintiff's status as a public official and the nature of the information at issue. Also, government and public figures in the United States, must expect "vehement, caustic, and sometimes unpleasantly sharp attacks" on them in debates on public issues. They are further required to meet a higher burden of proof than "private figures" to prevail in a libel action. The United Kingdom, on the other hand, relied heavily on public interest considerations and less on the status of the plaintiff. So, defamation law in the United Kingdom, unlike the test in the United States, fails to distinguish "political" libel from a "private" one on the basis of plaintiff's status.

While allowing newspapers to criticize freely governmental policy and activities, the qualified privilege standard requires the press and citizens to separate what is public from the personal and truth from falsehood. In this vein, whether it is for the common convenience in the United Kingdom or free interchange of ideas for democratic self-governance, both countries concur that speech concerning public interest should be paramount. Unlike the United States, the United Kingdom gives little special protection in political defamation cases.

POLITICAL DEFAMATION IN THE ECHR AND ITS RELATIONSHIP WITH THE OTHER JURISDICTIONS

The historical background to the institution and jurisprudence of ECHR is essential for understanding its standard of political defamation. The Court's historical foundation shapes its purpose, principles and approach to free political speech. Its history determines the impact and level of the Court's relationships with the United Kingdom, the United States and Australia.

After the Second World War, European leaders created the Council of Europe. From the experience of the war, the Council of Europe was concerned with rule of law and European unity. The European leaders believed "that as long as human rights are respected democracy is secure and the danger of dictatorship are the gradual suppression of individual rights ... and that once this process has started it is increasingly difficult to bring it to a halt."[134] Thus, the Council wanted to establish a mechanism that would ensure respect of human rights and prevent recurrence of dictatorship in Western Europe. In May 1948, a Congress of Europe met at Hague, the Netherlands, with delegates from sixteen European countries and observers from ten others.[135] The delegates adopted a resolution calling for a Charter of Human Rights and a Court of Justice with authority to implement the Charter.[136] A draft of European Convention on Human Rights and a draft statute for a European Court were prepared by Pierre-Henri Teitgen (former French Minister of Justice), Sir David Maxwell-Fyfe (later Lord Chancellor Kilmuir) and Professor Fernand Dehousse (later President of the Consultative Assembly).[137] The draft was submitted to the Committee of Ministers of the Council of Europe in July 1949. In August 1950, the Committee of Ministers substantially accepted a revised text of the draft. The Convention was ratified in 1950 by eight countries,[138] and its Court sits in Strasbourg. The Convention came into force in September 1953. The Court began its role in 1959 when its first judges were appointed. The European Convention on Human Rights became an offshoot of the Council.[139] Forty-one European countries, as of November 2000, had ratified the Convention and consented to its control mechanism.[140] The European Convention on Human Rights was therefore

[C]onceived as a bulwark against totalitarianism and the atrocities committed by the fascist regimes in Europe in the 1930s and 1940s. As such, it provides protection against bad-faith abuse of governmental power ... [and] provides a second level of protection: against limitations on liberty of the community with a legitimate objective but which nevertheless places a proportionate or unfair burden on the individual concerned.[141]

The Convention contains only civil and political rights. It provides for human rights obligations that are legally enforced through an international treaty. About enforceability of the Convention's provisions, "Member-states are required by international law to honor the decisions of the European Court of Human Rights and eventually to implement those decisions under domestic law and practice."[142]

To keep its proper role in relation to member states of the Convention, the Court has developed a set of principles to review cases referred to it.[143] It has now built an important body of precedents that reflects its jurisprudence, for example, on political defamation. The Court's jurisprudential approach is often characterized as:

An evolutive interpretation [that] allows variable and changing concepts already contained in the Convention to be construed in the light of the modern-day conditions ..., but it does not allow entirely new concepts or spheres of application to be introduced into the Convention: that is a legislative function that belongs to the Member States of the Council of Europe.[144]

By doing so, the Strasbourg judges enforce obligations that are expressly stated or are implicit in the provisions of the Convention by following some doctrines in a balancing test. Article 10 of the Convention is a freedom of expression provision.[145] Under this article, the Court has developed doctrines that help it to determine whether: the interference with the freedom of expression corresponded to a "pressing social need;" the member state had reasons "relevant and sufficient" to outweigh the public interest in freedom of expression; the interference was "proportionate to the legitimate aim pursued" under Section Two of Article 10 (deciding whether a restriction upon a non-absolute right is permissible); the interference was "within the margin of appreciation" accorded the member state in assessing Convention rights and the necessity of interference with those rights to achieve legitimate objects "prescribed by law" in a manner consistent with "necessity in a democratic society."[146]

ECHR emphasizes freedom of expression as an indispensable means of attaining a democratic society.[147] Over the years, decisions of ECHR, mostly involving criminal libel, have shown the inhibiting effect of defamation law on political speech. For example, in *Lingens v Austria*, a journalist wrote an article that criticized the then Austrian Chancellor, Bruno Kreisky. The Court scrutinized the contents of the criticisms, their purpose, contexts and the requirements under Austrian national law. The Court said that political speech is at the core of the concept of democratic society, which is included in the Convention, and the press plays a special role in that regard. Also, the Court distinguished politicians from nonpoliticians in libel law. It held:

> The limits of acceptable criticism are accordingly wider as regards a politician as such than as regards a private individual … [T]he former inevitably and knowingly lays himself open to close scrutiny of his every word and deed by both journalists and the public at large, and he must consequently display a greater degree of tolerance.[148]

Similarly, ECHR granted the highest protection to political speech in *Castells v Spain*,[149] where Castells complained that his conviction for defaming the government was a violation of freedom of expression. The Court held that the limits of criticism were wider regarding the government than a private citizen or a politician.

In its case law, ECHR argues from the principle of democracy as its basis for protecting free speech. The Court strongly recognizes this rationale and is highly protective of the criteria of "necessity in a democratic society" in assessing a member state's justification for restricting political speech.[150]

Interaction of ECHR with the United Kingdom

While the Convention requires that all restrictions on freedom of speech should only be such as are "necessary in a democratic society," the United Kingdom rejects the principle that political speech should be specially privileged.[151] So, for the United Kingdom to retain strict liability in political defamation contradicts this Convention requirement.[152]

From February 1975 through June 1996, the United Kingdom was found 41 times to have violated the European Convention on Human Rights, over one-third of which concerned freedom of expression.[153] One would attribute such failings of the United Kingdom to lack of a Bill of Rights and absence of a constitutional judicial review such as found in the United States. Though there is a judicial review procedure in the United Kingdom, its content is quite different. In the United Kingdom, the judicial review practice refers to the process by which those aggrieved by actions of public authorities may challenge those authorities in the High Court because the authorities have abused or exceeded their legal powers.[154] In this way, the British "[j]udicial review is concerned not with the decision, but with the decision making procedure."[155]

Until recently when the United Kingdom incorporated fully the Convention rights into English domestic law, the United Kingdom believed that "treaties and domestic law are distinct legal entities, and that treaties do not become directly binding on the domestic legal order unless Parliament passes enabling legislation that specifically makes it so."[156] As a result:

> [U]sually even a clear violation of the European Court of Human Rights has no remedy in British courts. There have been a few instances in which British courts have found support for rights in the common law, but usually the only resort has been an application ... to the European Court of Human Rights. [In fact] decisions of ... the European Court of Human Rights are binding on the United Kingdom as international treaty obligations.[157]

Before the United Kingdom adopted the European Convention jurisprudence through the Human Rights Act 1998, some observers concluded that ECHR already had a great impact on the United Kingdom. As the editorial of the launch issue of *European Human Rights Law Review* noted:

> The influence of the Convention on the law of the United Kingdom is nowadays undeniable. A growing list of remedial statutes owe their origins directly to the European Court of Human Rights. The Law Commission has begun to use conformity with the Convention as one of its key criteria for assessing current and proposed legislation. And the European Court of Justice has held that the Convention is an implicit part of Community law. Within the sphere of Community competence at least, the Convention now has a form of direct applicability in the domestic courts of this country [the United Kingdom].[158]

The *Derbyshire* decision was also an important development about the impact of ECHR on English common law. Lord Keith and the four Lords of the House held unanimously that English common law embraces a right to freedom of expression and of the press. Lord Keith commented that he reached his conclusion "upon the common law of England without finding any need to rely on the European Convention."[159]   However, John Gardner's essay on *Freedom of Expression* disputed Lord Keith's claim, arguing that there is no such thing as a general legal right to freedom of expression in English domestic law.[160]

Despite one's doubts about the accuracy of Lord Keith's conclusion that English courts have found human rights under the common law, rather than under ECHR, the *Derbyshire* decision anticipated the adoption of the European Convention as part of United Kingdom domestic law. Progressing in the effort, the law lords passed the Human Rights Bill on February 6, 1998, and it was introduced into the House of Commons as the Human Rights Act 1998. The act, which took effect in October 2000, allows English courts to use the Convention and its case law in the determination of disputes that raise questions of violation of Convention rights.[161]   The act requires judges to review legislation and public acts in such a way that they be compatible with the Convention, particularly as provided in Clauses Three and Seven of the Human Rights Bill.[162]   The government white paper accompanying the Human Rights Bill clarified the intention behind the act. It said, the Bill provided, that legislative interpretation be compatible with the Convention. So the Human Rights document

> [G]oes far beyond the present rule which enables the courts to take the Convention into account in resolving any ambiguity in a legislative provision. The courts will be required to interpret legislation so as to uphold the Convention rights unless the legislation itself is so clearly incompatible with the Convention that it is impossible to do so.[163]

The incorporation can bridge Convention requirements and the United Kingdom law.[164] However, the Human Rights Act reserves for the United Kingdom the right of margin of appreciation under the Convention.[165] According to Article 2(1)(a) of the Human Rights Act 1998, legal arguments by lawyers before English courts and judgments of the courts "must take into account" any relevant judgment, decision, declaration or advisory opinions of the ECHR.[166] But, the courts are not bound by the jurisprudence and decisions of the ECHR and the European Court of Human Rights. As the Lord Chancellor explained the intention behind the expression "must take into account:"

> We believe that Clause 2 gets it right in requiring domestic courts to take into account judgments of the European Court but not making them binding ... The Bill would ... permit United Kingdom courts to depart from existing Strasbourg decisions and upon occasion it might well be appropriate to do so and it is possible they might give a successful lead to Strasbourg. For example, it would permit the United Kingdom courts to depart from Strasbourg decisions where there has been no precise ruling on the matter ... [W]here it is relevant we would ... expect our courts to apply convention jurisprudence and its principles to the cases before them.[167]

Lord Irvin also clarified the intention behind the Article. He said, "The United Kingdom is not ... bound in international law to follow the court's judgments in cases to which it has not been a party and it would be strange to require courts in the United Kingdom to be bound by such decisions."[168]

However narrow the interpretation of qualified privilege by the majority, the House of Lords' October 1999 decision, *Reynolds v Times Newspapers Ltd.* [HL], anticipated the European Convention's impact on freedom of expression in English law:

> [T]he court is required, in relevant cases, to have particular regard to the importance of the right to freedom of expression. The common law is to be developed and applied in a manner consistent with art[icle] 10 of the European Convention for the Protection of Human Rights and Fundamental Freedom ...and the court must take into account relevant decisions of the European Court of Human Rights ...[169]

Unlike the common law defenses available to defendants under English law, the respondent at ECHR has only to prove that a pressing social need motivated the interference of the political speech. Also, the respondent must justify that the need outweighed public interest in freedom of expression, and that the objective for the interference was prescribed by law that is necessary in a democratic society.[170]

For the common law to develop political defamation jurisprudence along ECHR lines, it must accept the vital public role of the press in self-governance, recognize a wider protection for political speech, and allow greater criticism of politicians than of private individuals. To this effect, the Human Rights Act which recently incorporated the European convention provisions into the domestic legal system of the United Kingdom also makes the ECHR an integral part of the United Kingdom jurisprudence. So, as the United Kingdom departs from the traditional rules of statutory interpretation and accepts the convention provisions and jurisprudence, one can say that the jurisprudence of both the United Kingdom and the ECHR are converging.

Differences between ECHR and the United States Defamation Law

ECHR has more in common with the United States jurisprudence on political defamation than differences, but the two regimes have different historical foundations. Defamation law in the United States originated from the English common law. But, distrust of government influenced the United States to develop the First Amendment case law that in 1964 helped it depart from the common law.[171] On the other hand, the case law of political libel in ECHR is founded on transnational law. It was born in the aftermath of the Second World War to check member states from reneging on their acceptance of the Convention obligations, and turning into non-democratic regimes.[172]

The historical differences aside, the balancing test for political defamation case law in ECHR and the actual malice standard of the United States differ. However, both jurisdictions agree that government and politicians must expect that debate on public issues "may include vehement, caustic, and sometimes unpleasantly sharp attacks" on them.[173] Though the tests are different, the ECHR criteria of "necessity in a democratic society" is similar to the actual malice standard of the United States in relation to decisions on free speech matters. Both regimes make distinctions about the status of the defamed person and the nature of the defamatory statements.[174] While ECHR distinguishes between government or politicians and private persons, the actual malice rule is wider as it requires the same burden from public figures as government and politicians. Also, both protect public interest in political speech because of its value in democratic self-governance. Additionally, they believe that protection of political speech has value for self-fulfillment, and it promotes the free interchange of ideas.

The judicial review system in the Supreme Court of the United States is essentially similar to ECHR which has the ultimate power of decision about human rights cases originating in member states.[175] The judicial review role and, therefore, decisions that the judges of the Court make are comparable to those of the justices of the United States Supreme Court.[176]

Though their historical differences may set them apart, ECHR and the United States defamation laws converge on their liberal positions. They are similar in the judicial review systems. They also concur in securing the public interest in the protection of free political speech. The jurisprudence of both regimes appears press-friendly, and they distinguish types of defamatory statements and status of the defamed.

DEFAMATION LAW OF AUSTRALIA AS IT RELATES TO THE OTHER JURISDICTIONS

Prior to the United States Supreme Court "actual malice" rule in 1964, the libel laws of the United States and Australia shared the English common law. Because defamation law in the countries developed along separate paths after the United States's 1964 ruling, this part of the historical analysis is broken into two parts. The first analyzes the development of Australian defamation law as it relates to the United Kingdom and the United States until the 1980s. The second section considers their differences in the 1990s, and shows how recent Australian jurisprudence of qualified political defamation borrows some concepts from ECHR.

Development of Australian Defamation Law

Like the United States, the territories occupied by Australia were inhabited originally by aboriginal peoples, and European settlers took control of them. Immigrants from England, Spain and France settled in the United States in the 1600s and 1700s. As the French settlers were later integrated into the mainly Anglophone culture, most of them adopted English as their primary language. Similarly, England colonized Australia in the 1700s; however Australia served as a continent where European outcasts and prisoners could be sent.[177]

Through a revolution, the United States declared its independence from England in 1776, ratified its Constitution in 1789, and its Bill of Rights became effective in 1791. The provision of the First Amendment became the constitutional basis for free speech protections. In contrast, Australia peacefully gained its independence; the *Commonwealth of Australia Constitution Act* was passed by the British Parliament in 1900.[178] The Constitution came into force in January 1901. Nonetheless, Australia kept constitutional links with the British monarchy and is part of the British Commonwealth, a relationship an Australian referendum of November 1999 retained.[179]

In terms of legal culture, Australia and the United States inherited the English common law when each was colonized. Australian courts loyally followed English legal authorities. Since the 1980s, Australia has moved toward a distinctive understanding of the common law, particularly about qualified privilege, while maintaining English case law as a major source of persuasive authority.[180] Thus, Australian courts remained with the United Kingdom, in contrast to the United States, because "all the common law and statute law which existed in

England ... was treated as being the law of the colony [Australia]."[181] The United States courts, on the other hand, cite English precedents occasionally but not in political defamation.[182]

The Australian judicial system is similar to that of the United States, having lower and higher courts at the state and federal levels. The High Court of Australia functions as an equivalent of the United States Supreme Court.[183] Despite this structural similarity, the constitutional and statutory modifications of the common law underline the major differences between the United States and Australian defamation laws. Like the United Kingdom, Australia does not have explicitly written constitutional guarantees of free speech and freedom of the press.[184] So free political speech was not protected in defamation law. As the Australian Privy Council said in 1936: "Free speech does not mean free speech; it means speech hedged in by all the laws against defamation, blasphemy, sedition and so forth."[185] The United States Constitution, in contrast, has these guarantees under the First Amendment: Congress shall make no law ... abridging the freedom of speech, or of the press.[186]

The constitutional protection provided in the First Amendment marks a major contrast between Australian common law libel and the American actual malice rule. For, Australia has no equivalent provision to the First Amendment, either as a matter of federal or state constitutional or statutory law.[187] From the 1960s, the two countries have differed in how to strike a balance between the value of protecting a person's reputation and the value of freedom of expression. The case law and scholarly writings on political defamation in both countries show that Australian courts placed more emphasis on protecting reputation,[188] while American courts were more concerned with protecting freedom of expression.[189]

Now, the United States' political libel doctrine tilts the balance in favor of free political speech over individual reputation, especially when the criticism concerns public officials and their official actions. According to Smolla, the backbone of *New York Times* "is that, when the plaintiff is a public official using the common law of libel in a case arising from the discussion of the official's performance in or fitness for office, the common law is being used to effectuate governmental policy and to chill dissent."[190] Following English common law,

Australian jurisprudence keeps strict liability in political defamation.[191] In contrast, as a result of the *New York Times* decision, strict liability in political defamation ceased in the United States. In the United States, public figure plaintiffs have to prove "knowing falsity or reckless disregard of the truth." In Australia, the plaintiff has to prove that the publication was actuated by common law malice in government and political matters. But, while the United States emphasizes a distinction of status of persons, Australia emphasizes only the type of speech.

Both countries accept common law defenses like absolute privilege, qualified privilege, fair comment or justification.[192] While in Australia truth is a defense that must be raised by the defendant and on which he has the burden of proof, the position is different in the United States because of a formal shift that began in *New York Times*. In this regard, the media in the United States are more protected than their counterparts in England and Australia as defendants in libel cases.

Both Australia and the United States accept the defense of fair comment in libel cases, but they handle the defense differently. Whereas the defense of fair comment is of central importance to defendants in Australia,[193] the application of the First Amendment makes it almost irrelevant in the United States.[194] In Australia, the defendant must prove that the comment was on a matter of public interest,[195] that it was fair,[196] that the words complained of were comment rather than statement of fact[197] and were not made with express malice.[198] In the United States, fair comment protects "the honest expression of the communicator's opinion on a matter of public interest based upon facts correctly stated in the communication."[199] However, if the comment is based on a major factual error, the defense would fail in most states "unless the factual basis for the opinion is disclosed with it or generally known to the audience."[200] Additionally, the defense of fair comment has become unnecessary in the United States because the wide scope of the actual malice rule protects untrue statements of fact and comment. Fair comment was absorbed into "opinion" when the United States Supreme Court in *Milkovich v Lorain Journal* decided not to require a different privilege from the actual malice rule for opinion involving allegedly defamatory statements.[201] This makes the United States more liberal than Australia in relation to defenses in defamation cases.

Each country handles the qualified privilege defense differently. In Australia, qualified privilege protects a defendant from liability only if he or she acts in good faith and without improper motive, and if society's interest in having the communication made outweighs the possibility of it turning out to be wrong.[202] In both Australia and the United States, qualified privilege defense, also known as the "fair report" defense, protects defendants from liability for reports on official proceedings of governmental bodies and sometimes for reports based on records produced by those bodies if the reports are accurate, fair or balanced, substantially complete and not motivated by malice.[203]

Unlike the United Kingdom, Australia and the United States have similar federal systems. But, divergences between common law and "code" states in Australia further complicate its defamation law.[204] The Code States, for example, Queensland, Tasmania (in 1895),[205] and West Australia (in 1902)[206] adopted the Queensland Defamation Law of 1889.[207] The *Queensland Code* provisions were also in force in New South Wales from 1958 to 1974.[208] New South Wales, however, perceived the Code provisions as unsatisfactory. Under the *Queensland Code*, statutes modify the common law defenses of truth and qualified privilege.[209] While at common law, truth is a defense in libel suits, under the *Queensland Code* true defamatory statements are protected only when they are made for the public benefit.[210] Also, reciprocity of interest and duty is not required under the Code as under common law. So, under the Code, public interest alone or the media's duty alone suffices for the defense.[211] According to a Melbourne media law attorney, Anthony Smith, the media have not successfully raised the defense of qualified privilege since the 1960s, partly because the common law did not recognize the press as having sufficient reciprocal duty and interest relationship with its readers to support qualified privilege.[212] Thus, publication in a newspaper was considered excessive and the occasion of publication not protected by qualified privilege, unless the publication was a rejoinder to or correction of previously published information.[213]

As a result of its dissatisfaction with the Code provisions, the New South Wales Law Reform Commission in 1968 issued a discussion paper on defamation to the state Parliament and some legal scholars.[214] The Commission made recommendations in a report on defamation reform,[215] which later led to the passage of the state's *Defamation Act 1974*.[216] The Act abolished the Code provisions that applied to both civil and criminal liabilities for defamation.[217] For example, qualified privilege under Section 22 of the Act provided greater freedom to publish material in New South Wales that involved matters of public concern.[218] Defendants could use the defense where the recipient had an interest in receiving the information, the publication was made in the course of giving information, and the conduct of the defendant was reasonable in the circumstances. However, the defense would not apply if the plaintiff proved that the defendant was motivated by malice, unless the defendant showed that the imputation was substantially true.[219]

New South Wales was not alone in attempts at reforming defamation law in the 1970s. The Law Reform Committee of South Australia also issued a report on defamation in 1972, although the law in that state has not changed as a result.[220] The Western Australia Law Reform Commission, too, issued a working paper in 1969[221] that produced reports in 1972[222] and 1979.[223] Considering the developments, the Commonwealth Attorney General R. J. Ellicott, in 1976 called on the Australian Law Reform Commission to consider a national defamation law. In response, delegates at the Australian Constitutional Convention that year voted in favor of national defamation legislation.[224] These actions led to three discussion papers issued by the Australian Law Reform Commission in 1977[225] and a report on reform in 1979.[226] The 1979 report of the Commission drew attention to lack of uniformity in Australian defamation laws. It said, in addition, that the different laws do not protect either the interest of plaintiff or defendant, and the laws are archaic.[227] Consequently, the Australian Law Reform Commission proposed ways in which Federal Parliament could enact laws under the Australian Constitution, but it expressed doubt about the precise scope of Commonwealth power in that regard.[228]

In defamation cases, the High Court of Australian has original jurisdiction under Sections 75-76 of the Constitution in matters involving constitutional interpretation, or in which the Commonwealth is a party, or in actions between residents of different States, or between a State and a resident of another State.[229] Also, the *Judiciary Act of 1903*, Section 79, makes the laws of each State binding in federal courts, except in matters which the Constitution or the Commonwealth has provided otherwise. This indicates "that the High Court when sitting in a particular jurisdiction applies the law of that jurisdiction including its conflict of laws rules."[230] Considering these constitutional difficulties, the proposal of the Australian Law Reform Commission failed to achieve an enactment of uniform defamation laws.[231]

The diversity in the laws of defamation among the various Australian jurisdictions caused problems in cases of interstate defamation.[232] *Renouf v Federal Capital Press*[233] was a typical case that exposes the difficulties. The Federal Capital Press was sued in the Australian Capital Territory concerning an article published in all eight Australian jurisdictions. The Federal Capital Press was held liable in every jurisdiction, except New South Wales where the law of defamation gave a partial defense. About this, Justice Blackburn said: "The result, presumably, is that the total effect of the article is less defamatory in New South Wales than in the Territory. This anomaly does not surprise me; the interstate diversity of the law of defamation is a matter of familiar dismay in this court."[234]

Since the late 1960s, the United States jurisprudence on political defamation has become a challenge for reform in Australia.[235] However, many influential advocates for reform in Australian defamation law objected to the actual malice type of free speech protection. As John G. Fleming wrote in his treatise on Australian tort law, "In contrast to American law, our own has steadfastly declined to sacrifice individual reputation to recurrent demands by the press for privileged dissemination of so-called 'news.'"[236] Those in Australia who shared Fleming's view, believed that requiring defamation plaintiffs who are public figures to show a higher burden of proof would disturb the proper balance between protecting reputations from false statements and promoting speech. In light of such arguments against the adoption of the actual malice test for public figures, the Australian Law Reform Commission explained the rationale for protecting reputational interests of public figures. The Commission declared:

> [I]t is wrong in principle to deny legal protection to persons who are prominent in public affairs simply because of that fact. Persons in public life necessarily expose themselves to public criticism. They generally accept comment which would be deeply resented by a private citizen. They accept public interest in their activities and considerable interference with their home life and leisure pursuits. Nonetheless there is a point at which any person, however prominent in public

affairs, is entitled to protection against defamatory statements and the retailing of private information which has no relationship to those public affairs. The American experience has not been satisfactory ....[237]

Notwithstanding, critics of the Australian defamation law believed that it restrained media speech and prevented a free and full discussion of matters of public interest.[238] The debates bore fruit in a way in the 1990s.

Australian Defamation Law: Relationship with the United Kingdom and the United States in the 1990s

Just as prior to *New York Times*, the United States did not apply the First Amendment to the defamation laws of its states, divergences of defamation law existed in Australia before the High Court ruling in *Australian Capital Television Pty Ltd v Commonwealth of Australia*[239] and *Nationwide News Pty Ltd v Wills*.[240] Defamation law in Australia was modified when the High Court extracted from the structure and provisions of the Australian Constitution an implied protection for free political speech. The Court found that, because the Commonwealth Constitution provides for a system of representative government, the Constitution implies a guarantee of freedom of political communication. This holding about implied constitutional mechanism brought uniformity in protecting freedom of speech on government and political matters.

The decisions of *Australian Capital Television* and *Nationwide News* created the constitutional and political path for change. Afterwards, the High Court of Australia considered adopting the actual malice standard but decided against it.[241] In *Theophanous v The Herald and Weekly Times Limited*, the majority of the High Court took the view that the "actual malice" test in *New York Times v Sullivan* "tilts the balance unduly in favor of free speech against the protection of individual reputation."[242] Other reasons for the High Court's rejection of the public figure test were that: the decisions following *New York Times* expanded the privilege to publish false statements, the United States Supreme Court further extended it to candidates for public office and government employees who are in a position significantly to influence the resolution of public issues, and still further extended it to cover "public figures" who do not hold official or government positions.[243] While the plaintiff bore the burden of proving falsity in the United States as a result of the *New York Times* decision, the defendant in Australia bore this burden until the 1994 *Theophanous* defense, and the new extended common law qualified privilege defense under *Lange*.

Theophanous and its companion case *Stephens v West Australian Newspapers Ltd*[244] held that the implied freedom of communication decided in *Australian Capital Television* and *Nationwide News* applied to communication on political matters. *Theophanous* and *Stephens* created a constitutional defense that applied where the defamatory publication concerned a matter of political discussion which included discussion of the conduct, policies or fitness of office of government, political parties, public bodies, public officers and suitability of candidates seeking public office, discussion of political views and public conduct of people whose activities have become the subject of political debate.[245] Such publication would be protected from liability in defamation provided the publisher established that "it was unaware of the falsity of the material published," that "it did not publish the material recklessly, that is, not caring whether the material was true or false," and that "the publication was reasonable in the circumstances."[246] The defense was applied in all Australian jurisdictions, whether the basis of defamation law in that jurisdiction was common law or statute. Moreover, the decisions of the High Court expanded "duty-interest" in common law qualified privilege to protect a publisher who published defamatory material to the public in general in the course of political discussion.[247] The Court held that defamation in the course of discussing political matters in a newspaper would satisfy the reciprocal duty and interest relationship between a newspaper and its readers. This relationship would be an occasion of extended qualified privilege because "[t]he public at large has an interest in the discussion of political matters such that each and every person has an interest, of the kind contemplated by the common law, in communicating his or her views on those matters and each and every person has an interest in receiving information on those matters."[248]

Lange v Australian Broadcasting Corporation[249] revisited the two issues the High Court decided in *Theophanous* and *Stephens*: the constitutional defense in defamation law and the extension of qualified privilege. The Court decided unanimously that the constitutional defense created in *Theophanous* was wrong in law. Though the High

Court in *Lange* acknowledged that the freedom of communication of government and political matters is an "indispensable incident" of the system of representative government created by the Constitution,[250] it said that the implied constitutional provisions "do not confer personal rights on individuals."[251]   *Lange* held that there is no specific constitutional guarantee of the right of free communication as *Theophanous* suggested.   However, *Lange* said that freedom of communication can be implied from the structure and text of the Australian Constitution.[252] In answering the second question, the High Court unanimously held that the defense of qualified privilege pleaded about the publication complained of in New South Wales was good in law. According to the Court, "the right to remedy," under common law and the statute law, "cannot be admitted ... if its exercise would infringe upon the freedom to discuss government and political matters which the Constitution impliedly requires."[253]   As *Lange* found that the common law defenses were deficient in providing adequate protection for the implied freedom, it extended the common law qualified privilege defense into a new expanded common law defense of qualified privilege.[254] This Court stated:

> [E]ach member of the Australian community has an interest in disseminating and receiving information, opinions and arguments concerning government and political matters that affect the people of Australia ... The interest that each member of the Australian community has in such a discussion extends the categories of qualified privilege. Consequently, those categories now must be recognized as protecting a communication made to the public on a government or political matter.[255]

The Court accepted the extended qualified privilege in *Theophanous* but added a requirement of reasonableness. *Lange* said that a defendants's conduct will be reasonable if he or she:

> [H]ad reasonable grounds for believing that the imputation was true, took proper steps ... to verify the accuracy of the material and did not believe the imputation to be untrue ... [and] sought a response from the person defamed and published the response made (if any) except in cases where the seeking or publication of a response was not practicable or it

was unnecessary to give the plaintiff an opportunity to respond.[256]

Thus, the Court in *Lange* refined the expanded defense of qualified privilege created by the majority in *Theophanous*. *Lange* established that discussion of government or political matters on the federal, state, or local level can receive protection by satisfying requirements under the new extended qualified privilege.

The Distant Relationship between Australia and ECHR Protection of Political Defamation

Australia, unlike the United Kingdom, which is a member state of the European Convention, has no direct relationship with ECHR. However, Australian courts sometimes find support from precedents in other common law jurisdictions of the British Commonwealth. As Lord Keith of Kinkel argued in *Derbyshire* that there was no difference in principle between English law and the European Convention on Human Rights on the subject of freedom of speech, Australia can take inspiration from ECHR jurisprudence on Article 10 which guarantees the right of freedom of expression.[257]

Australia and ECHR show some similarities in their use of terms for the defense of political speech. Australia seems to have borrowed from ECHR, for example in *Lange*, as the High Court of Australia profusely used expressions found in ECHR jurisprudence on political defamation. The expressions include, "what is necessary for ... system of representative and responsible government"[258] as the basis for free political speech. This resembles what is "necessary in a democratic society" in ECHR.[259] *Lange* also mentioned "reasonably appropriate and adapted to serve a legitimate end ... for the maintenance of ... representative democracy,"[260] which compares with the ECHR principle of "proportionate and legitimate aim pursued."[261]

Another similarity is in the ECHR principle of "limits of acceptable criticism"[262] and the element of "reasonableness" under the Australian High Court's new extended qualified privilege.[263] While the two regimes use these principles to evaluate and protect legitimate criticism, they differ on distinguishing the status of persons. The High Court makes no distinctions about the status of persons, but dwells on the type of speech and its communication in order to protect political discussion. ECHR, on the other hand, emphasizes interest in open discussion of political issues and allows wider criticism as regards government and politicians than as regards a private individual.[264]

CONCLUSION

Social and political conditions that affected the jurisprudential history of the United States, the United Kingdom, and Australia combined with the concepts of representative government and democracy to inspire shifts in constitutional and common law understandings that supported reforms of the countries' defamation laws. The need to protect democracy guided ECHR interpretation of Article 10 of the European Convention on Human Rights to suit the changing times and allow free political discussion while it supervised member states against undesirable and unnecessary fetters on this freedom.

Considering the extent the jurisdictions protected political speech, the United States seemed the most liberal. The ECHR appeared less liberal than the United States but more liberal than Australia. The United Kingdom was least liberal largely because its weighing of interests in political speech and reputation was unpredictable. The jurisprudence of the United States and ECHR are closer in balancing free political speech against individual reputation. They both make distinctions in the type of speech and status of persons. Though Australia does not make status distinctions, its recent decisions have expanded qualified privilege to give more protection to government and political discussion. With the decision of *Derbyshire*, the United Kingdom also gave more protection to political speech. However, subsequent decisions on qualified privilege in the United Kingdom Court of Appeal and the House of Lords did not grant any special protection of political speech. As the United Kingdom has recently incorporated the European Convention into its domestic law, constraints imposed by Article 10 of ECHR should accelerate its convergence with the Court's jurisprudence. Because this chapter linked the past and the present defamation case laws of the four regimes, the next dwells on purposefully sampled cases that reflect prevailing political libel jurisprudence in those jurisdictions.

Chapter Four

Synthesis of Political Speech Cases in the Four Jurisdictions

To establish meaningful relationships in the high courts of the United States, the ECHR, the United Kingdom, and Australia, this study takes an analogical analysis of three purposefully selected cases from each regime as they reflect the current jurisprudence in each jurisdiction.[1] Cases selected for the United States' jurisdiction are *New York Times v Sullivan*,[2] *Gertz v Robert Welch, Inc.*,[3] and *Dun & Bradstreet v Greenmoss*.[4] For the ECHR jurisprudence, *Lingens v Austria*,[5] *Castells v Spain*,[6] and *Bladet Tromso and Stensaas v Norway*[7] are analyzed. *Derbyshire County Council v Times Newspapers Ltd.*,[8] *Reynolds v Times Newspapers Ltd.*,[9] and *Reynolds v Times Newspapers*[10] are cases taken to represent the study of the United Kingdom jurisdiction. Finally, for the case studies of the Australian jurisdiction, *Nationwide News Party Ltd. v Wills*,[11] *Theophanous v Herald & Weekly Times Ltd.*,[12] and *Lange v Australian Broadcasting Corporation*[13] are examined.

The legal analysis looks for critical facts, holdings, reasoning, and any rules articulated in the decisions of the various Courts to enable identifying any common denominator and comparing the regimes. After the case-law analysis of the jurisdiction, cases examined are further subjected to a qualitative content analysis as part of the technique of multiple methods used in the present study. Categories for the qualitative content analysis are "issue," "identity," "interest," "rationale" and "doctrinal approach." These categories are developed to help organize critical facts to reflect various authorities in the different jurisdictions. So, this chapter discusses similarities and differences in critical facts of the jurisdictions.

THE UNITED STATES: THE CONSTITUTIONAL STANDARD OF "ACTUAL MALICE"

As a forerunner in its break from the common law of defamation, the United States Supreme Court decision in *New York Times*[14] established a constitutional test for the protection of freedom of speech. In subsequent cases, the Court followed and interpreted the constitutional test to balance political speech against individual reputation. Analysis of the following United States Supreme Court decisions indicates the Court's controlling opinion on political debate and discussion of matters of public concern.

New York Times v Sullivan

During racial conflict in the American South, demonstrators asked for full implementation of the United States Supreme Court decisions in civil rights cases like *Brown v Board of Education.*[15] Segregationists and state officials in the South resisted, sometimes violently, and sought to silence criticism and discussion of racial integration.[16] Three weeks after Martin Luther King, Jr.'s arrest in Alabama in 1960, the *New York Times* ran an editorial that supported the efforts of the civil right movement, and called on Congress to "heed their rising voices, for they will be heard." This editorial phrase was used later by the *Committee to Defend Martin Luther King* in a full page paid advertisement published in the *New York Times.*[17] L. B. Sullivan, an elected city commissioner in Montgomery, Alabama, in charge of the police, sued the *New York Times* because the advertisement included alleged false statements about police action directed against students who took part in a civil rights action and against Martin Luther King, Jr., the leader of the civil rights movement.[18] Though some of the statements were inaccurate,[19] the advertisement generally mentioned "Southern violators" and did not criticize anyone by name. But, Sullivan claimed that the word "police," as mentioned in a paragraph about Montgomery, referred to him because he supervised the police department.[20] The trial judge instructed the jury to decide whether the statements in the advertisement were "of and concerning" Sullivan; if yes, they should award him compensatory damages. The jury in the trial court awarded Sullivan $500,000 for injury to his reputation, and the Supreme Court of Alabama affirmed.[21] The Alabama Supreme Court said that "[w]here the words published tend to injure a person libeled by them in his reputation, profession, trade, or business, or charge him with an indictable offense," the statements are "libelous per se;" so "the matter complained of ... is libelous per se, if it was published of and concerning the plaintiff."[22] Thus, the Alabama Supreme Court held: "In measuring the performance or deficiencies of [municipal agents], praise or criticism is usually attached to the official in complete control of the body."[23]

However, the United States Supreme Court reversed the decision of the Alabama courts.[24] Justice William Brennan writing the Court opinion, first determined whether public speech on public issues was constitutionally protected. Not satisfied that the defense of truth alone was sufficient to protect freedom of speech, the Court borrowed the conditional privilege of *Coleman v MacLennan*,[25] and merged it with common law doctrine of fair comment,[26] to argue a First Amendment basis for more protection for political speech. The Court restricted a public official's capacity to claim defamation damages for publications that examine the official's political beliefs and behavior. The Court said:

> The constitutional guarantees require ... a federal rule that prohibits a public official from recovering damages for a defamatory falsehood relating to his official conduct unless he proves that the statement was made with "actual malice" -- that is, with knowledge that it was false or with reckless disregard of whether it was false or not.[27]

While holding that the First Amendment protects defamatory falsehoods of the defendants, the Court stressed the "marketplace of ideas" theory of free speech.[28] The Court wrote that the First Amendment guarantees that fear of government related suppression must not hamper the people's ability to check government abuse of power.[29] To this end, the Court found: "The maintenance of the opportunity for free political discussion to the end that government may be responsive to the will of the people and that changes may be obtained by lawful means, an opportunity essential to the security of the Republic, is a fundamental principle of our constitutional system."[30] As a result, the Court explained, the First Amendment embodies "a profound national commitment to the principle that debate on public issues should be uninhibited, robust, and wide open, and that may include vehement, caustic, and sometimes unpleasantly sharp attacks on government and public officials."[31]

Having established that criticism of official conduct is constitutionally protected, the Court next held that libel rules should not restrict the free exercise of public criticism no matter how adversely it affects the reputation of public officials. Justice Brennan drew from the lessons of the Sedition Act of 1798 and viewed political libel action as a way of intimidating the press and citizens into silence. In terms of political communication, he did not find much difference between the effect of criminal libel laws and civil ones. For the First Amendment to ensure more protection for political speech, the Court said that "[e]rroneous statement is inevitable in free debate," and added that "it must be protected if freedoms of speech are to have the 'breathing space' that they 'need ... to survive.'"[32]

Thus, the Court found that the Alabama rule permitting only the defense of truth for public criticism did not give free speech enough breathing space, and the huge damages that libel judgments awarded created self-censorship that discouraged vigorous and free political discussion.[33] Therefore, to safeguard public interests in political speech, Justice Brennan said: "If neither factual error nor defamatory content suffices to remove the constitutional shield from criticism of official conduct, the combination of the two is no less inadequate."[34] As a consequence, the Court formulated a new theory:[35]

> The constitutional guarantees require, we think, a federal rule that prohibits a public official from recovering damages for a defamatory falsehood relating to his official conduct unless he proves that the statement was made with actual malice -- that is, with the knowledge that it was false or with reckless disregard of whether it was false or not.[36]

Moreover, to win a libel suit, the Court said, the public official or politician has to prove actual malice with "convincing clarity," a standard higher than the normal one of preponderance of the evidence in civil actions.[37] Though the Court agreed that the *New York Times* failed to check the facts in the ad against its own files and did not retract, the Court held that those failures did not constitute "actual malice."[38] Further, the Court held that the statements in the ad were not a personal attack on Sullivan, and so the Court could not find the libelous publication to be "of and concerning" Sullivan.[39] In effect, the Court also upheld the well-established rule that impersonal criticism of governmental agencies can never be considered defamatory of the public official in charge of them.[40]

The actual malice standard established in *New York Times* demonstrated a willingness to pay a price for free expression. As Kalven said: "Speech has a price. It is a liberal weakness to discount so heavily the price. It is not always a 'witchhunt,' it is not always correct to win by showing danger has been exaggerated."[41] However, the standard did not protect knowing falsehood. If a newspaper knowingly disseminates lies, it does not serve any useful public purpose but undermines the basis of informed consent on which the democratic process is built.[42] A later Supreme Court decision clarified that the showing of reckless disregard of truth or falsity requires that the statements be made with a high degree of awareness of their probable falsity.[43] In a still further explanation, the Court held in *St. Amant v Thompson*[44] that:

[R]eckless conduct is not measured by whether a reasonably prudent man would have published or would have investigated before publishing. There must be sufficient evidence to permit the conclusion that the defendant in fact entertained serious doubts as to the truth of his publication. Publishing with such doubts shows reckless disregard for truth or falsity and demonstrates actual malice.[45]

Also, the Supreme Court's new constitutional standard created in the *New York Times* rejected the "clear and present danger" test, the "balancing" test, and the absolutist stance of Justices Black, Douglas and Goldberg.[46] Nevertheless, as the Court in *New York Times* applied the new constitutional privilege to defamatory falsehoods concerning a "public official" and his "official conduct,"[47] a difficulty with the two concepts remained. *Curtis Publishing Co. v Butts*[48] and *Associated Press v Walker*[49] extended the actual malice rule to protect speech about public figures[50] "with respect to public issues and events."[51] In 1974, the dichotomy between public and private figures was settled in *Gertz v Welch, Inc.*[52]

Gertz v Robert Welch, Inc.

The late Elmer Gertz, a well-known Chicago attorney, brought a libel action against the publisher of the monthly magazine *American Opinion*, a publication of the John Birch Society. The article about the murder trial of Richard Nuccio, a police officer, associated the case with an alleged nationwide communist conspiracy to undermine local law enforcement. Its allegation suggested that this conspiracy would support a national police force to enforce a communist dictatorship.[53] The article mentioned Gertz, the co-counsel of the victim's family, who was pursuing civil remedies against Nuccio, as a member of the conspiracy. It also described Gertz, among several slurs, as a "Communist-fronter," a "Leninist" and a "Marxist."[54] *American Opinion* claimed protection of the *New York Times* actual malice standard. The Seventh Circuit Court of Appeals affirmed the district court's judgment that the actual malice standard applied to media discussion of a public issue without regard to whether the person was a public official or a public figure. However, the Supreme Court reversed the decision.

In an opinion written by Justice Lewis Powell, the Supreme Court repeated its earlier rejection of the traditional rule of strict liability for defamation that required a speaker to "guarantee the accuracy of his factual assertions" as an "intolerable self-censorship."[55] However, the Court noted that avoiding self-censorship was not the only value for society, and to grant news media absolute protection would be overly compromising other societal interests represented by that law of defamation.[56] With this in mind, the Court tried to resolve the conflict between free speech and protection of reputation. Simply, the holdings of the Court were the following: (1) Because private persons have not voluntarily exposed themselves into the public arena and matters, they are more vulnerable to injury and more deserving of recovery than public figures who have thrust themselves into social prominence and have more access to media to rebut accusations against them;[57] (2) Gertz was a private figure, and that in private figure cases, the actual malice standard was not required by the First Amendment;[58] (3) Whereas public officials and public figures must always meet the *New York Times* actual malice standard to recover for damages,[59] states could set for themselves the proper standard of liability in private plaintiff defamation suits;[60] while the Court gave states the option to set for themselves the fault standard, most states chose negligence; (4) Because the states' interest in protecting reputation must only compensate for actual injury, any award of punitive damages to private figures requires a proof of actual malice.[61]

One of the significant aspects of *Gertz* is the distinction it made between public figures and private figures. The Court's first justification of the distinction concerned "access to the media." It argued that "public officials and public figures usually enjoy significantly greater access to the channels of effective communication and hence have a more realistic opportunity to counteract false statements than private individuals enjoy."[62] Though the access for rebuttal has its limits, as the Court acknowledged, it insisted that the inadequacy of this self-help remedy does not make it irrelevant.[63]

The second rationale assumed that people who voluntarily take roles of prominence in society or seek public spotlight expose themselves to a greater public scrutiny as a contingent cost. The Court held: "[T]he communications media are entitled to act on the assumption that public officials and public figures have voluntarily exposed themselves to increased risk of injury from defamatory falsehood concerning them. No such assumption is justified with respect to a private individual."[64]

The Court in *Gertz* divided the public figures into three categories: "pervasive" public figures, "limited" voluntary public figures, and limited "involuntary" public figures. The first category includes persons who occupy positions of great power or are so pervasively involved in the affairs of society that they become public figures for all purposes.[65] Also, persons who by the "notoriety of their achievements" have attained "general fame or notoriety in the community" come within the category of pervasive public figures.[66] However, most public figures are in the voluntary limited public figure category. Of this second category, the Court said that persons who are commonly "classed as public figures have thrust themselves to the forefront of particular public controversies in order to influence the resolution of the issues involved."[67] Since they are involved in a particular public controversy, for a limited range of issues,[68] "[i]t is preferable to reduce the public figure question to a more meaningful context by looking to the nature and extent of an individual's participation in the particular controversy giving rise to the defamation."[69] Other aspects of their lives stay private and may receive compensation by a showing of negligence, though states may require more.[70]   The Court's third category, the limited involuntary public figures, rarely emerges.   The Court said that, despite the rarity, it is possible to have a person "become a public figure through no purposeful action of his own."[71]

Unlike public officials and public figures, private individuals do not voluntarily expose themselves to the risk of reputational injury. Neither do they have sufficient access to the media to rebut defamatory falsehoods. Hence, the Court said that "private individuals are not only more vulnerable to injury ... they are also more deserving of recovery ... for defamatory falsehood injurious to the reputation of a private individual."[72]

The basic issue that the Court in *Gertz* resolved was the level of constitutional protection to give the media when they defame private individuals. The Court repeated its decisions in *New York Times* and *Butts*.   In the process, the Court categorized plaintiffs into public officials, public figures and private individuals. It suggested that there can be no private defamation of public figures, but upheld the availability of presumed damages to plaintiffs who can show actual malice.   While the *Gertz* fault requirement offered media defendants greater protection under the First Amendment, negligence became the rule in most states for nonmedia defendants.[73]   The next case, *Dun & Bradstreet, Inc. v Greenmoss Builders*,[74] addressed the application of the fault requirement in libel action against nonmedia defendants, an issue untouched in *Gertz*.

Dun & Bradstreet v Greenmoss

A credit reporting agency, Dun & Bradstreet, issued an erroneous credit report showing that Greenmoss Builders, a construction contractor, had willfully filed a petition for bankruptcy. The report was an unintended attribution of a bankruptcy petition by a former Greenmoss employee to Greenmoss itself.   Because Greenmoss was in sound financial condition, the report falsely and grossly misrepresented its assets and liabilities. Though Dun & Bradstreet usually practiced prepublication verification before issuing a report, it did not verify the accuracy of the information in the Greenmoss report.   The president of Greenmoss became aware of the credit report during a meeting with the company's principal creditor concerning its future financing. Although the bank's president did not believe the report, the bank discontinued Greenmoss' credit. So Greenmoss brought suit against the credit reporting agency. The jury returned a $350,000 verdict ($50,000 compensatory damages and $300,000 punitive damages) for Greenmoss.   The trial court, recognizing that its instructions to the jury to award presumed and punitive damages were inconsistent with *Gertz*,[75] granted Dun & Bradstreet's motion for retrial. The Vermont Supreme Court reversed, holding not only that Dun & Bradstreet, which was not a member of the "media," did not deserve First Amendment protection,[76] but also that *Gertz* is inapplicable to nonmedia actions.[77] The United States Supreme Court affirmed, in a 5-to-4 ruling, a decision that was not based on the media and nonmedia distinction. The Court held that "permitting recovery of presumed and punitive damages in defamation cases absent a showing of 'actual malice' does not violate the First Amendment when the defamatory statements do not involve matters of public concern."[78]

Considering whether the rule of *Gertz* applied when the false and defamatory statements do not involve matters of public concern, the Court ruled that it had "never considered whether the *Gertz* balance obtains when the defamatory statements involve no issue of public concern."[79] The Court opinion, which Justice Lewis Powell wrote, argued from the enlightenment purpose of the First Amendment in promoting self-governance. The Court said, "speech on 'matters of public concern' that is 'at the heart of the First Amendment's protection' was fashioned to assure unfettered interchange of ideas for the bringing about of political and social change."[80] However, "speech on matters of purely private concern is of less First Amendment concern."[81] Whereas interest in speech at the core of First Amendment concerns overrides state interest in awarding presumed and punitive damages, speech of private concern or of less constitutional interest does not. So Justice Powell added: "The rationale of the common-law rules has been the experience and judgment of history that 'proof of actual damage will be impossible in a great many cases where, from the character of the defamatory words and the circumstances of publication, it is all but certain that serious harm has resulted in fact.'"[82] In this vein, "courts for centuries have allowed juries to presume that some damage occurred from many defamatory utterances and publications."[83] Supporting this common law rule, Justice Powell said that the "rule furthers the state interest in providing remedies for defamation by ensuring that those remedies are effective."[84] As a result, the Court decided that in "the reduced constitutional value of speech involving no matters of public concern, we hold that the state interest adequately supports awards of presumed and punitive damages -- even absent a showing of 'actual malice.'"[85] Holding that speech concerning "matters of public concern must be determined by [the expression's] content, form and context ... as revealed by the whole record,"[86] the Court said that Dun & Bradstreet's credit report was not speech about a matter of public concern.[87] Justice Powell described the credit report as speech that was "solely in the individual interest of the speaker and its specific business audience."[88] Also, the "credit report was made available to only five subscribers, who, under the terms of subscription agreement, could not disseminate it further," and so it did not concern any "strong interest in the flow of commercial information."[89] In the light of the individual interests of the speaker and its audience, the limited dissemination of the credit report, and its defamatory falsehood, the Court maintained that it did not warrant any special protection to ensure uninhibited, robust and wide-open debate on public issues.[90]

While *New York Times* set the constitutional standard that required public officials to prove actual malice, *Gertz* tried to resolve problems associated with the distinction between public officials or public figures and private persons in requiring prove of actual malice. So *Gertz* established a fault requirement for the media when they defame private persons. *Dun & Bradstreet, Inc. v Greenmoss Builders* addressed the application of the fault requirement in libel action against nonmedia defendants. The Court did not use the public figure and private individual distinction to determine the fault requirement; rather it found "matters of public concern" as the essential element for protection of speech under the constitutional privilege of the First Amendment. As a negligence case, the Court demonstrated that fault was still required in cases of private speech. By doing so, the Court did not depart from *Gertz*, and yet showed the special importance it attaches to the protection of political speech. To sustain this protection, the Court held in *Philadelphia Newspapers, Inc. v Hepps*[91] that the First Amendment prohibits liability for defamation unless the plaintiff in a media libel action also proves that the defamatory statement was a false statement of fact where the defamatory story concerns a matter of public concern. Also, the Court's interest in protecting matters of public concern extends to the protection of genuine opinion or nonfact, requiring that actionable speech be factual speech.[92]

ECHR: FREEDOM OF EXPRESSION AS NECESSARY FOR A DEMOCRATIC SOCIETY

The term "freedom of expression" in the European Convention on Human Rights comprises the expression of opinion and receiving and imparting information and ideas.[93] The provision is both an end and a means. It is an end because it ensures open communication, which is a condition of self-realization. And, it is a means because it allows claims to be made and so ensure the protection of other rights.[94] However, Mark Janis, Richard Kay and Anthony Bradley wrote that the nature of "expression protected by Article 10 is not always self-evident, because problems can arise in distinguishing expression from action involving communication of viewpoint."[95] Yet, the case law of the ECHR has not focused on questions of its definition. Rather, the Court states that any limitation on freedom of expression must be prescribed by law, necessary in a democratic society, and for the protection of one of the interests in Article 10 (2). Also, the Court has concerned itself with how states operate within those limits of interference.[96] This test requires states to show that any restrictions on free expression were lawful, that a pressing social need prompted the interference, and that the restrictions were proportional to the interest served.[97]

The Court's aim is to find a balance between protecting free expression and protecting the rights and freedoms of others. In this way, the Court allows states a margin of appreciation.[98] The Court assumes that states can determine whether a restriction is necessary within the local circumstances. The necessity may vary according to the state and to changing situations. Notwithstanding, the Court oversees legal conflicts that follow restrictions states may impose which may threaten a democratic society as a result.[99]

Because of the centrality of free political speech in democratic self-government, the Court interprets free expression narrowly and shows greater preference for political speech as necessary for a democratic society.[100] A prelude to the argument for political speech in the ECHR should be the Court's 1976 judgment in *Handyside v the United Kingdom* that affirmed the value of free expression. Though it was about a prosecution for possessing an alleged obscene publication, *Handyside* stated:

Freedom of expression constitutes one of the essential foundations of a [democratic] society, one of the basic conditions for its progress and for the development of every man. Subject to Article 10 (2), it is applicable not only to "information" or "ideas" that are favorably received or regarded as inoffensive or as a matter of indifference, but also to those that offend, shock or disturb the State or any sector of the population. Such are the demands of that pluralism, tolerance and broadmindedness without which there is no "democratic society."[101]

By this decision the Court recognized a link between freedom of expression and democracy. It held that free speech extends to unfavorable information or ideas, as well as those that are popular or inoffensive.[102] However, freedom of expression is subject to Article 10 (2) and that suggests that the right is not absolute.[103] The following cases, therefore, indicate the scope and limits of political speech as developed in the case law of ECHR.

Lingens v Austria

Lingens v Austria[104] involved ECHR's determination of the extent of permissible and impermissible political speech. Peter Lingens published in a magazine two articles critical of the Austrian Federal Chancellor, Bruno Kreisky, and accused him of protecting and assisting former members of the Nazi SS. The alleged defamatory comments about Kreisky included statements that described Kriesky's political behavior as "basest opportunism" and "immoral and undignified." The Federal Chancellor brought a private prosecution for criminal libel. Under the Austrian criminal code, defamation of an officeholder was punishable and proof of truth was the only defense available. Because Lingens could not prove the truth of his value judgments, he was convicted and fined. The European Court unanimously held that Lingens' freedom of expression was breached.

The European Court said that "freedom of expression ... constitutes one of the essential foundations of a democratic society and one of the basic conditions for its progress and for each individual's self-fulfillment."[105] One could imply that the Court recognized individuals' self-fulfillment and their full potential through communication of feelings, ideas, and opinions. Adding to it, the Court held that the right of free expression is essential to the functioning of a democratic society, for political representatives can only understand and represent the views of their constituents through an open exchange of views, opinions and facts.[106] In this view, the Court emphasized the news media's important role in reporting matters of public interest. According to the Court, freedom of the press provides citizens "one of the best means of discovering and forming an opinion of the ideas and attitudes of political leaders."[107] In emphasizing the important place of political speech in self-governance, the Court observed: "More generally, freedom of political debate is at the core of the concept of a democratic society which prevails throughout the Convention."[108]

After establishing that political speech possessed "core" status, the Court showed that this status had profound implications for the Convention's member states in the ways that they interfere with political speech. Though the Court did not deny that politicians deserve reputational protection, it held that politicians should not be treated as "private citizens" by the defamation laws of their countries. In this reasoning, the Court concluded:

> The limits of acceptable criticism are accordingly wider as regards a politician as such than as regards a private individual. Unlike the latter, the former inevitably and knowingly lays himself open to close scrutiny of his every word and deed by both journalists and the public at large, and he must consequently display a greater degree of tolerance. No doubt Article 10(2) enables the reputation of others ... to be protected, and this extends to politicians too, ... but in such cases the requirements of such protection have to be weighed in relation to the interests of open discussion of political issues.[109]

Underlying *Lingens* is the distinction that speech about political matters has higher value than speech about private lives of politicians. In addition, the Court pointed out that political speech is not limited to facts which are verifiable, but it includes value judgments that are impossible to prove. So the Court drew a line between the expression of a personal opinion and facts that affect the reputation of persons. It said: "The existence of facts can be demonstrated, whereas the truth of value judgments is not susceptible of proof."[110] As the Court found that the good faith of Lingens and the facts on which he based his value judgments were undisputed, it held that it was not "necessary in a democratic society ... for the protection of others" for journalists to prove the truth of their opinions and value judgments about political figures.[111]

The decision in *Lingens* demonstrated that the Court has greater preference for political speech. The Court supported the role of the press in maintaining democratic self-governance. Then, in a liberal approach, it held that communication on matters of public concern and about political figures promotes individual self-fulfillment, and it serves a central role in the functioning of democratic societies. To decide permissible and impermissible political speech, the Court allowed a wider criticism of political figures than private plaintiffs, and it also distinguished between facts and opinions. The next case dealt with the effect that libel laws can have on political discussion, and the European Court's preference for substance over form of speech.

Castells v Spain

In *Castells v Spain*,[112] Miguel Castells, a lawyer and an elected senator supporting Basque independence, wrote some newspaper articles which suggested that the government applied different standards in prosecuting left-wing extremists and right-wing ones. One of the articles accused unnamed government officials of involvement in the murders of several Basque separatists. After an investigation on a charge that he insulted the government, Castells was prosecuted and convicted of criminal libel under Article 161 of Spain's Criminal Code.[113] Castells argued that his prosecution by the government and the conviction served no legitimate aim under Article 10 of the European Convention. ECHR overturned the conviction.

The Court found that the government's purpose was not to protect any person's reputation but to preserve public order. Recognizing the considerable turmoil in the Basque area when the articles were published in 1979, the Court said it was legitimate that Spain imposed criminal law sanctions on persons who published lies or accusations "formulated in bad faith."[114] In Castells' case, however, such sanctions were inconsistent with Article 10 of the ECHR because the government did not make available the defense of truth.[115] Castells neither had the opportunity to show the good faith of his motives nor prove the accuracy of his stories. Thus, the Court held that the restraints on free political discussion were more severe than those justified by protection of reputation and the government's interest to preserve public order.[116] The Court maintained:

> [T]he preeminent role of the press in a State governed by the rule of law must not be forgotten ... Freedom of the press affords the public one of the best means of discovering and forming an opinion on the ideas and attitudes of their political leaders. In particular, it gives politicians the opportunity to reflect and comment on the preoccupations of public opinion; it thus enables everyone to participate in the free political debate which is at the core of the concept of a democratic society.[117]

Castells extended the liberality states must give to criticism of politicians. The Court suggested that domestic legal systems should make a threefold distinction among political libel plaintiffs: government, politician and private citizen.[118] The Court believed that the "limits of permissible criticism are wider with regard to governments [and its institutions] than in relation to a private citizen, or even a politician."[119] Government and politicians must tolerate more criticism than private citizens. Whereas governmental organs and activities must be subject to close scrutiny by the press and citizens, "the dominant position which the Government occupies makes it necessary for it to display restraint in resorting to criminal proceedings."[120]

Castells demonstrated the Court's strong protection of free political speech in a representative democracy, and confirmed its earlier principles stated in cases such as in *Lingens*. Like *Lingens*, *Castells* held that freedom of political speech is at the core of the concept of a democratic society, and so government and politicians must tolerate wider criticism than private citizens to ensure a responsible and representative government. But it went further to make a threefold distinction among libel plaintiffs. In addition, the Court said that, as regards political criticism, criminal law must be the remotest remedy, for government must exercise restraint in using criminal proceedings to control political speech. Recently the European Court upheld the protection of political expression in *Bladet Tromso and Stensaas v*

Norway,[121] a case involving defamatory statements of public concern and newspaper allegations of fact.

Bladet Tromso and Stensaas v Norway

A newspaper publisher and its editor published statements that were defamatory, "unlawful" and not proven to be true about a seal hunting inspector and some seal hunters. Though the impugned statements did not concern the private affairs of private persons, they apparently accused some unnamed crew members of cruel and unlawful behavior during the hunt. The 17 seal hunters brought a defamation action against the newspaper. Bladet Tromso and Stensaas contended that the articles were intended to initiate a debate about the proper means of ensuring the seal hunting industry's survival through compliance with the relevant regulations and possibly amending those rules to improve seal hunting and its image.[122] So, Bladet Tromso and Stensaas argued that the impugned articles were not aimed at defaming the reputation of crew members of the seal hunting industry. They also argued that they relied on a report by an appointed official of the Norwegian Ministry of Fisheries. The Nord-Troms District Court declared the statements null and void.[123] It said that the newspaper acted negligently and instructed the newspaper to pay compensation to the 17 crew members. Applying its test of "necessity in a democratic society,"[124] ECHR declared that the State violated Bladet Tromso and Stensaas' right of freedom of expression.

Considering the wider context of the newspaper coverage,[125] the Court found that "the impugned articles were part of the ongoing debate of evident concern to the local, national and international public, in which the views of a wide selection of interested actors were reported."[126] While the Court acknowledged that the press has duties and responsibilities, the Court likewise reaffirmed the latitude of freedom it consistently affords the press.[127] As a result, the Court observed that governmental restrictions that can discourage the participation of the press in debates over matters of legitimate public concern need the most careful scrutiny.[128]

On the issue involving Bladet Tromso and Stensaas' factual statements, not value judgments, the Court held that the newspaper had a reasonable basis for its factual allegations. The Court came to this conclusion by examining three factors: the nature and degree of the defamation, and the trustworthiness of the source of the information.[129] Concerning the nature and degree of the defamation, the Court found that four statements alleging that certain seal hunters' behavior was cruel and unlawful imputed reprehensible conduct, but were not particularly serious.[130] It considered the other two allegations as more serious, but said they "were expressed in rather broad terms and could be understood by readers as having been presented with a degree of exaggeration."[131] Also, because Bladet Tromso and Stensaas did not mention the names of any crew member, "the potential adverse effect of the impugned statements on each seal hunter's reputation or rights was significantly attenuated .... In particular, the criticism was not an attack against all the crew members or any specific crew member."[132]

As regards the trustworthiness of the information Bladet Tromso and Stensaas received from an appointed official of the Ministry of Fisheries, the Court said: "[T]he press should normally be entitled, when contributing to public debate on matters of legitimate concern, to rely on the contents of official reports without having to undertake independent research. Otherwise, the vital public-watchdog role of the press may be undermined."[133] As the Court did not require the newspaper to do its independent research into the accuracy of the facts, given the various limiting factors, the Court found no basis to doubt that the newspaper acted in good faith.[134] Therefore, the Court concluded that the vital public interest in ensuring an informed public debate outweighed the interest of protecting the crew members' reputation.[135]

The European Court has clearly preferred political speech by affirming its well-established case law concerning Article 10. The Court's rulings in favor of political expression follow the test of "necessary in a democratic society." By doing so, the Court has balanced political speech, expressed largely through the news media, against other compelling interests. The Court distinguishes the nature and degree of libel, and the status of the complainant. Essentially, the Court holds that speech involving political issues and political leaders or arms of government fulfills a central function in democratic societies. Besides, the standard for political defamation in the European Court is less protective of the reputation of political figures than private persons. Also, the Court makes the distinction between statements of fact and opinion judgment. *Bladet* Tromso added that the ECHR protects speech that displays the vital public interest in ensuring an informed public debate. In sum, the ECHR deals favorably with the news media, and its view of the essential role played by political speech in a democratic society resembles the First Amendment doctrine on political defamation. Thus, the case law of ECHR and the United States Supreme Court decisions on political defamation are converging. Both Courts have laid down legal measures that impede rather than ease government institutions and politicians' capacity to stifle public discussion through libel action.

THE UNITED KINGDOM: THE COMMON LAW DEFENSE OF QUALIFIED PRIVILEGE

The defense of qualified privilege in Great Britain protects "a person acting in good faith and without any improper motive [or malicious intent] who makes a statement about another person even when that statement is in fact untrue and defamatory."[136] For an occasion to merit qualified privilege at common law, the defendant must establish "an interest or a duty, legal, social, or moral" to communicate the relevant material to a recipient or others, and the recipient of the material must have "a corresponding interest or duty to receive it."[137] For example, the news media would have the duty to publish credible information that a minister pilfered public funds from his office into his private project, and the audience would have a corresponding duty to receive it.[138] This duty principle shows that political speech is protected because a representative government involves open discussion and debate of political affairs. At the same time, the defense recognizes that political communication must be a reciprocal duty. However, the plaintiff can remove the privilege by proving that the alleged defamatory statements were published with intentional malice.[139] This section considers how recent House of Lords and Appeal Court decisions in Great Britain interpret the qualified privilege test in cases involving political defamation.

Derbyshire County Council v Times Newspapers Ltd

Determination of the present English law and political defamation should begin with the *Derbyshire County Council v Times Newspapers Ltd*,[140] a landmark decision of the House of Lords. In *Derbyshire*, the *Sunday Times* published three articles in September 1989 that questioned the propriety of investments made by the Derbyshire County Council and its control of the corporation's pension fund. The articles were headlined, "Revealed: Socialist Tycoon's Deals with a Labor Chief," "Bizarre Deals of a Council Leader and the Media

Tycoon" and "Council Share Deals under Scrutiny." The county
council alleged that the *Sunday Times*'s articles were defamatory of it.
It brought a suit, alleging that the libel brought the county council into
"public scandal, odium and contempt."[141] A judge of the Queen's
Bench found in the council's favor. But it was reversed by the Court of
Appeal. The House of Lords dismissed the appeal to the lords.

In deciding whether a local authority could sue for libel, the House
of Lords identified two conflicting common law precedents. The first,
Manchester Corporation v Williams,[142] had decided that a municipal
corporation could not receive damages in a libel action involving
charges of bribery and corruption because these crimes could not be
committed by a corporation, only by its individual members or
officials. The second, *Bognor Regis Urban District Council v
Campion*,[143] had held, to the contrary, that a local government
corporation could obtain damages to its reputation, if the libel reflected
on its "governing" reputation as distinct from the reputations of its
members. Though the Court of Appeal rejected the *Bognor* decision, it
depended mostly on Article 10 of the European Convention on Human
Rights because it found neither a controlling higher court precedent nor
a "pressing social need that a public authority should have the right to
sue in damages for protection of its reputation."[144]

However, Lord Keith, writing the opinion of the House, noted that
the same conclusion could be reached under the "common law of
England without finding any need to rely upon the European
Convention."[145] After citing *New York Times Co v Sullivan*[146] and *City
of Chicago v Tribune Co*,[147] Lord Keith still argued that the common
law of England provided sufficient basis for protecting free speech. He
wrote:

> While these decisions were related most directly to the
> provisions of the American Constitution concerned with
> securing freedom of speech, the public interest considerations
> which underlaid them are no less valid in this country. What
> has been described as the 'chilling effect' induced by the
> threat of civil actions for libel is very important.[148]

So, the House of Lords decided that a local authority, as an organ of government, could not sue for libel.[149]   The House argued that it would be against the public interest, and would place an undesirable burden on freedom of speech to allow governmental organs to sue.[150] Also, "It is of the highest public importance that a democratically elected governmental body, or indeed any governmental body, should be open to uninhibited public criticism.   The threat of civil action for defamation must inevitably have an inhibiting effect on freedom of speech."[151]

The decision in *Derbyshire* was an attempt to remove unreasonable fetters on freedom of speech imposed by the common law of defamation.   It said that the common law rules that required defendants to prove the truth of allegations of libel exercised an undesirable "chilling effect" on free speech.[152]   This decision would shape subsequent rulings involving political defamation.   Not only is the *Derbyshire* decision reflected in *Reynolds v Times Newspapers*[153] at the Court of Appeal, but it also was a forerunner for the latter to extend the scope of qualified privilege defense.   Though the *Derbyshire* decision would shape subsequent rulings involving political defamation, *Derbyshire*'s liberality would not be extended toward libel of government agencies to libels of individuals.

Reynolds v Times Newspapers Ltd (Court of Appeal)

In *Reynolds*, an elected politician brought an action of defamation against *The Sunday Times* for defamatory words relating to a political crisis in the Republic of Ireland.   Albert Reynolds, the plaintiff, was a member of the Irish Parliament starting in 1977 and he became Prime Minister in 1997.   He headed a coalition of his own party and Labor, under Dick Spring.   Reynolds and Spring promoted greatly the Northern Ireland peace process, so the future of the coalition was a matter of public interest in Great Britain and Ireland.   Spring decided to end the coalition because of a political crisis caused by the appointment to the office of President of the High Court of a former Attorney General and the handling of an extradition of a priest from Eire to Northern Ireland to answer charges of sexual abuse of children.   When Reynolds resigned as Prime Minister soon after, Times Newspapers published an article in the British mainland edition of its Sunday newspapers about the political crisis and Reynolds' resignation. Reynolds sued Times Newspapers for damages, claiming the alleged defamatory words in the article had deliberately and dishonestly misled the Irish Parliament, his cabinet colleagues and Spring.   Reynolds contended that Times Newspapers gave the impression he withheld from the Parliament and his cabinet information about the handling of the extradition request, and that he had lied to Parliament about when the information came into his possession. Times Newspapers claimed qualified privilege at common law on grounds that the article served the public interest in communication and discussion about political issues and elected politicians' public conduct. Times Newspapers also argued that its defense would be protected by Article 10 of the European Convention on Human Rights. The trial judge ruled that the defendants could not rely on qualified privilege. While the jury awarded Reynolds one pence in compensation, he was ordered to pay Times Newspapers' legal cost from the time the case entered the court. Reynolds appealed for a new trial and Times Newspapers cross-appealed.

Drawing support from authorities in domestic cases, the United States, the Commonwealth and ECHR jurisdictions, Times Newspapers submitted in the cross-appeal that qualified privilege should protect publication of material that concerns political matters to the public; that the qualified privilege defense be available to defendants in circumstances where the defamatory statements relate to the elected official's public conduct rather than his private or personal life; and that the qualified privilege defense arises because of the threat of defamation law placing an undesirable fetter on freedom of expression.[154]

However, Lord Bingham of Cornhill, Chief Justice, outlined a three-part test as the criteria by which the news media could successfully claim qualified privilege defense. The test questioned: (1) whether the publisher was under a legal, moral or social duty to those to whom the material was published (the duty test); (2) whether those to whom the material was published had an interest to receive the material (the interest test); and (3) whether the nature, status and source of the material, and the circumstances of the publication, were such that the publication should in the public interest be protected in the absence of proof of express malice (the circumstantial test).[155]

The court believed that modern conditions make the duty and interest tests "rather more readily held to be satisfied" than in the past.[156] While the two tests seemed to favor Times Newspapers, the circumstantial test depended on whether judges believed it could have a chilling effect on freedom of expression. A reasonableness test recently adopted by the High Court of Australia in *Lange v Australian Broadcasting Corporation*[157] influenced the circumstantial test of *Reynolds*.[158]

Applying the principles, the court decided that Times Newspapers had a duty to inform the public, and so it satisfied the duty test. The court argued that the publication of the circumstances in which the plaintiff's government had fallen from power were matters of public interest in Great Britain.[159] The interest test was also met since the public had a corresponding interest to receive the information.[160]

The court in *Reynolds*, however, held that Times Newspapers' publication failed the circumstantial test given "the nature, status and source"[161] of Times Newspapers' information, and all the circumstances of the publication.[162] The court observed:

> While those who engage in public life must expect and accept that their public conduct will be the subject of close scrutiny and robust criticism, they should not in our view be taken to expect or accept that their conduct should be the subject of false and defamatory statements of fact unless the circumstances of the publication are such as to make it proper, in the public interest, to afford the publisher immunity from liability in the absence of malice.[163]

In the Court of Appeal's opinion, Times Newspapers was unjustifiably negligent in the source attribution and in checking credibility of the source. The court considered it irresponsible for Times Newspapers to judge the statement of Reynolds' chief political opponent as an authoritative source for a serious factual allegation.[164] Moreover, Times Newspapers had reasonable time to either investigate serious factual allegations or alert Reynolds to their highly damaging allegations about him, but they failed to do so. Also, Times Newspapers failed to record Reynolds' account of his conduct in its publication. Furthermore, the court found that Times Newspapers failed to resolve whether Reynolds was a victim of circumstance, as conveyed to Irish readers in one article, or a devious liar, as conveyed in another article to readers in the British mainland. The court believed that Reynolds could not be both.[165] For these reasons, the Court of Appeal allowed Reynolds' appeal and dismissed the defendants' cross-appeal.

Left at *Reynolds* interpretation of the readily satisfied duty and interest tests, the decision would have marked a shift in qualified privilege approaching the liberality of the United States' "actual malice" standard. Yet, it introduced a third element, the circumstantial test. While the standard set forth in *Reynolds* did not regulate free speech or the practice of journalism, the circumstantial test was wider than the Australian reasonable test it was intended to follow.[166] Also, the court did not recognize special protection of political speech. Neither did it remove the chilling effect that English defamation law may have on political speech.[167] However, it was important in interpreting the common law qualified privilege. Like *Derbyshire* before it, *Reynolds* represented a development of the United Kingdom law in favor of free political expression provided that the three conditions are fulfilled. Also, *Reynolds* prepared the ground for further deliberation of ECHR's impact on freedom of political speech in British law. The House of Lords decision that followed examined the legality of the circumstantial test and the call to extend qualified privilege for political speech.

Reynolds v Times Newspapers (House of Lords)

The facts of *Reynolds v Times Newspapers*[168] before the House of Lords remained the same. It involved Reynolds, who resigned as Prime Minister of Ireland and leader of his party in November 1994 because of a political crisis. The defamation action followed *Sunday Times'* reporting this matter of political importance. Reynolds complained that the article reported that he had deliberately and dishonestly misled the Irish House of Representatives and his coalition cabinet colleagues, especially the Deputy Prime Minister.[169] While the jury at trial rejected Times Newspapers' (publishers and editor of the newspaper, and the author of the article) plea of justification, it decided that the author did not act maliciously, and so awarded no damages. The judge awarded Reynolds one penny in compensation, and rejected Times Newspapers' defense of qualified privilege. Both parties were dissatisfied with the judge's decision: while Reynolds claimed that the judge misdirected the jury, Times Newspapers cross-appealed against the judge's decision on qualified privilege. The Court of Appeal allowed Reynolds' appeal, but denied Times Newspapers' claim of qualified privilege. Times

Newspapers appealed, arguing that a libelous statement of fact made in good faith in the course of political discussion is free from liability. Thus, Times Newspapers sought a "generic" qualified privilege of political speech. Also at issue was whether the Court of Appeal correctly held that the test for qualified privilege included a "circumstantial test" separate from, and additional to, the conventional "duty-interest" test.[170]

In a divided (3-2) opinion, the House of Lords rejected Times Newspapers' argument that the political information should be privileged in English common law. The law lords also held that, although the circumstantial test should not be considered separately from duty-interest test, it was necessary for determining whether the public was entitled to know the particular information.

Lord Nicholls, writing the majority opinion, tracked the history of common law defamation and qualified privilege defense. He noted that the defense applied to comment on a matter of public interest and not defamatory statements of fact, and concluded that the common law should not develop a generic qualified privilege of political speech like the *New York Times* rule in the United States' law.[171] He elaborated that developing a special category of political speech would not provide adequate protection for reputation, which was an integral and important part of the dignity of the individual.[172] In the majority opinion, Lord Nicholls wrote:

> Protection of reputation is conducive to the public good. It is in the public interest that the reputation of public figures should not be debased falsely. In the political field, in order to make an informed choice, the electorate needs to be able to identify the good as well as the bad ... [H]uman rights conventions recognize that freedom of expression is not an absolute right. Its exercise may be subject to such restrictions as are prescribed by law and are necessary in a democratic society for the protection of reputations of others.[173]

While "it would be unsound in principle to distinguish political discussion from discussion of other matters of serious public interest," Lord Nicholls added, "the common law approach to misstatements of fact remains essentially sound."[174] He explained:

> The elasticity of the common law principle enables interference with freedom of speech to be confined to what is

necessary in the circumstances of the case. This elasticity enables the court to give appropriate weight, in today's conditions, to the importance of freedom of expression by the media on all matters of public concern.[175]

Important as the circumstances must be considered by the judge, the majority of the law lords stated that a list in the circumstantial test is not exhaustive and the value to be placed on any relevant circumstantial factor will vary from case to case.[176] However, Lord Nicholls noted that the circumstances should not be taken separately from the duty-interest test because it can create "conceptual and practical difficulties."[177]

The majority acknowledged that the European Convention on Human Rights should be particularly important to the United Kingdom law as the Human Rights Act 1998 requires, but it concluded that, in the present ECHR case law, "no trace is to be found of endorsement of a generic privilege in the political context."[178] Adding to it, Lord Nicholls emphasized:

[T]he court should have particular regard to the importance of freedom of expression. The press discharges vital functions as a bloodhound as well as watchdog. The court should be slow to conclude that a publication was not in the public interest and, therefore, the public had no right to know, especially when the information is in the field of political discussion. Any lingering doubts should be resolved in favor of publication.[179]

Lord Nicholls's final note about the vital role of the press makes the dissenting opinion of Lords Steyn and Hope worth considering. Lord Steyn reasoned that the anticipated incorporation of the Human Rights Act 1998 strengthened "constitutional dimension of freedom of expression."[180] Criticizing the majority for failing to consider this reality, Lord Steyn remarked:

The new landscape is of great importance inasmuch as it provides the taxonomy against which the question before the

House must be considered. The starting point is now the right
of freedom of expression, a right based on a constitutional or
higher legal order foundation .... [F]reedom of expression is
the rule and regulation of speech is the exception requiring
justification.[181]

Moreover, Lord Steyn stressed "the public watchdog role of the
press" and wrote that the liberal approach of the ECHR in balancing
free political speech against the right of reputation must be the basis of
English law on qualified privilege of political speech.[182]

Siding with Lord Steyn, Lord Hope argued that the increased
recognition of free speech and the changed nature of the electoral
process in the United Kingdom strongly favor "wider availability of the
qualified privilege for free political speech."[183] Contending that the
United Kingdom law should have qualified privilege of political
speech, Lord Hope observed:

There are powerful dicta to the effect that there is no
inconsistency between art[icle] 10 of the European
Convention ... and the English common law on freedom of
speech .... But there can be no doubt that the incorporation of
the convention into English law by the Human Rights Act
1998 has strengthened the arguments in favor of the principles
which are set out in that article.[184]

Unlike *Derbyshire*, the decisions in *Reynolds* (both the Court of
Appeal and House of Lords) did not take a liberal approach to free
political speech. Because the majority of the lords in *Reynolds* refused
to endorse the "generic privilege" for political speech, they failed to
remove the potential of English defamation law to stifle robust public
debate. Though the lords acknowledged the right to criticize freely and
publicly the institutions and officials of government as an essential
element in the maintenance of a representative democracy, they were
not ready to bear the probable cost of free speech. For the law lords,
political speech does not need special protection from unwarranted
constraints of political defamation.   However, the conservative
arguments of the majority conflict with the liberal views of the dissent.
So, the split decision of the lords in *Reynolds* shows the struggle among
the United Kingdom jurists about balancing free speech and
reputational interest. As it stands now, qualified privilege in *Reynolds*
cases does not secure unimpeded criticism of politicians. While the

United States libel and United Kingdom laws differ in their doctrinal approaches to political speech and in distinguishing among the status of libel plaintiffs, they agree on rationales that justify protection of free speech as well as public interest in matters of public concern. Similar differences exist in the relationship between the ECHR and the United Kingdom. However, the ECHR is close to the United States in its jurisprudence. Moreover, because the Human Rights Act 1998 has since October 2000 incorporated human rights under the European Convention into the United Kingdom domestic law, the Act should bolster free political speech and induce the law lords to modify *Reynolds*. Until the United Kingdom's compliance with the Convention's requirement, the United Kingdom will remain far from convergence with the United States and the ECHR. Because the Human Rights Act makes the European Convention provisions and jurisprudence part and parcel of the United Kingdom legal system, one can say that the United Kingdom jurisprudence and those of the ECHR, the United States and Australia are converging.

AUSTRALIA: THE IMPLIED FREEDOM OF COMMUNICATION

As a member of the British Commonwealth, Australia has historical, political and legal affiliation with the United Kingdom. Thus, English common law affected Australian defamation jurisprudence. Like in the United Kingdom, defendants in Australia could use common law qualified privilege defense to protect the publication of defamatory matter where the publisher had a duty to publish the material and the recipient had a reciprocal interest in receiving it, or where the material was published according to a common interest between the publisher and the recipient.[185] In the United Kingdom and Australian jurisdictions, the defense of qualified privilege protects "a person acting in good faith and without any improper motive [or malicious intent] who makes a statement about another person even when that statement is in fact untrue and defamatory.[186] At common law, a defendant had to satisfy the duty interest test of qualified privilege, otherwise a plaintiff who was publicly defamed received damages for injury to his or her reputation.[187] So, political expression did not receive special protection in Australia until shifts in the 1990s, beginning with *Nationwide News Party Ltd. v Wills*[188] and its companion case, *Australian Capital Television Pty. Ltd. v The Commonwealth of Australia.*[189] As two companion decisions, *Nationwide News* and *Australian Capital Television* represent the first freedom of communication cases in which the Australian High Court made a landmark ruling that the Australian Commonwealth Constitution protects the right of freedom of political communication by implication. In both freedom of communication cases, a majority in the Australian High Court extracted from the body of provisions and structure of the Australian Federal Constitution an implication that national legislation unacceptably interfered with free political speech.

Nationwide News Pty Ltd. v Wills

In *Nationwide News* an officer of the Australian Federal Police charged in Australian Federal Court that the newspaper published an article criticizing the Australian Industrial Relations Commission and accused the Commission members of corruption contrary to Section 299(1)[190] of the Commonwealth *Industrial Relations Act* 1988. The newspaper article accused the Commission and its members of, among other things, being regulated "by a mass of official controls, imposed by a vast bureaucracy in the ministry of labor and enforced by a corrupt and compliant 'judiciary' in the Soviet-style Arbitration Commission." *Nationwide News* challenged the constitutionality of the provision, arguing that the Constitution implicitly allowed citizens to reasonably criticize governmental institutions without restraint. The Australian High Court unanimously found the provision to be constitutionally invalid.

Chief Justice Anthony Mason, and Justices Daryl Dawson and Michael Hudson McHugh based their decisions on analysis of the "incidental" scope of the industrial relations power, and held that the public interest in public scrutiny and freedom to criticize outweighed the reputational interest of the Commission and its members.[191] The majority decision, however, depended on an implied constitutional guarantee of freedom of communication.[192] The majority held that free political discussion is based on the principle of representative democracy enshrined in the Constitution. As the guarantee of free political discussion must be understood in the constitutional context, Justices William Deane and Leslie Toohey argued, the implied freedom arises from "the doctrines of government upon which the Constitution as a whole is structured and which form part of its fabric."[193]

In his contribution to the majority opinion, Justice Gerard Brennan wrote that the Australian governmental power, which receives its legitimacy from the principle of representative democracy or a universal franchise, must by the same democratic principle afford extensive protection to free political discussion.[194] This implied freedom is not absolute,[195] yet it goes beyond a mere privilege and "is inherent in the idea of a representative government" and its "effective maintenance."[196]

Relying on this implied constitutional freedom, the majority of the High Court held that the act of the Federal Parliament, which prohibited criticism likely to bring the Australian Industrial Relations Commission into disrepute, was invalid. According to the majority, the range of conduct that might be protected by the implied freedom includes "political and economic matters,"[197] "governments and political matters,"[198] "information and opinions about matters relating to the government of the Commonwealth,"[199] "public affairs and political discussion,"[200] and "political discourse."[201]

Nationwide News is the first case to decide that freedom of communication is implied in the Australian Commonwealth Constitution. But it did not decide the effect the implied freedom of political speech could have on the libel law in Australian common law or statutes. However, the High Court of Australia decisions in the joined cases of *Theophanous v Herald & Weekly Times Ltd*[202] and *Stephens v West Australian Newspapers Ltd*[203] addressed the issue.

Theophanous v The Herald & Weekly Times Ltd

Andrew Theophanous, the plaintiff, born an Australian of Greek origin, was a member of the House of Representatives, the lower house of the Federal Parliament, and chairperson of a parliamentary committee on immigration regulations. In October 1992, another member of the House criticized his views and conduct about immigration issues, and the criticism received media publicity. A month before a federal election, the Herald & Weekly Times Ltd published in its newspaper, *The Sunday Herald Sun*, a letter written by the second defendant entitled "Give Theophanous a shove." Theophanous brought a libel action against the defendants claiming that the publication contained imputations that he "showed a bias toward Greeks as migrants," that he "stood for things that most Australians were against," and that he "was an idiot and his actions were the antics of an idiotic man."[204] The Australian High Court found that defamatory criticism was protected by the implied constitutional freedom to discuss government and political matters.

The narrow majority comprising Chief Justice Mason and Justices Toohey, Mary Genevieve Gaudron and Deane,[205] applied *Nationwide News*[206] and *Australian Capital Television*[207] and held that there is implied in the Australian Constitution a freedom to publish matters that discuss government and political issues, performance of politicians' official duties, and suitability of persons for public office.[208] However, the implied freedom of political communication did not extend to freedom of communication generally. Commercial speech would ordinarily fall outside the Australian constitutional protection unless it contained also some political content.[209] Speaking of freedom of communication not only as a negative restriction on legislative power, but also as a source of individual citizens's positive rights,[210] the majority referred to free political speech "as an implication rather than as a guarantee of freedom."[211] About the implied freedom and its effect on libel law, the majority noted:

> [I]t is incontrovertible that an implication of freedom of communication, the purpose of which is to ensure the efficacy of representative democracy, must extend to protect political discussion from exposure to onerous criminal and civil liability if implication is to be effective in achieving its purpose.[212]

In the light of the implied freedom of political communication and its underlying objective of ensuring efficacious working of the representative democracy,[213] the majority established a new qualified privilege defense. According to the new defense, a publication would not be actionable under defamation law if the defendant established that: (a) it was unaware of the falsity of the material published; (b) it did not publish the material recklessly; that is, not caring whether the material is true or false; and (c) the publication was reasonable in the circumstances.[214] To satisfy the test of acting reasonably, the defense would require the defendant to show that "it acted reasonably, either by taking some steps to check the accuracy of the impugned material or by establishing that it was otherwise justified in publishing without taking such steps or steps which were adequate."[215]

Nationwide News created the implied freedom of communication rule, but *Theophanous* applied the implied freedom to qualified privilege defense and its effects on Australian political libel laws. The *Theophanous* decisions significantly modified both the law of defamation in Australia and the way in which plaintiffs in defamation actions involving "political discussion" are treated in Australian courts. The High Court of Australia recognized that it is fundamental to the principle of representative democracy, as established in the Australian Constitution, that the people enjoy the implied constitutional right of political speech in order to exercise their free and informed role in the democratic process. Though the new defense still placed the burden of publishing in good faith on the defendant, it gave publishers greater freedom to publish material about political matters. At the same time, the defense encouraged responsible journalism as it required publishers to act reasonably. In the following case, *Lange v Australian Broadcasting Corporation,*[216] the High Court revisited its decisions in *Nationwide News* and *ACTV,* and *Theophanous* and *Stephens,* which held that there is implied in the Constitution the freedom to publish defamatory matters about government and political issues, and determined whether those decisions were correct.

Lange v Australian Broadcasting Corporation

David Russell Lange, former Prime Minister of New Zealand, brought a defamation action in the Supreme Court of New South Wales against the Australian Broadcasting Corporation (ABC). He accused the ABC of broadcasting a documentary made in New Zealand, which alleged improper dealings by him when he was a member of the New Zealand Parliament. The ABC relied on the decisions in *Theophanous* and *Stephens* to plead immunity from liability, arguing that "the matter complained of was published pursuant to a freedom guaranteed by the Commonwealth Constitution to publish material in the course of discussion of governmental and political matters."[217] The ABC also pleaded common law defense of qualified privilege, contending that the matter complained of related to subjects of public interest and political matters. The corporation also pleaded that it had a duty to publish the material to viewers of the program who had a legitimate and reciprocal interest in receiving the information. On the other hand, Lange claimed that the two defenses pleaded were bad in law. Because this raised a constitutional question, the case was taken to the High Court of Australia.

Though the *Lange* decision overturned the *Theophanous* defense *de facto*, the High Court did not overrule it *de jure*.[218] Rather, the Court questioned the circumstances of the weak majority in *Theophanous* and *Stephens* in order to revisit the principles established in those cases. First, *Lange* took an unanimous decision that the constitutional defense ABC pleaded was bad in law,[219] because freedom of communication is not expressly guaranteed under the Constitution of Australia. As the Court said, freedom of communication could only be implied from several sections of the Constitution,[220] as an "indispensable incident" of the system of representative government created by the Federal Constitution.[221] In this vein, federal legislation as well as State and Territory legislation and the common law must maintain free political communication, which is intended to ensure responsible and representative government in Australia.[222] Thus, some provisions of the "Constitution necessarily protect freedom of communication between the people concerning political or government matters which enables the people to exercise a free and informed choice as electors, those provisions do not confer personal rights on individuals."[223] Apart from this implied freedom, "the Constitution itself confers no personal right of defense."[224] But, because of the implied freedom, a right of action or remedy, whether it is in the common law or in a statute, cannot be allowed "if its exercise would infringe upon the freedom to discuss government and political matters which the Constitution impliedly requires."[225]

The High Court in *Lange*, again unanimously, held that the defense of qualified privilege pleaded in respect of the publication complained of in New South Wales was not bad in law, "[b]ut that the particulars given [by the defendant] do not bring the publication within that defense."[226] The qualified privilege defense applied in *Lange* was not the traditional common law qualified privilege defense, but a new and expanded one. *Lange* refined the expanded defense established in *Theophanous*. The expanded defense of qualified privilege, first, establishes an "area of immunity which cannot be infringed by a law of the Commonwealth, a law of a State or a law of those Territories whose residents are entitled to exercise the federal franchise."[227] Second, the implied freedom of communication is not absolute, and its exercise is "limited to what is necessary for the effective operation of that system of representative and responsible government provided for by the

Constitution."[228] Third, the scope of the implied freedom is determined by "the common convenience and welfare of society" which "requires an examination of changing circumstances and the need to strike a balance in those circumstances between the absolute freedom of discussion of government and politics and the reasonable protection of the persons who may be involved, directly or incidentally, in the activities of government or politics."[229] Fourth, its exercise is not confined to giving and receiving information during an election period.[230]

The High Court further created a test to determine whether the exercise of legislative or executive power violated the "area of immunity" provided by the implied freedom. The test considers two questions: (a) in its terms, operation or effect, does the law burden the implied freedom? (b) if so, is the law reasonably appropriate and adapted to serve a legitimate end, the fulfillment of which is compatible with the maintenance of the system of representative and responsible government established by the Australian Constitution?[231] Applying the test to the traditional defamation law, the Court found that the common law of defamation burdened the implied freedom in so far as it "requires electors and others to pay damages for the publication of communications concerning [government or political matters relating to the Commonwealth] ... or leads to the grant of injunctions against such publications..."[232] Also, the Court applied it to determine whether the defamation law of New South Wales violated the "area of immunity" as provided by the implied freedom. The Court said that, without the statutory defense of qualified privilege in section 22 of the *Defamation Act 1974* (NSW),[233] the traditional defenses of justification, fair comment, fair report of parliamentary and similar proceedings and qualified privilege provided "no appropriate defense for a person who mistakenly but honestly publishes government or political matter to a large audience."[234] As the Court wrote: "As long as the publisher honestly and without malice uses the occasion for the purpose for which it is given, that person escapes liability even though the publication is false and defamatory."[235] Thus, noting that the traditional Australian defamation law "would impose an undue burden on the required freedom of communication under the Constitution,"[236] the Court held that "the common law doctrine as expounded in Australia must now be seen as imposing an unreasonable restraint on [the implied] freedom of communication."[237] For the traditional defamation law to conform to the implied freedom, the Court held that the implied freedom required the extension of traditional qualified privilege.[238] In support of this need, the Court declared:

> [E]ach member of the Australian community has an interest in disseminating and receiving information, opinions and arguments concerning government and political matters that affect the people of Australia .... The interest that each member of the Australian community has in such a discussion extends the categories of qualified privilege[239]

As a result, "those categories now must be recognized as protecting a communication made to the public on a government or political matter."[240] About the ambit of the new extended qualified privilege defense, the Court noted: "[D]iscussion of government or politics at State or Territory level and even at local government level is amenable to protection by the new extended category of qualified privilege, whether or not it bears on matters at the federal level."[241]

Whereas the traditional qualified privilege defense could be pleaded in publications to one or few people, the *Lange* qualified privilege could be pleaded in publications to a wider audience. In explaining the parameters of the *Lange* form of qualified privilege defense, the High Court distinguished a publication about a government or political matter published to one or few people that would plead a common law qualified privilege from a publication about government and political matters published to a wider audience that would attract the new extended qualified privilege defense. The High Court observed that "a test devised for situations where usually only one person receives the publication is unlikely to be appropriate when the publication is to tens of thousands, or more, of readers, listeners or viewers."[242] In this sense, "The damage that can be done when there are thousands of recipients of a communication is obviously so much greater than when there are only a few recipients."[243] Therefore, the High Court decided that, for the new extended common law defense of qualified privilege, "a requirement of reasonableness ... which goes beyond mere honesty, is properly to be seen as reasonably appropriate and adapted to the protection of reputation, and thus not inconsistent with the freedom of communication which the Constitution requires."[244]

To distinguish different occasions at which the traditional qualified privilege and the *Lange* qualified privilege can be pleaded, the Court used an example. It said: when a member of the public who publishes a complaint that contains false and defamatory material to a Minister concerning the administration of his or her department, the publisher can successfully claim ordinary common law qualified privilege if the statement is published honestly and without malice.[245] While a person can successfully use ordinary common law qualified privilege in a communication to a limited audience, a publisher of a defamatory matter in a national newspaper or on radio or television will rather succeed by claiming the extended qualified privilege defense if his or her conduct is regarded as reasonable by a judge.[246] As the Court put it: "Reasonableness of conduct is an element for the judge to consider only when a publication concerning a government or political matter is made in circumstances that, under the English common law, would have failed to attract a defense of qualified privilege."[247]

While recognizing that reasonableness of a defamatory publication must depend upon "all the circumstances of the case,"[248] the High Court gave some specific conditions of reasonableness. The Court said that a defendant's conduct in publishing material giving rise to a defamatory imputation will only be reasonable if the defendant: (1) was unaware of the falsity of the matter published, and (2) did not act recklessly in making the publication.[249] The Court later added that, as a general rule, the imputation will not be reasonable unless the defendant:

(1) had reasonable grounds for believing that the imputation was true; (2) took proper steps, so far as they were reasonably open, to verify the accuracy of the material; (3) did not believe the imputation to be untrue, and (4) had sought a response from the person defamed and published the response made (if any) except in cases where the seeking or publication of a response was not practicable or it was unnecessary to give the plaintiff an opportunity to respond.[250]

However, the High Court in *Lange*, declared that the new extended qualified privilege "defense will be defeated if the person defamed proves that the publication was actuated by common law malice to the extent that the elements of malice are not covered under the rubric of reasonableness."[251]   For the Court, communications involving government and political matters should be regarded as "actuated by malice" if the publication was "made not for the purpose of communicating government or political information or ideas, but for some improper purpose."[252] Notwithstanding, "the existence of ill will or other improper motive will not itself defeat the privilege," because "[t]he plaintiff must prove that the publication of the defamatory matter was actuated by that ill will or other improper motive."[253] The Court explained further that "the motive of causing political damage to the plaintiff or his or her party cannot be regarded as improper. Nor can the vigor of an attack or the pungency of a defamatory statement, without more, discharge the plaintiff's onus of proof ... [that the publication of the defamatory matter was actuated by that ill will or other improper motive]."[254]

The *Lange* decision is important because of the unanimity of all seven High Court justices sitting. They held that freedom of political discussion in Australia is embodied in Australian Constitution, and so they modified Australian defamation law. The new extended qualified privilege defense covered discussion of government and political matters. The decision concerned the nature of discussion and did not suggest that such protection involved whether the plaintiff is a politician or a public figure.   But, it could discourage many potential politician plaintiffs from seeking remedies for defamatory publications concerning government and political matters. It favored free flow of information, opinion and arguments about government and political matters that affect the Australian people by giving publishers of political communication an immunity from defamation actions provided they act reasonably and without malice.   However, the requirements of reasonableness in the *Lange* decision can threaten the ethical codes of journalists who rely on the *Lange* defense. For example, in determining reasonableness, a court may require a journalist to identify his or her confidential source against his or her ethical obligations. Also, a defense under the new extended qualified privilege can burden a publisher because he or she may be required to show that he or she believed in the truth of the defamatory material and that he or she verified the accuracy of the material before publication.[255]

CONCLUSION

Analysis of the cases suggests the following. The United States Supreme Court's main justification in political defamation cases rests on self-expression, self-government and, above all, the marketplace of ideas principles. The Court holds that free interchange of ideas has an enlightenment function that promotes self-governance and can bring about political and social change. In light of the marketplace of ideas rationale, the Court shows greater interest in political speech than individual reputation in matters of public concern and governance. To promote free public discussion in self-governance, the Court makes distinctions among libel plaintiffs and asks public officials and public figures to tolerate more criticism than private plaintiffs.[256] By using the constitutional standard of "actual malice," the United States Supreme Court takes the approach of heightened scrutiny as its dominant balancing method. By doing so, the Court prefers free, uninhibited, robust, and wide-open discussion of public issues, and says that protected speech may include vehement, caustic, and sometimes unpleasantly sharp attacks on government and public officials.[257]

In quite similar terms, the ECHR shows greater interest in political speech than individual reputation regarding discussion of matters of public concern. The ECHR believes in the marketplace of ideas principle as one of its free speech justifications just as in the United States, but the European Court uses multiple rationales for protecting free political speech. Not only does the ECHR base its justification of the core status of political speech on open exchange of views, opinions and facts, but also the Court balances political speech against reputation because political speech can contribute to the self-fulfillment of citizens and can help maintain democratic self-governance. Though the ECHR has a different test of "necessary in a democratic society," it is similar to the United States' test in that it takes a heightened scrutiny approach in favor of political speech against other competing interests.[258] What is more, the ECHR is comparable to the United States in making status distinctions in freedom of expression cases. The ECHR expects governments or state institutions to accept wider criticism than politicians and private citizens from the press and public opinion. Likewise, the European Court requires politicians to tolerate more criticism than private citizens.

As the Human Rights Act 1998 requires the domestic law of the United Kingdom to take the European Convention and the ECHR jurisprudence into account, the United Kingdom law is likely to undergo considerable change as a result of the incorporation. Now, however, the decisions of the English Court of Appeals and the House of Lords examined indicate a jurisprudence that follows an *ad hoc* balancing approach of resolving political defamation issues. Despite the elasticity of this approach, the decisions depend on public interest in the information. The English regime has interest in speech involving matters of public concern and weighs political speech against reputation when it is published without intentional malice. Though this jurisprudence can chill speech because of its concern for personal reputation, it claims to protect uninhibited speech and robust criticism for the maintenance of a representative democracy. Unlike the United States and ECHR, the duty-interest standard of qualified privilege and the case-by-case approach of the English jurisprudence make no distinctions of political defamation plaintiffs.

Similar to English jurisprudence, the High Court of Australia does not make any distinctions in regard to public figures. However, its implied constitutional freedom of communication that led to an extended qualified privilege departs from the United Kingdom jurisprudence and gets closer to the United States Supreme Court and the ECHR in protecting political speech. In view of its special interest in political speech, the Australian High Court protects discussion and criticisms involving political and government matters when the test of reasonableness is satisfied. So, the High Court of Australia uses preferred position balancing of political speech against interest in reputation. Because political speech helps the exercise of free and informed citizenry in the democratic process, the Court bases its preference for political speech on the principle of responsible and representative democracy and free interchange of ideas.

Taking all in all, the United States Supreme Court, the ECHR and the High Court of Australia believe that political speech is not absolute, but they essentially converge on the preferred position of weighing political speech as a higher value in the balance against reputation. The United Kingdom seems to give less weight to political speech against other competing interests. However, as it is required to incorporate the ECHR case law, it must soon make modifications that will bring it closer to convergence with the other jurisdictions. All four regimes agree on protecting political speech because of its nature as it pertains to issues of public concern. They also accept the need for uninhibited and robust criticism in a democratic society. Moreover, they agree on multiple principles to justify free political speech. While the United States Supreme Court and the ECHR make distinctions in the status of plaintiffs, the regimes in the United Kingdom and Australia do not. The next section involves qualitative content analysis as part of the multiple techniques to subject the findings in the historical and case analyses to scrutiny as well as enhance confidence in this study.

SYNOPSIS OF CASES

The following section categorizes the content of cases studied. It is a summation as well as a comparison of findings as revealed in the selected jurisdictions under study.

Issue of Public Versus Private Concern

This study considered "issue" as facts or subject matter of a libel action, i.e., publication of an alleged defamatory statement could be either a public or private affair. The publication involving a public matter has to show such characteristics as a contribution to political deliberation, opinion about government, discussion and criticism of matters of public concern. On the other hand, speech about a purely private matter pertains to one's personal intimacy. A matter that involves neither corruption nor injustice in the public figures' official function can also be considered private. Also, a private affair concerns a publication that has no direct value to the democratically informed public and the governing process. Findings from cases studied show that the United States, the ECHR, the United Kingdom, and Australia consider political speech as involving matters of public concern, expression of opinion about government, discussion and criticism of issues found in political deliberation, and behaviors relating to governance or impacting the well-being of the citizenry. All the jurisdictions distinguish issues of public concern from purely private matters. The subject matter that pleads protection relates to issues of public concern rather than personal affairs that have no value for an informed public and the governing process.

In the United States, public and political affairs are described in the Supreme Court decisions as matters that concerned "official conduct," "official actions," "public contempt," "public office," "public trust," "public questions," "public discussion of public issues," "free debate," "free and open discussion," "political conduct of officials," "criticism of government and public officials," "public criticism," "discussing public affairs," "issue of public interest and concern," "discussion and communication involving matters of public or general public concern," "governmental office," "impersonal attack on governmental operations," "debate on public issues," "public scrutiny," and "official's fitness for office." The Court used such terms as "public" and "official" to characterize most of the issues involving the conduct of government and its officials. In defamation cases, where the matters exhibited public or official characteristics, the Court upheld criticisms, discussion or debates as legitimate. It considered such concerns in political deliberation to be free, open and protected. For example, in *New York Times*, the Court held that the "publication ... communicated information, expressed opinion, recited grievances, protested claimed abuses, and sought financial support on behalf of a movement whose existence and objectives are matters of the highest public interest and concern."[259] When the issue has a legitimate public concern, it can be protected regardless of the disturbing nature of the expression.

Also, on the subject of public questions, for example, the Court included "defamatory criticism of nonpublic persons who are nevertheless intimately involved in the resolution of important public questions or, by reason of their fame, shape events in areas of concern to society at large."[260]

One can draw from the indicators that the subject matter for protection in the United States relates to public issues and concerns. Purely private affairs are not considered issues within the ambience of political speech. So political speech in the form of open debates, discussion, and criticisms concerning public issues and political conduct of government, public officials and public figures receive protection.

Like the United States, issues of public concern come within the subject matter that often qualifies for protection in the ECHR. For the ECHR, the issues may involve an election process that aroused great public interest.[261] Other issues may concern open discussion and criticisms of a politician's behavior, "[fitness for office as] a member of Parliament, a politician and a member of government," "political criticism of politicians on political questions," "value judgments" or "freedom of opinion of an individual," "insults in political discussion," "criticism uttered in political controversy ... not on [a person's] private life," "political debate," "[criticizing] the action of the government," "discussion related to a matter of public interest," and "public discussion of issues affecting the life of the community." These terms reveal that the subject matter for political speech must be public in nature. The ECHR considers issues and the extent the issues relate to the governing process and life of the society. Thus, the ECHR protects defamation in the process of discussing or criticizing governmental or a politician's conduct. For example, "articles dealt with political issues of public interest in Austria which had given rise to many heated discussions concerning the attitude of Austrians in general -- and the Chancellor in particular -- to National Socialism and to the participation of former Nazis in the governance of the country."[262]

In addition to matters related to the political process, the ECHR considers issues that bear on the life and well-being of citizens as legitimate public concern and worth discussing. An example was the ECHR's finding "that the statements ... bore on a matter of serious public concern .... In publishing those statements ... the applicants assumed their role as representatives of a free press acting as a forum for an open discussion in which ... crew and their spokesmen were able to participate."[263]

Similar to the United States, the ECHR protects political speech because it involves open discussion and criticisms of government and a politician's behavior. Where the subject matter is not directly a political matter, it must at least be an issue related with serious public concern.

The study found that the United Kingdom, the United States, the ECHR and Australia agree on protecting issues that involve matters of public concern. In the United Kingdom, occasions of common convenience and welfare of society are the subject matter that embraces issues concerning "public interest," "governmental and administrative functions," criticism of "an inefficient or corrupt government," "conduct of public affairs," "political crisis," "matter affecting the public at large," "reporting matters of public importance," "political discussion," "comment, not imputations of fact," "a matter of serious public concern," "issues of general interest," "fitness for office of candidates," "communications to the general public on government or political matters," and "information, opinion and arguments concerning government and political matters that affect the people of the United Kingdom." These terms characterize protected speech as opinion or criticism of the governing process and discussion of matters of general public interest. On the public interest to criticize the conduct of government, for example, Lord Keith of Kinkel said in *Derbyshire*: "[N]ot only is there no public interest favoring the right of organs of government, whether central or local, to sue for libel, but that it is contrary to the public interest that they should have it. It is contrary to the public interest because to admit such actions would place an undesirable fetter on freedom of speech."[264]

Believing that political criticism was an issue of public interest, Lord Steyn argued that "publication by a newspaper to the public at large of factual information, opinions and arguments concerning government and political matters that affect the people of the United Kingdom" must be protected.[265] In a different view, Lord Cooke said that "matters other than those pertaining to government and politics may be just as important in the community; and they may have as strong a claim to be free of restraints on freedom of speech."[266] But, relating the issue of public concern to political speech, Lord Hope pointed out: "[W]here the category involves communication to the public, the question must be whether the public interest in the receipt of the information will always outweigh the general public interest in protecting the individual."[267]

Like in the United States and the ECHR, the United Kingdom jurisdiction gives indications that the subject matter of political speech must be one involving public concerns, government performance and suitability for office of public officials and politicians. They are issues of public interest and therefore are described as occasions that promote the common convenience of society.

Similar to the other jurisdictions, Australia's subject matter for protection under political speech is discussion and criticism of issues of public concern, government and political matters. Expressions that show such concern in Australia include "disparagement and criticism of a Commission or its members into disrepute," "freedom of expression in relation to public affairs and freedom to criticize public institutions," "public discussion of migration issues," "discussing government and political matters," "the suitability of persons for office as members of Parliament," and "whether [implied freedom] extends to the publication of matter concerning members of Parliament relating to the performance by such members of their parliamentary duties and their suitability for parliamentary office." The terms demonstrate common characteristics that first indicate that the subject matter of political speech in Australia involves discussion and criticisms of government, or parliamentarians and politicians' performance, and their suitability for office. Second, the political speech is protected when the case concerns political matters that includes information for citizens' participation in the election process and issues that affect their well-being.

Like the other jurisdictions, Australia protects public interest in political speech. However, the indicators in Australia demonstrate that the subject matter must be only discussion and criticism in relation with government and political matters.

Identity of Plaintiff

"Identity" as a category in this study referred to the status of the libel complainant. Here, three persons were distinguished: government or state institution, a politician or public official and non-political public figures, and private citizen. Unlike the similarities among the jurisdictions as regard issues of public concern that plead protection, the jurisdictions differ on making distinctions in the status of political libel plaintiffs. While the United States and the ECHR jurisdictions make such distinctions, the United Kingdom and Australia do not.

United States case law, since *New York Times*, makes distinctions in the status of political libel plaintiffs. According to the United States Supreme Court, such a distinction is necessary "to determine ... the extent to which the constitutional protections for speech limit a State's power to award damages in libel brought by a public official against critics of his official conduct."[268] As a result of this public official and public figure-private person distinction, the Court described "public officials" in other terms like "public servants," "state authorities," "government officials," and "public employees." These terms suggest that people who perform executive, legislative or judicial functions of government and those who are employed by national or local government have public official status. Also, within the public official status are "public persons" or "public men."[269]

While the Supreme Court extended its initial public official and private persons distinctions to cover "public figures,"[270] it did not "apply *New York Times* to the private individual."[271] However, the "actual malice" standard protects defamatory falsehood relating to limited purpose public figures that concerned matters of general or public interest.[272]

The descriptive terms cited indicate that the United States adjudicates political libel cases by distinguishing among the status of plaintiffs. Those distinguished are the public government or public institutions and officials, public figures and private individuals. Protection of political speech is stringent when it involves public officials or institutions and public figures.

Both the ECHR and the United States agree on permitting more protection for private affairs and private persons. They also require the government and politicians to expect more criticism of their public conduct. However, unlike the United Kingdom, but similar to the United States, the ECHR makes status distinctions.[273] The Court said that "the limits of permissible criticism are wider with regard to government than in relation to a private citizen, or even a politician."[274]

The examples indicate that, like the United States, the ECHR makes status distinctions in reviewing political defamation cases. The ECHR gives a threefold distinction according to the limits of acceptable and wider criticism, namely government, a politician, and a private individual. The government must expect more criticism than the politician, and the politician should tolerate more criticism than a private citizen.

In contrast with the United States and the ECHR, the cases studied show that the common law jurisprudence of the United Kingdom does not make any distinction in the status of political libel plaintiffs. However, decisions of the Appeal Court and the House of Lords indicated that governmental organs and officials should tolerate more criticism than the rest of the society. As Lord Keith put it: "In a democratic society, it is almost too obvious to need stating that those who hold office in government and who are responsible for public administration must always be open to criticism. Any attempt to stifle or fetter such criticism amounts to political censorship of the most insidious and objectionable kind."[275] According to the United Kingdom jurisdiction, it would be quite contrary to the common law tradition to make status distinctions. For, "What matters is the subject matter of the publication and how it is treated, rather than who happens to be the subject of the allegations."[276]

Aside from the *Derbyshire* case, which gives an indication of a distinction, decisions that came later do not make any distinctions in the status of plaintiffs. *Reynolds* objected to any distinctions in the status of libel plaintiffs.

At variance with the United States and the ECHR jurisdictions, Australian case law does not make distinctions in the status of political libel plaintiffs. This study found that the Australian avoidance of subject distinctions in defamation cases is the same as its English counterpart. The position in Australia is based on the belief that "following the long tradition of the common law, [Australians] have accepted that personal reputation is a proper subject of protection, no less for those in public office as for private citizens."[277]

In the only clear comment on status distinctions, Australia rejects such distinction as found in the United States and the ECHR. Like the United Kingdom, Australia maintains the common law tradition of protecting the reputation of all citizens alike. By doing so, Australia evaluates the nature of the defamatory material without regard to the status of the defamed. The following schematic table discusses the conclusions of the critical facts of the cases under the four jurisdictions.

Political Expression Versus Reputation

This study defined "interest" as the consideration that weighed heavily in the court's decision -- political expression against reputational interest or vice versa. The Court could show its concern in protecting political expression such as a matter of public concern and an opinion on public matter, or opinion on an individual's private affair, or personal reputation. With the exception of the United Kingdom, political speech weighs heavily in the decisions of the jurisdictions.

From the findings of cases analyzed, interest in political speech weighs more heavily than individual reputation in the United States Supreme Court. For the Court, "freedom of expression on public questions [is]secured."[278] It added: "The maintenance of the opportunity for free political discussion to the end that government may be responsive to the will of the people ... is a fundamental principle of our constitutional system."[279]

Justice Arthur Goldberg explained the Court's interest in political speech: "In a democratic society, one who assumes to act for the citizens in an executive, legislative, or judicial capacity must expect

Table: Critical Facts by Jurisdiction

Jurisdiction	Issue	Identity	Interest	Rationale	Approach
United States	Subject matter involved public concern: Discussion and criticism of issues of public concern, political deliberation, opinion about government	Status of libel plaintiff was important; divided into (1) Public official (2) Pervasive public figure (3) Voluntary limited purpose public figure (4) Involuntary limited purpose public figure *Government agencies have no reputation and so cannot sue (5) Private person or ordinary citizen	The consideration that weighed heavily in libel decisions concerned political speech, public concern, public matter, or governmental matters	Multiple rationales -- Free speech justifications used: - Search for truth - Self-expression - Democratic self-government	Heightened scrutiny: "Actual malice" test
ECHR	Subject matter involved public concern: Discussion and criticism of issues of public concern, political deliberation, opinion about government	Status of libel plaintiff was important; divided into (1) Government, state institution (2) Politician (3) Private person or ordinary citizen	The consideration that weighed heavily in libel decisions concerned political speech, public concern, public matter, or governmental matters	Multiple rationales -- Free speech justifications used: - Search for truth - Self-fulfillment - Democratic self-government	Heightened scrutiny: Test of "necessity for a democratic society"

Continuation of Table: Critical Facts by Jurisdiction

Jurisdiction	Issue	Identity	Interest	Rationale	Approach
United Kingdom	Subject matter involved public concern: Discussion and criticism of issues of public concern, political deliberation, opinion about government	No differentiation of status of libel plaintiff *Government agencies cannot sue	Balancing of the interest of political speech and that of reputation was elastic and uncertain	Multiple rationales -- Free speech justifications used: - Search for truth - Democratic self-government	Ad hoc balancing: "Duty-interest" test
Australia	Subject matter involved public concern: Discussion and criticism of issues of public concern, political deliberation, opinion about government	No differentiation of status of libel plaintiff	The consideration that weighed heavily in libel decisions concerned political speech, public concern, public matter, or governmental matters	Multiple rationales -- Free speech justifications used: - Search for truth - Democratic self-government	Heightened scrutiny: Test of "reasonableness"

that his official acts will be commented upon and criticized. Such criticism cannot ... be muzzled or deterred by the courts at the instance of public officials under the label of libel."[280] Not only did the Court weigh political speech against individual reputation in relation to public officials or public figures, it also held:

> States should retain substantial latitude in their efforts to enforce a legal remedy for defamatory falsehood injurious to the reputation of a private individual .... [But] a private individual whose reputation is injured by defamatory falsehood that does concern an issue of public or general interest has no recourse unless he can meet the rigorous requirements of New York Times.[281]

The examples demonstrate that, for the United States jurisdiction, the interest in political speech outweighs that of an individual's reputation. It warrants that the special interest in political speech serves democratic goals of the society.

As with the United States Supreme Court, political speech weighs heavily in ECHR decisions. According to the ECHR, "[I]t is incumbent ... on [particularly the press] to impart information and ideas on political issues just as on those in other areas of public interest. Not only does the press have the task of imparting such information and ideas: the public also has a right to receive them."[282] Also, about the Court's interest in political speech over individual reputation, it said: "[T]he Court cannot find that the crew members' undoubted interest in protecting their reputation was sufficient to outweigh the vital public interest in ensuring an informed public debate over a matter of local and national as well as international interest."[283]

Similar to the United States, the statements of the ECHR indicate that the ECHR's interest in political speech outweighs that of individual reputation. According to the ECHR, the interest in political speech serves the public interest in information and ideas that are at the core of the democratic society.

Unlike the United States and the ECHR jurisdictions where political speech outweighs individual reputation, the balance is not clear-cut in the British jurisdiction. While the British jurisdiction protects political speech because of public interest considerations, it is reputation-protective. Where public concern outweighs the individual reputation, British case law would accept Lord Keith's argument that "[i]t is of the highest public importance that a democratically elected governmental body, should be open to uninhibited public criticism. The threat of a civil action for defamation must inevitably have an inhibiting effect on freedom of speech."[284] In like reasoning, Lord Bingham of Cornhill wrote:

> People are entitled to hold and to express freely on matters of public interest strong views, views which some of you, or indeed all of you, may think are exaggerated, obstinate, prejudiced, provided -- and this is the important thing -- that they are views which they honestly hold.[285]

However, Lord Bingham refused to provide any special protection for political speech because such protection would "[expose] those who are properly the subject of political speech to false and defamatory factual statements about them with no protection save on proof, which will often be difficult or impossible, that the publisher lacked an honest belief in the truth of the statements."[286]

Despite the democratic value of political speech, the British jurisdiction follows a reputation-protective principle. As Lord Nicholls stated:

> The common law has long recognized the 'chilling' effect of this rigorous, reputation-protective principle. There must be exceptions. At times people must be able to speak and write freely, uninhibited by the prospect of being sued for damages should they be mistaken or misinformed. In the wider public interest, protection of reputation must then give way to a higher priority.[287]

Some statements of Lord Nicholls suggested that political speech would weigh heavily against individual reputation. Instead of supporting political speech as the rule, he shifted to defending protection of reputation. Contending that the protection of reputation is of the public interest, he reasoned:

> Reputation is an integral and important part of the dignity of the individual. It also forms the basis of many decisions in a democratic society which are fundamental to its well-being .... Once besmirched by an unfounded allegation in a national newspaper, a reputation can be damaged for ever, especially if there is no opportunity to vindicate one's reputation. When this happens, society as well as the individual is the loser. For it should not be supposed that protection of reputation is a matter of importance only to the affected individual and his family. Protection of reputation is conducive to the public good. It is in the public interest that the reputation of public figures should not be debased falsely.[288]

However, the other side of the divided House showed interest in public speech that would weigh against individual reputation. For example, Lord Steyn believed: "Exceptions to freedom of expression must be justified as being necessary in a democratic society. In other words, freedom of expression is the rule and regulation of speech is the exception ... only ... justified if it is underpinned by a pressing social need."[289]

The reputation-protective argument and the free speech stance of the lords demonstrate the fluidity of balancing the interests of reputation and political speech in the United Kingdom. The interest of the Court in every case would seem unpredictable and uncertain.[290]

The common law solution in the United Kingdom jurisdiction, as regards weighing of interests, is more unpredictable and uncertain. For a court to decide that a publication is privileged, the court has to consider all the circumstances and determine whether the quality and subject matter of a published material has value to the public. While one may describe the United Kingdom as reputation-protective, the weighing of interest in public concern and that of personal reputation depends on the circumstances of each case.

In the High Court of Australia, political speech weighs heavily in the balance against reputation under the principle of implied freedom, provided that "the defendant is genuinely exercising the right of criticism and not acting in malice or attempting to impair the administration of justice ...."[291] In safeguarding the nation's interest in political speech, Chief Justice Anthony Mason explained: "Public acceptance of the Commission's determinations is essential to the stability of industrial peace and harmony. But no less important is the interest of the public in ensuring that the Commission and its activities should be open to public scrutiny and criticism."[292] For, the reputation of the Commission "is in any event outweighed by the strength of the public interest in public scrutiny and freedom to criticize."[293] The statements demonstrate the High Court's position that public interest in political speech must weigh more in the balance than individual reputation. The High Court showed interest in protecting political speech as it relates to, at least "'public affairs and political discussion,' 'freedom ... to discuss governments and political matters,' 'freedom of communication about the government of the Commonwealth which extends to all political matters, including matters relating to other levels of government,' 'freedom of political discourse,' and 'freedom of participation, association and communication in relation to federal elections.'"[294] These terms describe characteristics of expressions that involve government and political matters. According to the High Court, "criticism of the views, performance and capacity of a member of Parliament and of the member's fitness for public office, particularly when an election is in the offing, is at the very center of the freedom of political discussion."[295] The High Court reversed the situation where reputation weighed against the interest in political speech, because the Court believed

> [T]he common law defenses which protect the reputation of persons who are the subject of defamatory publications do so at the price of significantly inhibiting free communication. To that extent, the balance is tilted too far against free communication and the need to protect efficacious working of representative democracy and government in favor of the protection of individual reputation.[296]

Explaining its interest in political speech, the Australian High Court held that "[t]he law of defamation, whether common law or statute law, must conform to the implication of freedom, even if conformity means that plaintiffs experience greater difficulty in protecting their reputations."[297]

Whereas the jurisdictions demonstrate similarities in their views about the subject matter, they are equally divided on the status distinctions. Though Australia concurs with the United Kingdom in rejecting status distinctions in defamation cases, Australia departs from the United Kingdom in weighing political speech against reputational interests. The terms and statements in the High Court decisions indicate that Australia weighs political speech against the right of individual reputation where government and political matters are concerned.

Rationale

"Rationale" concerned the reasoning of the court, i.e., the value the court used for justifying any protection of speech in the case. The values included self-fulfillment (self-identity, self-expression), search for truth, and democratic self-government (political participation, deliberation, democratic value in general). The jurisdictions studied do not use a single rationale to justify interest in political speech. Rather, they employ multiple rationales. Common to all are the "search for truth" and "democratic self-government."

In the cases studied, United States Supreme Court commonly used the marketplace of ideas and democratic self-government rationales for protecting free political speech in defamation cases. The Court at times used the self-expression argument. Using the enlightenment principle, the Court said: "The constitutional safeguard, we have said, 'was fashioned to assure unfettered interchange of ideas for the bringing about of political and social changes desired by the people.'"[298] To this end, the Court explained: "[T]he First Amendment presupposes that right conclusions are more likely to be gathered out of a multitude of tongues, than through any kind of authoritative selection."[299]

Though the Court gave extensive protection to information relevant to self-government,[300] it warned against false statements of fact, intentional lies, and careless errors as of such slight social value to the search for truth. But, concurring in *Dun & Bradstreet v Greenmoss*, Justice White said: "In a country where the people purport to be able to govern themselves through their elected representatives, adequate information about their government is of transcendent importance. That flow of intelligence deserves full First Amendment protection."[301]

The Court believed that the enlightenment function of free speech would help maintain the goals of representative democracy. Apart from the marketplace of ideas rationale, the Court justified protection of political speech by arguing from the democratic self-government or political participation rationale. The United States Supreme Court said that elected "officials are responsible to the people for the way they perform their duties."[302] It argued that "freedom to discuss public affairs and public officials is unquestionably ... the kind of speech the First Amendment was primarily designed to keep within the area of free discussion."[303] Another explanation was that "freedom of press and of speech insures that government will respond to the will of the people and that changes may be obtained by peaceful means."[304]

Also, Justice William Brennan used both the political participation rationale and the self-expression argument. He wrote: "The free speech guarantees gives each citizen an equal right to self-expression and to participation in self-government."[305]

The statements of the justices of the United States Supreme Court are illustrations that the jurisdiction justifies protection of political speech based on three rationales. The rationales that the United States Supreme Court uses are the marketplace of ideas, self-fulfillment and democratic self-government arguments. The Court offers this multiple rationales to allow a special protection for political speech.

The pervading rationales for protecting free speech in the United States are the same as those used in the ECHR. The ECHR employs multiple rationales of search for the truth, self-fulfillment and democratic self-government to justify protection of political speech in defamation cases. Several statements of the ECHR illustrate this position. For example, the Court said that "freedom of expression ... constitutes one of the essential foundations of a democratic society and one of the basic conditions for its progress and for each individual's self-fulfillment."[306] This pronouncement indicates the Court's belief that democratic self-governance and the self-fulfillment rationales form the root and survival of the system of representative democracy.

To stress the political participation principle, *Castells* added to the reasoning of *Lingens*: "In particular [freedom of the press] gives politicians the opportunity to reflect and comment on the preoccupations of public opinion; it thus enables everyone to participate in the free political debate which is at the very core of the concept of a democratic society."[307] In addition to the democratic self-government and self-fulfillment rationales, democracy thrives on the search for the truth principle by creating informed citizenry. According to the Court, "Freedom of the press furthermore affords the public one of the best means of discovering and forming an opinion of the ideas and attitudes of political leaders."[308]

Like the United States, pronouncements of the ECHR demonstrate that the principles of search for the truth, democratic self-governance and individual self-fulfillment guide the decisions of this European Court. So the ECHR is similar to the United States in using multiple rationales in favoring political speech in mostly criminal defamation cases.

Similar to the United States and the ECHR, the United Kingdom jurisdiction uses the democratic self-government and search for the truth rationales for the protection of political speech. In the United Kingdom, Lord Bingham said, for example:

> We do not for an instant doubt that the common convenience and welfare of a modern plural democracy such as ours are best served by an ample flow of information to the public concerning, and by vigorous public discussion of, matters of public interest to the community. By that we mean matters relating to the public life of the community and those who take part in it, including within the expression "public life" activities such as the conduct of government and political life, elections ... and public administration .... Recognition that the common convenience and welfare of society are best served in this way is a modern democratic imperative which the law must accept .... It would be strange if the law in this country -- the land of Milton, Paine and Mill -- were to deny this recognition ....[309]

While the term "ample flow of information to the public" illustrates Lord Bingham's belief in the search for truth argument, "vigorous public discussion of matters of public interest" indicates his justification of the political participation idea. In a similar vein, Lord Nicholls spoke of the search for the truth and political participation rationales. In his rendering of the majority, he wrote: "At the pragmatic level, freedom to disseminate and receive information on political matters ... enables those who elect representatives to Parliament, and those elected to make an informed choice, regarding individuals as well as policies, and those elected to make an informed decisions."[310] Lord Nicholls' statement implies that the search for the truth enables citizens and representatives of their constituents to make better political choices in a representative democracy. About this search for the truth, Lord Cooke cited Justice Oliver Wendell Holmes, Jr.'s statement that "the best test of truth is the power of the thought to get itself accepted in the competition of the market ...."[311]

Lord Hobhouse, in his opinion, emphasized the political participation rationale. He wrote: "The citizen is at liberty to comment and take part in free discussion. It is of fundamental importance to a free society that this liberty be recognized and protected by law."[312] This illustrates Lord Hobhouse's view that criticism and discussion of matters of public interest are permissible in the United Kingdom.

The case indicators suggest that the United Kingdom at least believes in the democratic self-governance and search for the truth principles. In relation to the rationales for justifying free speech, the United Kingdom shares common understandings with the United States and the ECHR.

Like the other jurisdictions in this study, the High Court of Australia uses more than one rationale to justify protection of political speech. The Court justifies the protection of political speech in the Australian Commonwealth by synthesizing two principles, namely the "marketplace of ideas" and "democratic self-government" rationales. For example, in Australia, "the principle[s] of responsible government are constitutional imperatives which are intended ... to make both the legislative and executive branches of the government of the Commonwealth ultimately answerable to the Australian people."[313] This statement illustrates Justice Gerard Brennan's opinion that the principle of self-governance makes the government responsible to the sovereign people of Australia. It permits citizens to freely and openly discuss political and economic matters of the country. Thus, he added:

> To sustain a representative democracy embodying the principles prescribed by the Constitution, freedom of public discussion of political and economic matters is essential: it would be a parody of democracy to confer on the people a power to choose their Parliament but to deny the freedom of public discussion from which the people derive their political judgments.[314]

The principle of representative government itself is the source of political speech. So far as this principle is recognized as firmly entrenched in the Australian Constitution, freedom of political speech can achieve its purpose of the efficacious working of representative democracy.[315]

Using both the search for the truth and political participation rationales, the majority in *Theophanous* observed:

> Because the system of representative government depends for its efficacy on the free flow of information and ideas and of debate, the freedom extends to all those who participate in political discussion. By protecting the free flow of information, ideas and debate, the Constitution better equips the elected to make decisions and the electors to make choices and thereby enhances the efficacy of representative government.[316]

Similar to the other jurisdictions, the Australian case indicators demonstrate that the jurisdiction also uses multiple rationales for protecting political speech in Australia. The marketplace of ideas and democratic self-governance rationales are mentioned as the basis and principle of Australian representative democracy.

Doctrinal Approach

This study considered "doctrinal approach" as the method the court used to balance free speech and personal reputation. The method could be any of the three dominant approaches in free speech jurisprudence, namely "absolutism," "ad hoc balancing," and "heightened scrutiny." Absolutism referred to the method of resolving free speech problems that gave unconditional (absolute) protection of speech against any restriction by government. The "*ad hoc* balancing" method involved the approach of weighing competing interests in every speech conflict by balancing the importance of the competing interests in a specific case. It does not give a fixed doctrinal rule. The "heightened scrutiny" or "the preferred position balancing" gives slightly less protection to free speech than absolutism, yet it is much more protective of free speech than ad hoc balancing. It weighs free speech interest against other interests. So it places a heavy burden on government whenever a governmental action is challenged as a violation of free speech protection, and it makes it difficult for politicians and public figures to win a defamation suit.

None of the jurisdictions guarantees absolute protection of speech or reputation. However, apart from the United Kingdom, which uses an *ad hoc* balancing approach, the other jurisdictions rely on preferred position balancing that favors political speech.

The actual malice test, rooted in the First Amendment jurisprudence, is a preferred-position balancing approach (approach of heightened scrutiny) ingrained in the United States Supreme Court decisions studied. Though the Court held that "libel can claim no talismatic immunity from constitutional limitations,"[317] it maintained that "debate on public issues should be uninhibited, robust, and wide-open, and that it may well include vehement, caustic, and sometimes unpleasantly sharp attacks on government and public officials."[318] The approach of heightened scrutiny, under the actual malice standard, considered restraint on criticism of government and public officials as inconsistent with the First Amendment. The Court believed that "the pall of fear and timidity imposed upon those who would give voice to public criticism is an atmosphere in which the First Amendment freedoms cannot survive."[319]

As a result, the Court demarcated the State's power to penalize good-faith critics of government by prohibiting a public official from recovering damages for a defamatory falsehood relating to his official conduct unless he proves that the statement was made with "actual malice" -- that is, with knowledge that it was false or with reckless disregard of whether it was false or not.[320] This position offers slightly less protection than the absolutist stance suggested by Justices Hugo Black and William O. Douglas,[321] and Justice Goldberg.[322] But, the heightened scrutiny is more protective of free political speech than *ad hoc* balancing.

Because an "ad hoc resolution of the competing interests at stake in each case is not feasible,"[323] the Court established the actual malice test as a general rule of application.[324] As a result, the Court's heightened scrutiny gives more protection to political speech by removing the specters of presumed and punitive damages in the absence of *New York Times* malice and eliminates significant and powerful motives for self-censorship that otherwise were present in the traditional libel action.[325]

The Court's doctrinal approach, simply put, showed that the "interest of the public [to criticize their governors] outweighs the interest of appellant or any other individual."[326] The United States

Supreme Court pronouncements as exemplified in the cases studied show that the method of heightened scrutiny was the doctrinal approach that the Court followed. The Court applies the "actual malice" test established in *New York Times* as the controlling authority in its balancing approach that supports its preference for political speech.

The ECHR is close to the United States and Australian jurisdictions in its preferred-position balancing approach in political defamation cases. The ECHR protects more political speech than the *ad hoc* balancing offered in the United Kingdom jurisdiction. The ECHR's test of "necessity in a democratic society" is a balancing exercise that "requires the Court to determine whether the 'interference' complained of corresponded to a 'pressing social need,' whether it was proportionate to the legitimate aim pursued and whether the reasons given by the national authorities to justify it are relevant and sufficient."[327] This rule of categorization is the ECHR's well-established case law, and it maintains that "interferences with the freedom of expression ... call for the closest scrutiny on the part of the Court."[328]

Put in another way, protection of freedom of expression is the rule and any interference that passes the strict scrutiny of the Court is an exception. For example, in *Bladet Tromso*, the preferred-position balancing approach of the Court demonstrated its favor for public interest speech. The preference for political speech, however, met the criticism of the joint dissent of Judges Elizabeth Palm, Willi Fuhrmann and Andras Baka, who said: "It is the right to the protection of reputation aspect of the present case which has been given insufficient attention in the Court's judgment and which motivates the present dissent."[329] The dissenting view represented an objection to the Court's doctrinal approach in favor of free speech as applied in this case. While the Court was more protective of the public interest, the joint dissent reasoned: "[T]he fact that a strong public interest is involved should not have the consequence of exonerating newspapers from either the basic ethics of their trade or the laws of defamation."[330] But, the Court's opinion illustrates its position that the defamation of the individuals involved was not as grave as to override the importance of protecting public interest speech.

Similar to the United States, statements in ECHR decisions studied demonstrate that the ECHR employs a heightened scrutiny approach to weigh political speech against individual reputation. However, the doctrinal approach in the ECHR uses a different test, i.e., the rule of "necessity in a democratic society."

In contrast to the United States Supreme Court that employs a heightened scrutiny in its approach to political speech, the United Kingdom jurisdiction uses the *ad hoc* balancing method "to protect publications to the general public in the particular circumstances of the case."[331] The "duty-interest" requirement of the United Kingdom courts considers "whether the occasion of the particular publication, in the light of its particular circumstances, contains the necessary ingredients to give rise to [qualified] privilege."[332] Concerning this common law approach, Lord Nicholls argued: "[T]he common law principle enables interference with freedom of speech to be confined to what is necessary in the circumstances of the case ... The weight to be given to [the circumstances] and other relevant factors will vary from case to case."[333] This approach under common law qualified privilege contrasts with generic privilege as applied in *New York Times*. The *ad hoc* balancing under the English common law can stifle free political speech.[334]

Despite the resemblance of the jurisdictions in their democratic ideals, the United Kingdom differs from the others in its balancing method. The United Kingdom is different in its doctrinal approach from the others because, while the other jurisdictions rely on the heightened scrutiny method of balancing political speech against personal reputation, the United Kingdom uses an *ad hoc* balancing method. The United Kingdom's "duty-interest" test as applied in the *ad hoc* approach does not give any preference for political speech, and the balancing is unpredictable.

Though they follow different tests, Australia, the ECHR and the United States are close in using the preferred balancing approach in weighing the interests of political speech against reputation. According to the High Court of Australia, the interest of Australian people in political communication "extends the categories of common law qualified privilege. Consequently, those categories now must be recognized as protecting a communication made to the public on a government or political matter."[335] As the Court noted, "the category of political speech amenable for protection" includes "discussion of the conduct, policies or fitness for office of government, political parties, public bodies, public officers and those seeking public office ... discussion of political views and public conduct of persons who are engaged in activities that have become the subject of political debate...."[336] In such situations involving government and political matters, the High Court gives greater preference for political speech. This doctrinal approach in Australia follows a test of "reasonableness" that gives less protection than absolutism, and yet it is more protective of political speech than *ad hoc* balancing in the United Kingdom jurisdiction.

According to the Court, the test of reasonableness requires the defendant to establish "that it was unaware of the falsity of the matter" and that it "did not act recklessly in making the publication;" that it "had reasonable grounds for believing that the imputation was true, took proper steps, so far as they were reasonably open to verify the accuracy of the material and did not believe the imputation to be untrue;" that "the defendant sought a response from the person defamed and published the response made (if any) except in cases where the seeking or publication of a response was not practicable or it was unnecessary to give the plaintiff an opportunity to respond."[337]

The Australian jurisdiction resembles the United States and the ECHR in the result of using the heightened scrutiny balancing method. The Australian High Court applies the test of "reasonableness" to protect political speech in relation to government and political matters.

In summary, all the jurisdictions accepted discussion and criticism of issues of public concern, political deliberation, or opinion about government as the subject matter that could plead for protection against individual reputation in political defamation cases. But, while the United States and the ECHR additionally recognize distinctions in the status of a political defamation plaintiff, the United Kingdom and Australia do not recognize such distinctions. According to the United Kingdom and Australia, the concern of any defamation action is the subject matter of the publication rather than the plaintiff. Aside from the United Kingdom, whose weighing of interests in political speech and reputation is unpredictable, the other jurisdictions are close in weighing political speech against individual reputation. So, the United States, the ECHR and Australia use a preferred-position balancing approach that favors political speech. On the other hand, the United Kingdom uses an *ad hoc* balancing approach that makes its decisions in balancing competing interests elastic and uncertain. However, the United Kingdom's incorporation of European Convention of Human Rights and its jurisprudence into the British legal system under the Human Rights Act 1998 is a turning for future convergence with the

ECHR. Finally, all four jurisdictions justify the protection of speech of public concern or political speech with a multiple rationale that embodies, in particular, the search for truth and democratic self-government arguments.

Chapter Five

Conclusion: Convergence of Political Speech Protections

The present study was designed to answer two questions on political defamation by comparing and contrasting the prevailing jurisprudence in the United States, the ECHR, the United Kingdom and Australia. First, it examined whether the jurisdictions are converging or diverging, and found that recent developments in political defamation laws in the jurisdictions are converging. Legal developments in Australia and the United Kingdom in the 1990s have produced more areas of convergence than divergence with the other jurisdictions regarding political speech. While the United Kingdom is at a turning point, Australia has established a defamation law that protects political speech in government and political matters. Second, concerning the extent to which rationales for protecting political speech justify restrictions on libel laws in a democratic society, all the jurisdictions offered multiple rationales that weighed speech of legitimate public interest against individual reputation.

The multiple methods used to analyze the four jurisdictions revealed that social and political conditions shaped the jurisprudential history of the United States, the ECHR, the United Kingdom, and Australia.[1] The social and political factors combined with the principles of democracy to inspire rationales for protecting free speech. In the United States, the United Kingdom and Australia, when arguments for protecting free speech became dominant at a point in the countries' history, shifts in constitutional and common law understandings brought reforms in the countries' defamation laws. In the United States, suppression of speech through criminal libel prosecutions tumbled as liberal ideas for speech opposed such prosecutions and argued for protection of political speech. The analyses indicated that the United States Supreme Court's main justification in political defamation cases rested on self-expression,

141

self-government and, above all, the marketplace of ideas principles. The United States jurisdiction believed that free interchange of ideas has an enlightenment function that promotes self-governance and can bring about political and social change. In light of the marketplace of ideas, self-fulfillment and self-governance rationales, the United States placed greater interest in political speech than individual reputation in matters of public concern and governance.

A quite different social and political history affected the ECHR. The need to protect democracy in Europe reinforced free political speech protection under the European Convention on Human Rights. As a result, Article 10 of the European Convention is interpreted by ECHR to allow free political discussion and check member states against undesirable and unnecessary fetters on this freedom. The ECHR considered the marketplace of ideas, self-fulfillment and democratic self-government principles as free speech justifications just as did the United States. For the ECHR, the core status of political speech required an open exchange of views, opinions and facts, and so contribute to the self-fulfillment of citizens and help maintain democratic self-governance.

The United Kingdom shared the history of common law defamation, and part of its social and political history with the United States and Australia. While the United States constitutionalized its defamation law under the First Amendment and abandoned the strictures of seditious libel, the United Kingdom made gradual modifications until criminal libel reforms in the 1980s and the Human Rights Act 1998. To curb infringement of the convention rights on its citizens, the United Kingdom responded to the need to incorporate the European Convention jurisprudence into its domestic law. By doing so, the United Kingdom establishes a new English law that should conform to the convention rights and repair its image on human rights. Like the United States and the ECHR, the United Kingdom depended on search for truth and democratic self-government to justify protection of public interest speech.

Unlike the United States, Australia remained loyal to the United Kingdom. Australia continues to use English case law as a major source of persuasive authority. Because Australia gives great weight to the United Kingdom law, change in the United Kingdom domestic law as a result of its incorporation of the European Convention on Human Rights provisions and jurisprudence will have a great impact on Australia's jurisprudence as well. For example, the United Kingdom and Australia are likely to make the ECHR type of status distinctions requiring governments to accept wider criticism than politicians, and politicians than private citizens.

Recently, Australia departed from the common law qualified privilege and established an extended qualified privilege for the protection of discussion of government and political matters. Australia relied on the principles of democratic self-government and search for truth to justify protection of political speech. Thus, the four jurisdictions justified the protection of speech of public concern or political speech with multiple rationales that embodied, in particular, the search for truth and democratic self-government arguments.

On issues for free speech considerations, all the jurisdictions accepted discussion and criticism of matters of public concern, political deliberation, or opinion about government as the subject matter that could merit protection against individual reputation in political defamation cases. Though the jurisdictions agreed on the subject matter of protection, they were split on categorizing status of plaintiffs. While the United States and the ECHR recognized distinctions in the status of political defamation plaintiffs, the United Kingdom and Australia rejected such distinctions. The United States made distinctions among libel plaintiffs and required public officials and public figures to tolerate more criticism than private plaintiffs. Similar to the United States, the ECHR made status distinctions in freedom of expression cases. The ECHR expected governments or state institutions to accept wider criticism from the press and the public opinion than politicians and private citizens. On the other hand, the United Kingdom and Australia did not make any distinctions in regard to public figures. According to the United Kingdom and Australia, the concern of any defamation action is on the subject matter of the publication rather than plaintiff. So, the decisions in the United Kingdom and Australia depended on public interest in information involving matters of public concern. However, the recent integration of the European Convention provisions and the ECHR jurisprudence into the United Kingdom domestic legal system means that the United Kingdom and Australia can expect government and politicians to accept wider criticism than private citizens.

This study found differences in the extent the jurisdictions protected political speech. The United States was the most liberal. The ECHR was less liberal than the United States but more liberal than

Australia. The United Kingdom was least liberal largely because its weighing of interests in political speech and reputation was unpredictable. The United States, the ECHR and Australia took greater interest in political speech than individual reputation regarding discussion of matters of public concern. Recent Australian High Court decisions, based on an implied constitutional freedom of communication, created an extended qualified privilege that departed from the United Kingdom jurisprudence and drew Australia closer to the United States and the ECHR in protecting political speech. The United Kingdom had an interest in speech involving matters of public concern, but its case-by-case weighing of speech against reputation gave no special preference for political speech. But the United Kingdom under the Human Rights Act 1998 incorporates ECHR jurisprudence; this new legal scheme makes the ECHR jurisprudence part and parcel of the United Kingdom domestic law in a way that will give preference for political speech.

Despite the differences in the extent to which the jurisdictions restrict libel laws by weighing political speech and reputation, all the jurisdictions are now coalescing. The jurisdictions that weighed the interest of political speech against individual reputation also used the heightened balancing approach. The United States, the ECHR and Australia used a preferred-position balancing approach that favored political speech. By using the constitutional standard of "actual malice," the United States Supreme Court took the heightened scrutiny approach as its dominant balancing method. By doing so, the Court prefers "that debate on public issues should be uninhibited, robust, and wide-open," and said that protected speech "may well include vehement, caustic, and sometimes unpleasantly sharp attacks on government and public officials."[2] Though the ECHR has a different test of "necessary in a democratic society," it is similar to the United States by taking a heightened scrutiny approach in favor of political speech against other competing interests. Also, the High Court of Australia used the extended qualified privilege test (test of reasonableness) under the implied freedom to grant preferred position balancing of political speech against interest in reputation because, it believed, political speech helps the exercise of free and informed citizenry in the democratic process. Unlike the tests of the United States, the ECHR and Australia, the duty-interest standard of qualified privilege of the United Kingdom followed a case-by-case approach. But with the present change to interpret the United Kingdom's domestic laws in light of the European Convention provisions and jurisprudence, the United Kingdom will shift from its traditional *ad hoc* balancing approach into a heightened scrutiny method of the ECHR. The findings have theoretical implications for free political speech. The study found that democratic jurisdictions give heightened protection for political speech by assimilating into their defamation laws values embodied in multiple rationales for protecting political speech. A similar finding was obtained in Rodrigo J. Bustos Sierra's comparative study of the United States and Spain jurisdictions. Bustos Sierra found that both legal regimes emphasized the preferred position of free speech.[3] The search for truth and for informed citizenry, individual self-expression and self-fulfillment, political participation, and open discussion and criticism of public affairs combined to offer stringent protection for political expression and restrict libel laws. They are not conflicting values, but rather, they are mutually sustaining and interrelated. They form a rich congruity of democratic values, and give the quintessential justification for heightened protection of political speech. This finding supports Rodney Smolla's position on multiple rationales for protecting political speech. He wrote: "Nothing in the self-governance rationale 'knocks out' the marketplace of ideas rationale or the self-fulfillment rationale .... There is, in sum, nothing *inside* the self-governance theory that disqualifies the marketplace of ideas or fulfillment theories, and nothing *outside* those two theories that limits them to self-governance issues."[4] For, there "is no logical reason why the preferred position of freedom of speech might not be buttressed by multiple rationales."[5] What is more, political speech receives stringent protection because it is grounded in what Cohen calls "the fact of reasonableness," respecting the citizen's freedom to receive, share, hold, modify or express opinions.[6] These values are democratic goals and free political speech, above all, promotes them concretely.

In addition, the findings of this study have implications for legal policy making in the United Kingdom. The United Kingdom weighing of political speech against other competing interests contrasted with the other jurisdictions. The practical ways by which it incorporates the ECHR case law and makes modifications will bring it closer to convergence with the other jurisdictions. With the landmark decision of *Derbyshire*, the United Kingdom progressed in protecting more political speech. But subsequent decisions of the Court of Appeal and the House of Lords did not follow that lead. But, as the Human Rights Act 1998 requires the domestic law in the United Kingdom to take the European Convention and the ECHR jurisprudence into account, the United Kingdom law will undergo extensive changes as a result of the incorporation. So, constraints imposed by Article 10 of ECHR are expected to accelerate its convergence with the ECHR jurisprudence.

Moreover, the Human Rights Act 1998 can have an impact on Australia and other emerging common law countries, which are part of the British Commonwealth. Legal experts and jurors in Commonwealth countries such as Australia, Ghana and Nigeria often cite English authorities in their legal practice. Because English precedents and those of Commonwealth countries have persuasive authority in the British Commonwealth, the Human Rights Act can have legal implications on member countries. Australia and the other Commonwealth countries can rely on legal insights the Human Rights Act establishes in British courts. What is more, emerging common law democracies belonging to the British Commonwealth can draw inspiration from Australia's implied constitutional protection of political speech. Particularly, where the constitutions of those countries do not have specific guarantees of freedom of speech and of the press, they can distill from sections of their constitutions an implication to protect freedom of communication as Australia did. In another way, those emerging democracies can create a bill of rights as the United Kingdom made of the Human Rights Act 1998.

Also, the findings of this study should inform policy makers in emerging common law democracies such as Ghana, Nigeria and Kenya about foundational values that sustain political speech in a representative government. In this regard, this study makes the following recommendations. First, emerging common law democracies should effectively eliminate threats of dictatorship through civic education in democratic values such as political participation and informed citizenry. Many people in emerging democracies seem politically "illiterate" and do not know that national sovereignty resides in citizens rather than the governors. Educating the people about their civil and political rights will help them preserve their system of representative democracy.

Second, common law emerging democracies should work for legal understandings that value the preeminent role of political speech in the survival of a democratic society. To achieve this, they must have a bill of rights that lays the strong foundation for the protection of citizens' rights and gives them an unambiguous claim for exercising freedom of political speech.

Third, as the common law democracies enact a bill of rights, they should make the protection of political speech the rule and any interference of this right an exception. As a result, interest in political speech should weigh against individual reputation in defamation cases.

Fourth, any exception can be gauged by using the preferred balancing approach. The common law emerging countries can find insights from the legal experience of the United States Supreme Court, the ECHR and the High Court of Australia. The jurisdictions agree that political speech is not absolute, but, with different tests, they essentially converge on the preferred position of balancing political speech against reputation. So, in considering a test for defamation cases, an emerging democracy should create defamation jurisprudence that follows a heightened balancing approach.

Fifth, common law emerging democracies should use multiple rationales for free speech to secure greater protection for political speech. According to this study, all regimes that agreed on the preferred balancing approach also used multiple rationales for protecting political speech in a democratic society.

Sixth, common law emerging democracies should note that principles regulating defamation laws need not be uniform to achieve protection of political speech. However, tests that emerging democratic jurisdictions establish should consider political speech in relation to a subject matter that involves discussion and criticism of issues of public concern, and opinion about government and political matters. Such matters of public concern must merit the heightened balancing approach and the multiple rationales that should govern the defamation jurisprudence of emerging democratic jurisdictions. As a result, the jurisdictions can have different tests as determined by their constitutions, statutes or common law to arrive at the heightened approach. For example, while the United States Supreme Court and the ECHR made distinctions in the status of plaintiffs, the regimes in the United Kingdom and Australia did not. Yet, Australia could create a preferred balancing test based solely on the subject matter of the defamatory publication to ensure protection for political speech. Thus, whether a jurisdiction considers distinctions in the status of political defamation plaintiffs or not, an interest in political speech as the subject matter requiring protection is paramount.

Seventh, because the exercise of freedom of political speech often involves issues that deal with governance and political matters, government agents and officials are most likely affected. To ensure more political speech, the defamation jurisprudence in emerging democracies should expect government and politicians to accept a wider criticism than private individuals. This will impede frequent defamation actions by government agents and politicians but help uninhibited political participation of citizens in the political process.

Eighth, emerging common law democracies need a system of judicial review such as those in the ECHR and the United States that are independent of the executive branch of government. Often the function of checks and balances among the executive, legislative and judicial branches of government in developing countries does not work as it should. The executive branch can overreach its authority and impair the powers of the judiciary. So, emerging common law countries should have a strong and independent judiciary with credible judicial review that can sustain legal interpretations consistent with democratic understandings.

Looking for a common ground, this study goes beyond common law to recommend a model for emerging democracies. Because the common law does not satisfactorily weigh political speech against an individual's reputation, jurisdictions such as the United States, Australia and lately the United Kingdom modified the traditional defamation laws. Thus, this study proposes the ECHR as the common ground for emerging democracies. The ECHR is a fitting common ground for several reasons. First, the ECHR is a reasonable synthesis of the jurisdictions that make status distinctions among political libel plaintiffs and those that do not. Though the ECHR accepts status distinctions, it does not make complex extensions of who comes within a "public figure" test as does the United States. It also satisfies jurisdictions like Australia and the United Kingdom that protect government and political matters but subject such protection to reasonable deference for personal reputation. Yet, the ECHR test of "necessity in a democratic society" takes a heightened scrutiny approach that protects the core status of political speech from unreasonable fetters and governmental interference.

Second, the ECHR can be the common ground because emerging common law countries can find in this model a legal regime directly influenced by the Universal Declaration of Human Rights. Also, the ECHR has an advantage of wider acceptability in Western European democracies. It is supranational in its jurisdictional impact and is tested as effective in promoting democratic values in forty-one European countries.

Third, threats to human rights and stability are readily recognizable social and political factors that challenge emerging democracies. Such threats are similar to totalitarianism in Europe in the 1930 and 1940s that led to the creation of the European Convention. As the need to protect democracy in Europe reinforced free political speech protection under the European Convention on Human Rights, so emerging democracies can allow free political discussion and check government against undesirable and unnecessary fetters on this freedom in their representative democracies.

Fourth, the ECHR can be the common ground model for emerging democracies because the incorporation of the ECHR into the United Kingdom law will have an impact on emerging democracies that are members of the British Commonwealth. As a result of the United Kingdom's incorporation of the ECHR provisions and jurisprudence, the United Kingdom develops a new body of law. This new law in the United Kingdom follows the test of "necessity in a democratic society" as in the ECHR and gives more protection to political speech. The Commonwealth member countries have strong affinity with the United Kingdom and its law has strong persuasive authority on them. The training of lawyers of the Commonwealth emphasizes British law. Also, some of the lawyers receive further training in British institutions to the extent that the legal minds of the emerging common law democracies are greatly influenced by the United Kingdom jurisprudence. What is more, lawyers in the emerging common law democracies read British legal journals and reporters for fresh perspectives and developments in the United Kingdom jurisprudence. As the United Kingdom law has strong persuasive authority in British Commonwealth nations, the new law in the United Kingdom that embodies the ECHR will also influence the emerging common law democracies.

For future research, one can bring civil law jurisdictions such as France and Germany into the sample and consider how common law and civil law jurisdictions will compare in restricting libel laws, the free speech rationales they will employ to justify such restrictions in relation to political speech, and determine whether they converge or diverge. Another study can involve analysis of political defamation jurisprudence in emerging Commonwealth democracies such as India and Ghana, and look at how they compare with the same in established democracies. Also, a future researcher can look at what happens to political defamation in the United Kingdom a decade after the incorporation of the European Convention through the 1998 Human Rights Act. The researcher should examine whether or not the United Kingdom is getting closer to the ECHR.

Notes

INTRODUCTION

[1] See an analysis of Dewey's idea of communication in Carl Bybee, *Can Democracy Survive in the Post-Factual Age?: A Return to the Lippmann-Dewey Debate about the Politics of News*, 1 Journalism and Mass Communication Monograph 1, 27-56 (1999). Bybee analyzed the ideas of both Lippmann and Dewey about democratic theory. He said both theorists agreed on the importance of communication. "For the public to act as a public requires open and free communication in order to inform itself of the current state of affairs and to debate the consequences of individual and associated behavior in order to judge their value in terms of the shared interests of the public" (at 55). Bybee added that Lippmann believed this role of communication no longer possible in the democracy because of the size and complexity of government and the basic irrationality of human action. But Dewey believed in the enduring relevance of the role communication is expected to play in the liberal theory of democracy.

[2] Rodney A. Smolla, *Free Speech in an Open Society* 3 (Alfred A. Knopf, Inc., 1992).

[3] For example, the United States' Constitution guarantees the right of freedom of speech in the First Amendment. In Britain, freedom of speech has nonconstitutional status as a legal principle, but it is an accepted political principle that affects the interpretation of statutes and the development of judicial doctrines.

[4] Amy Gutmann, *How Liberal Is Democracy?* in Douglas MacLean and Claudia Hills, eds, *Liberalism Reconsidered* 25-50 (Rowman & Allanheld 1983).

[5] Kent Greenawalt, *Speech, Crime, and the Uses of Language* 4 (Oxford University Press, 1989).

[6] Julianne Schultz, *Reviving the Fourth Estate: Democracy, Accountability and the Media* 70 (Cambridge University Press, 1998), said:

> In the United States, where rights to freedom of the press and expression and individual rights are explicitly stated ... the news media has used its constitutional authority to add force to the argument that it should operate unfettered. In countries such as Australia and Britain, where there is no constitutional acknowledgment of the right to freedom of speech and the press, the

Fourth Estate authority of the news media is informal and depends on custom, practice, and the common law. As a result the outcome of contests between major political institutions is less predictable and the need to find a balance between competing areas of authority and legitimacy subject to ongoing renegotiation.

[7] Randall P. Bezanson, *Libel Law and the Realities of Litigation: Setting the Record Straight*, 71 Iowa L Rev 226, 266 (1985).

[8] *Attorney-General v Guardian Newspapers Ltd.*, 1 WLR 1248, 1286 (1987). Similarly, Lord Oliver cited Blackstone's statement that the liberty of the press is essential to the nature of a free State (at 1320); also Eric Barendt, *Freedom of Speech* 1 (Clarendon Press, 1987) explained that, in Britain where fundamental liberties "lack constitutional protection, politicians and law reformers regard freedom of expression as a basic value which should always be respected. It is not an absolute right ... but powerful reasons are generally required before its restriction by legislation is accepted as justified."

[9] *Reno v American Civil Liberties Union*, 521 US 844, 885 (1997).

[10] Modern law does not protect the reputation of public institutions. But reputation of public institutions is included here because this study considers one such case in England.

[11] See *New York Times v Sullivan*, 376 US 254, 279-283 (1964).

[12] See *Hill v Church of Scientology of Toronto*, 126 DLR (4th) 129 (1995). The Court expressed its opinion about the public figure defense as it operates in the United States, though the case was not about political speech. Moreover, the Canadian Court has not had the opportunity to consider the issue of defamatory falsehood in political discussion.

[13] *Rajagopal v State of Tamil Nadu*, 6 SCC 632, 650 (1994).

[14] *Lange v Australian Broadcasting Corp.*, 189 CLR 520, 571-574 (1997).

[15] *Lingens v Austria*, 8 EHRR 407 ¶ 47 (1986).

[16] Id.

[17] Lammy Betten, ed, *The Human Rights Act 1998 What It Means: The Incorporation of the European Convention on Human Rights into the Legal Order of the United Kingdom* 6 (Kluwer Law International, 1999).

[18] Paul Mahoney, *Principles of Judicial Review As Developed by the European Court of Human Rights: Their Relevance in a National Context*, in Lammy Betten, ed, *The Human Rights Act 1998 What It Means: The Incorporation of the European Convention on Human Rights into the Legal Order of the United Kingdom* 65, 85 (Kluwer Law International, 1999).

[19] Hereinafter the European Court of Human Rights is written ECHR.

[20] Thomas Buergenthal, *International Human Rights in a Nutshell* 113 (West Publishing Co., 1988).

[21] Peter Cumper, *A Path to a Bill of Rights*, New L J 100, 100 (1991); see E. Jerald Ogg, Jr., *The European Convention and Freedom of Information: The*

Domestic Impact of a Human Rights Regime (Ph. D. diss., Southern Illinois University at Carbondale, 1993).
    [22] Alex S. Edelstein, *Comparative Communication Research* 131 (Sage, 1982).
    [23] Schultz, *Reviving the Fourth Estate* at 97 (cited in note 6).

CHAPTER ONE

    [1] Eric Barendt, *Freedom of Speech* 152 (Clarendon Press, 1987).
    [2] Cass R. Sunstein, *Democracy and the Problem of Free Speech* 130 (The Free Press, 1993).
    [3] Id at 131.
    [4] Jeremy Cohen and Timothy Gleason, *Social Research in Communication and Law* 65 (Sage, 1990).
    [5] Robert Trager and Donna L. Dickerson, *Freedom of Expression in the 21st Century* 106 (Pine Forge Press, 1999).
    [6] John Dewey, *Practical Democracy*, New Republic 52 (Dec 2, 1925).
    [7] On the theory of democracy see generally, for example, David Held, *Models of Democracy* (Stanford University Press, 2d ed 1996).
    [8] Thomas Christiano, *Freedom, Consensus and Equality in Collective Decision Making*, 101 Ethics 151 (1990).
    [9] Arthur Isak Applbaum, *Democratic Legitimacy and Official Discretion*, 21 (3) Phil & Pub Aff 240, 257 (Summer 1992), citing Joseph A. Schumpeter, *Capitalism, Socialism, and Democracy* (Allen & Unwin, 1976); Michael Walzer, *Philosophy and Democracy*, 9 Pol Theory 379-399 (1981); Amy Gutmann, *How Liberal Is Democracy?* in Douglas MacLean and Claudia Mills, eds, *Liberalism Reconsidered* (Rowman & Allanheld, 1983).
    [10] About 500 B.C., Athenians established the world's first democratic constitution. Pericles inherited this form of government half a century later, and he reformed the fragile democracy to mature into its classical form. "Although limited to adult parentage, Athenian citizenship granted full and active participation in every decision of the state without regard to wealth or class. The Athenians excluded women, children, resident aliens, and slaves from political life, but the principle of equality within the political community that they invented was the seed of the modern idea of universal egalitarianism that flowered during the French enlightenment." Donald Kagan, *Pericles of Athens and the Birth of Democracy* 1-2 (The Free Press, 1991).
    [11] Leo Bogart, *Media and Democracy*, in E. F. Dennis and R. W. Snyder, eds, *Media and Democracy* 3-11 (Transaction Publishers, 1998).
    [12] See Jeremy Waldron, *Liberal Rights* 35-62 (Cambridge University Press, 1993); see also John Rawls, *A Theory of Justice* 61 (Harvard University Press, 1971); and see the discussion of free speech as a consequent to the contract in Alan Haworth, *Free Speech* 70-83, 151-174 (Routledge, 1998).

[13] The consent of citizens to the institutional arrangement can be a tacit or written entering into the social contract.

[14] Unless otherwise stated, this study depended on Mel Thompson, *Ethics* 155-158 (NTC Publishing Group, 1994) for the discussion of the contractualists.

[15] Thomas Hobbes, *Leviathan*, ed. Richard Tuch (Cambridge University Press 1991), 89.

[16] Gregory S. Kavka, *Hobbesian Moral and Political Theory* 22 (Princeton University Press, 1986).

[17] David P. Gauthier, *Taming Leviathan*, 16 (3) Phil & Pub Aff 280, 296 (Summer 1987).

[18] See generally David P. Gauthier, *The Logic of Leviathan: The Moral and Political Theory of Thomas Hobbes* (Clarendon Press, 1969).

[19] Thompson, *Ethics* at 156 (cited in note 14).

[20] Id. See also David Wootton, ed, *Political Writings of John Locke* 309-327 (Penguin Books Ltd., 1993).

[21] See Jean-Jacques Rousseau, *The Social Contract*, trans G. D. H. Cole (J. M. Dent 1993), 105-133, 182-196.

[22] See generally Thomas Paine, *Rights of Man*, in Collected Writings (Literary Classics of the United States, 1995).

[23] John Stuart Mill, *On Liberty*, ed. David Spitz (W. W. Norton and Co., Inc. 1975), 78.

[24] Thompson, *Ethics* at 158 (cited in note 14).

[25] Rawls, *A Theory of Justice* at 240 (cited in note 12).

[26] Paul J. Weithman, *Contractualist Liberalism and Deliberative Democracy*, 24 (2) Phil & Pub Aff 314, 315 (Fall 1995).

[27] Id.

[28] Id at 316; see also James W. Nickel, *Free Speech, Democratic Deliberation, and Valuing Types of Speech*, in Simone Chambers and Anne Costain, eds, *Deliberation, Democracy and the Media* 3-10 (Rowman & Littlefield Publishers, 2000).

[29] Cass R. Sunstein, *The Partial Constitution* 135 (Harvard University Press, 1993).

[30] Id.

[31] See Locke, *The Second Treatise of Civil Government* ch VIII § 96. According to the Lockean theory, "the majority determines the direction of the whole group." David Esthund, *Beyond Fairness and Deliberation: The Epistemic Dimension of Democratic Authority*, in James Bohman and William Rehg, eds, *Deliberative Democracy: Essays on Reason and Politics* 173, 183 (The MIT Press, 1997). See also Gerald F. Gaus, *Reason, Justification, and Consensus: Why Democracy Can't Have It All*, in James Bohman and William Rehg, eds, *Deliberative Democracy: Essays on Reason and Politics* 205, 232-234 (The MIT Press, 1997).

[32] Thomas Christiano, *The Significance of Public Deliberation*, in James Bohman and William Rehg, eds, *Deliberative Democracy: Essays on Reason and Politics* 243-278 (The MIT Press, 1997).

[33] John B. Thompson, *The Media and Modernity: A Social Theory of the Media* 249-258 (Polity Press, 1995). For more general discussion of deliberative democracy see essays in James Bohman and William Rehg, eds, *Deliberative Democracy: Essays on Reason and Politics* 173, 183 (The MIT Press, 1997).

[34] Joshua Cohen, *Deliberation and Democratic Legitimacy*, in Alan P. Hamlin and Philip Pettit, eds, *The Good Polity* 17, 18 (Blackwell, 1989).

[35] Id.

[36] Id.

[37] Id at 19.

[38] Id.

[39] Kaarle Nordenstreng, *The Citizen Moves from the Audience to the Arena*, 18 (2) Nordicom Rev 13, 13 (Nov 1997).

[40] John Dewey, *Democracy and Education*. Edited by J. A. Boydston, Vol 9 the Middle Works 1916 (Southern Illinois University at Carbondale, 1980), 6.

[41] John Dewey, *The Public and Its Problems*, Edited by J. A. Boydston, Vol 2 the Later Works 1916 (Southern Illinois University at Carbondale, 1984), 332.

[42] Charlene Haddock Seigfried, *Socializing Democracy: Jane Addams and John Dewey*, 20 (2) Phil Soc Sci 207, 208 (June 1999).

[43] Id at 210, citing Dewey, *Democracy and Education* (cited in note 40); his *Human Nature and Conduct*. Edited by J. A. Boydston, Vol 14 the Middle Works 1922 (Southern Illinois University at Carbondale 1983); still see his *The Public* (cited in note 41); and his *Individualism Old and New 1929-1930*. Edited by J. A. Boydston, Vol 5 the Later Works (Southern Illinois University at Carbondale, 1984), 41-123.

[44] Seigfried, *Socializing Democracy* at 210 (cited in note 42).

[45] Id at 211. See also Dewey, *The Public* at 235-372 (cited in note 41); see also his *Liberalism and Social Action*. Edited by J. A. Boydston, Vol 11 the Later Works 1935-1937 (Southern Illinois University at Carbondale, 1987), 1-65.

[46] Richard Shusterman, *Putman and Cavell on the Ethics of Democracy*, 25 (2) Pol. Theory 193, 194 (April 1997).

[47] Hilary Putnam, *Renewing Philosophy* 182 (Harvard University Press, 1992).

[48] Id.

[49] Id at 180.

[50] Id at 186.

[51] Id.

[52] Id at 186-187.

[53] Id at 188.

[54] Shusterman, *Putman and Cavell* at 195 (cited in note 46)

[55] Id at 189.

[56] Id. A similar idea was reiterated in Putman's, *Word and Life*. Edited by James Conant (Harvard University Press, 1994), 217.

[57] Shusterman, *Putman and Cavell* at 202 (cited in note 46).

[58] Id at 202.

[59] Stanley Cavell, *Conditions Handsome and Unhandsome: The Constitution of Emersonian Perfectionism* 3 and 56 (Chicago University Press, 1990).

[60] See id at 12, 16 and 46.

[61] See id at 53, 125.

[62] Id at 125.

[63] Id.

[64] Thomas Christiano, *The Rule of the Many: Fundamental Issues in Democratic Theory* 15 (Westview Press, 1996).

[65] Id at 15-16.

[66] Trager and Dickerson, *Freedom of Expression* at 180 (cited in note 5).

[67] Id at 183.

[68] Eric Barendt, *Freedom of Speech* at 173 (cited in note 1).

[69] Id at 173 n 1. See also Van Vechter Veeder, *The History and Theory of the Law of Defamation*, 3 Colum L Rev 546, 550-551 (1903).

[70] Veeder, *Law of Defamation* at 546 (cited in note 69). For other discussions of the history of the law of defamation, see generally Frank Carr, *The English Law of Defamation* (pts 1-2), 18 L Q Rev 255, 388 (1902); W. S. Holdsworth, *Defamation in the Sixteenth and Seventeenth Centuries* (pts 1-3), 40 L Q Rev 302, 397 (1924), 41 L Q. Rev 13 (1925); Colin Rys Lovell, *The "Reception" of Defamation by the Common Law*, 15 Vand L Rev 1051 (1962); Jerome Lawrence Merin, 11 Wm & Mary L Rev 371 (1969).

[71] T. Plucknett, *A Concise History of the Common Law* 484 (Little, Brown and Co., 5th ed 1956).

[72] W. Prosser, *Torts* § 111 (4th ed 1971).

[73] Restatement (Second) of Torts § 558 (1977).

[74] See, for example, *Guccione v Hustler Magazine, Inc.*, 632 F Supp 313 (SDNY 1986), rev'd, 800 F2d 298 (2d Cir 1986), cert denied, 479 US 1091 (1987), a false statement that a married person had a live-in girlfriend implied that that person was engaged in sexual intercourse with someone other than his spouse, or was committing adultery, and, therefore the statement was libel *per se.*

[75] *Electric Furnace Corp. v Deering Milliken Research Corp.*, 352 F2d 761, 764-765 (6th Cir 1963).

[76] See Cal Civ Code §§ 45-46.

[77] On the four conditions, see Thomas L. Tedford, *Freedom of Speech in the United States* 83-86 (McGraw-Hill, Inc., 1993). In the United States, there is no federal law of defamation for all libel laws are at state level. For more

about federal-state distinction of libel laws, see Clifton O. Lawhorne, *The Supreme Court and Libel* 3-5 (Southern Illinois University Press, 1981).

[78] The fourth condition of fault that was added in *New York Times Co. v Sullivan* 376 US 254 (1964) as a constitutional overlay of the common law. Though it was restricted narrowly to public officials, it was later applied to public figures as well. No similar requirement was applied to private plaintiffs until the case of *Gertz v Welch, Inc.,* 418 US 323 (1974). Here, the Supreme Court expanded the condition of fault to include private plaintiffs who sue media defendants for defamation, and are so required to prove a minimum standard of fault known as "negligence."

[79] Tedford, *Freedom of Speech* at 86 (cited in note 77).

[80] Libel and Slander, 28 *Halsbury's Laws of England* ¶ 16 (Butterworths, 4th ed 1997); *Aldridge v John Fairfax & Sons Ltd.,* 2 NSWLR 544, 551 (1984).

[81] *Philadelphia Newspapers, Inc. v Hepps,* 475 US 767, 778 (1986).

[82] Restatement (Second) at §§ 558(d), 575 (cited in note 73). *Gertz* rule that requires plaintiffs to prove actual malice to recover presumed and punitive damages does not apply in cases where the alleged defamatory statements do not involve matters of public concern. *Dun & Bradstreet v Greenmoss Builders,* 472 US 749 (1985).

[83] Thomas Starkie, *A Treatise on the Law of Slander, Libel, Scandalum Magnatum and False Rumors* 16-17 (London: Printed for W. Clarke, 1813).

[84] *Uren v Fairfax,* 117 CLR 118, 150 (1966), *per* Windeyer, J.

[85] Tedford, *Freedom of Speech* at 88 (cited in note 77).

[86] Id. Punitive damages on media libel litigation remain contentious, see Dennis Hale, *The Impact of State Prohibitions of Punitive Damages on Libel Litigation: An Empirical Analysis,* 5 VandJ Ent L&Prac 96 (2003).

[87] Fair reportage is also a constitutional defense in jurisdictions which recognize it.

[88] Libel and Slander, 28 *Halsbury's Laws of England* ¶ 82 (cited in note 80).

[89] Restatement (Second) at § 559 (cited in note 73).

[90] *Medico v Time, Inc.,* 643 F2d 134, 137 (3d Cir 1981).

[91] David A. Elder, *The Fair Report Privilege* 5, 111-113 (1988).

[92] Libel and Slander, 28 *Halsbury's Laws of England* ¶ 82 (cited in note 80). As to details of the law of libel and its defenses see id ¶¶ 82-109.

[93] Id ¶ 16, citing *Bromage v Prosser,* 4 B & C 247, 255 (1825) *per* Bayley J., *Belt v Lawes,* 51 LJQB 359, 361 (DC 1882). Common law malice in a defamatory action is a claim that the statements "were published falsely and maliciously," implying that the libelous imputation was "a wrongful act done intentionally, without just cause or excuse." In this sense, "malice is presumed from the fact of publication and defamatory words, so that the plaintiff need not plead or prove it." Libel and Slander, 28 *Halsbury's Laws of England* ¶ 16 (cited in note 80). This is different from actual malice, that is knowing

falsehood or "reckless disregard" of truth. *New York Times v Sullivan*, 376 US 254, 279-280 (1964). Reckless disregard means that the plaintiff must prove that the press "in fact entertained serious doubts as to the truth" of the published statements. *St. Amant v Thompson*, 390 US 727, 731 (1968).

[94] See Robert D. Sack, *Libel, Slander, and Related Problems* 314-317 (Practicing Law Institute, 1980).

[95] Restatement (Second) at § 566 cmt. a (cited in note 73); *Restatement of Torts* § 606, art. 1 (1938); *Cassidy v Merin*, 582 A2d 1039, 1044-1048 (NJ Super Ct App Div 1990); William G. Hale, *The Law of the Press* 130 (West Publishing Co., 1923).

[96] *Toogood v Spyring*, 1 CM & R 181, 193 (1834).

[97] *Webb v Times Publ'g Co.*, 2 Q B 535, 565 (1960); see *Adam v. Ward*, 31 T L R 299 (1915), aff'd AC 309 (HL 1917).

[98] John G. Fleming, *The Law of Torts* 588 (The Law Book Co. Ltd., 8th ed 1992).

[99] See Theodore M. Benditt, *The Public Interest*, 2 (3) Phil & Pub Aff 291 (Spring 1973).

[100] See id at 306.

[101] Jeremy Bentham, *An Introduction to the Principles of Morals and Legislation*. Edited by J. H. Burns and H. L. A. Hart (Clarendon Press, 1996), 12.

[102] Id.

[103] Id at 12-13.

[104] Benditt, *The Public Interest* at 292 (cited in note 99).

[105] Jean-Jacques Rousseau, *The Social Contract and Discourse on the Origin of Inequality*. Edited by Lester G. Crocker (Pocket Books 1967), 27.

[106] Id at 30.

[107] See Benditt, *The Public Interest* at 310-311 (cited in note 99). The collective paradigm of the public interest is more agreeable than the distributive notion. For, the distributive conception of the public interest would consider a policy as in the public interest only when every member of the public benefits from it. However, there may be individuals who have the benefits in question already and, therefore, will not be improved by the policy under consideration. On the other hand, the collective idea of public interest has a value of allowing a policy in which actual improvements will come only to a minority of the public who are deficient in some areas, and so should be subject to public interest considerations.

[108] Id at 310.

[109] Barendt, *Freedom of Speech* at 25-27 (cited in note 1).

[110] See Benditt, *The Public Interest* at 298-303 (cited in note 99).

[111] Steven Helle, *Judging Public Interest in Libel: The Gertz Decision's Contribution*, 61 Journalism Q 117, 119 (Spring 1984), citing Alfred Hill, *Defamation and Privacy under the First Amendment*, 76 Colum L Rev 1205, 1229 n 113 (Dec 1976).

[112] Restatement (Second) § 611 (cited in note 73).

CHAPTER TWO

[1] Questions about the amount of protection that countries give to political speech have concerned legal experts. Studies reveal that jurisdictions are not uniform in requiring public officials and public figures to tolerate more criticism. And, in the 1970s, debate and studies on the scope of defamation law and proper balance between free speech and reputation intensified. For example, Clifton Lawhorne did an extensive analysis of the relationship between libel law and public officials from the settlement of New England until the 1970 (*Defamation and Public Officials: The Evolving Law of Libel*. Southern Illinois University Press, 1971). He observed that laws that restricted defamation of public officials were continually narrowed while the social and political changes allowed more discussion and criticism of government and government officials. His analysis included the constitutional guarantees of free speech and the press established in *New York Times v Sullivan* that prohibited public officials from recovering damages unless they proved actual malice (*New York Times v Sullivan*, 376 US 254, 285-286 [1964]). Lawhorne's study also considered the extension of the public official defense of actual malice to include public figures not holding governmental office in *Curtis Publishing Co. v Butts* and its companion *Associated Press v Walker* (388 US 130 [1967]). However, Lawhorne's analysis predated important decisions made in *Gertz v Welch, Inc* (418 US 323, 351-352 [1974]) that introduced complex distinctions between public figures and private persons, and the minimum constitutional requirements for recovering damages. Moreover, the analysis was limited for not considering the trend of political libel laws in some modern jurisdictions, such as Australia and the United Kingdom, which, until now, do not subscribe to the idea of public figures.

At least, until recent changes in the legal landscape of Australian defamation jurisprudence, elected officials and candidates for elective office in Australia, according to an Australian Law Reform Commission report, were the most litigious group of defamation plaintiffs (see Australian Law Reform Commission, Unfair Publication: Defamation and Privacy, Report No 11 at 20 [1979]). This report was similar to Geoffrey Palmer's finding from reported cases in Australia and New Zealand (*Defamation and Privacy Down Under*, 64 Iowa L Rev 1209, 1215 [1979]). But, comparing reported decisions of the same 25-year period, the Australian Law Reform Commission found that politicians in England seemed less often inclined than their counterparts in Australia to take libel actions (Australian Law Reform Commission, Unfair Publication: Defamation and Privacy, Report No 11 at 20 [1979]).

Other studies have shown the destabilizing effect of political defamation suits by public officials and public figures. Earliest of such empirical studies included two surveys conducted by Marc A. Franklin on United States defamation suits. Franklin's studies revealed that the reporting of appellate judgments of defamation cases could be selective (*Winners and Losers and*

Why: A Study of Defamation Litigation, 1980 Am B Found Res J 455-500; *Suing Media for Libel: A Litigation Study*, 1981 Am B Found Res J 795-831).

He noted that cases that involved prominent persons or those that drew public interest and involved constitutional issues were more likely to be reported. According to his data, taken together, elected and nonelected public officials were plaintiffs in about one-quarter of all libel litigations by individuals in the United States. If social prominence of defamation plaintiffs influenced reporting of judicial judgments, it could be that the data on which the Australian Law Reform Commission and Palmer based their studies accounted for public officials a little more than other categories of plaintiffs.

However, an empirical study conducted by the Iowa Libel Research Project found results similar to the Franklin studies (see Randall P. Bezanson, *Libel Law and the Realities of Litigation: Setting the Record Straight*, 71 Iowa L. Rev 226 [1985]; Gilbert Cranberg, *Fanning the Fire: The Media's Role in Libel Litigation*, 71 Iowa L. Rev 221 [1985]); John Soloski, *The Study of the Libel Plaintiff: Who Sues for Libel*, 71 Iowa L. Rev 217 [1985]. The study of the Iowa Libel Research Project consisted of surveys of reported decisions and interviews with plaintiffs, media defendants and media personnel. The researchers reported that about 43 percent of the plaintiffs surveyed were public employees that included elected officials or candidates for office before the libel occurred or when they sued (Randall Bezanson, Gilbert Cranberg and John Soloski, *Libel Law and the Press* 8 and 9 [1987]). This result was a larger percentage than the Franklin studies found. Politicians more readily initiated defamation actions against the media defendants than they did nonmedia persons. One may conclude that this study was not different from the Franklin research in finding that most defamation actions were taken by individuals who hold prominent and public positions.

Such conclusions about libel suits involving public figures induced debates about whether the United States' actual malice rule gave public figures enough protection (see, for example, Peter Stoler, *The War against the Press: Politics, Pressure and Intimidation in the '80s* 135-154 [Mead Dodd, 1986]; Richard Labunski, *Libel and the First Amendment: Legal History and Practice in Print and Broadcasting* 1-4, 111-145 [Transaction Books, 1987]). While commentators like Renata Adler considered the actual malice rule as overly protective of the press and the most stringent ever imposed by any judicial system in the world (*Reckless Disregard: Westmoreland v CBS et al.; Sharon v Time* 144, 335, and 242 [Alfred A. Knopf, Inc., 1986], see also F. Trowbridge Vom Baur, *The License to Defame Government Officials: New York Times Co v Sullivan Should Be Overruled*, 30 Fed B News & J 501 [Dec 1983]), Rodney Smolla advocated reform of the United States libel law to place more stringent restrictions on public figures' ability to sue (*Suing the Press: Libel, the Media and Power* 243 [1986]; see also Floyd Abrams, *Why We Should Change the Libel Law*, NY Times Mag 34 [Sept 29, 1985]).

Soon after the Iowa Libel Research Project, the Libel Defense Resource Center (LDRC) studied a time frame that began at the end of the period covered in Franklin's study (Libel Defense Resource Center, *Public Official Libel Action: A Comparison of Reported Cases 1976-1979 and 1979-1984*, LDRC Bull, No 16 [Winter 1986], cited in Michael Newcity, *The Sociology of Defamation in Australia and the United States*, 26 Tex Intl L J 1, 20-22 [1991]. While Franklin data covered reported judgments from January 1977 through mid-December 1980, the LDRC gathered data from reported decisions from mid-June 1979 through the end of 1984). Comparing its analysis of the Franklin study, the LDRC noted that reported libel suits by politicians and other public officials were on the rise. The rise in defamation suits by public officials as the LDRC determined could have overrepresented actual figures given the broader definition of "public official" that the study used in gathering its data. Aside from the difficulty in distinguishing elected and nonelected officials in comparing both data, the problem is worsened because LDRC considered nonelected plaintiffs as public officials, such nonelected plaintiffs as law enforcement personnel, public school personnel, judges and attorneys (see Newcity, *Sociology of Defamation* at 22).

However, the study of Judy D. Lynch found that plaintiffs who were low-ranking public employees sued for defamation more frequently than higher-level officials or candidates for prominent positions (*Public Officials, the Press, and the Libel Remedy: Toward a Theory of Absolute Immunity*, 67 Or L Rev 611, 618 [1988]). As she found, low-ranking public employees such as police officers accounted for one-third of the total number of defamation suits. So, Lynch concluded that defamatory statements about police officers could give problems for the press.

As the studies so far suggest, public figures frequently initiated defamation suits, but they do not always win. Where public figure plaintiffs often fail in libel litigations, the situation could hamper the rate at which public figures initiate defamation suits. This seemed the case found in Michael Newcity's study. Newcity explored sociological questions about Australian defamation litigations and compared the Australian data with the results of the previous studies by Franklin, the Iowa Libel Research Project and LDRC studies. His data suggested that Australian public officials and candidates for office more frequently initiated defamation suits than did politicians in the United States Newcity, *Sociology of Defamation* at 19. He also found that "elected public officials and nonincumbent candidates for office institute the vast majority of their defamation suits against media defendants" (Id at 43).

Also, Eric Barendt and his colleagues studied the impact of defamation law on the mass media in Great Britain and considered how the deterrent function of the law could exercise a "chilling" effect on free speech (see generally Eric Barendt et al, *Libel and the Media: The Chilling Effect* [Clarendon Press, 1997]). Their survey data were drawn from libel writs in the Royal Courts of Justice, some statistical information taken from the annual *Judicial Statistics*, questionnaires addressed to editors and lawyers, and interviews with some attorneys who have been involved with libel plaintiffs, as well as libel defendants. The researchers found that fear of libel suits deterred the national press from reporting on public figures' private lives and from scrutinizing their public lives (Id at 76). According to the study, interviewees in the United Kingdom "expressed particular concern about the propensity of police officers to sue for libel," and thereby inhibit the journalists and editors from "writing stories with allegations of excessive force or brutality on the part of the police" (Id at 118). This supported Lynch's finding that low-ranking public employees such as police officers frequently initiate defamation suits.

In a comparative study of the jurisprudence and socio-cultural influences of the United States Supreme Court and those of the Constitutional Court of Spain, Rodrigo J. Bustos Sierra found that both Courts emphasize the preferred position balancing that favors free speech and the press. But Bustos Sierra noted that United States jurisprudence is more protective of the press than its Spanish counterpart. Cultural understandings, according to Bustos Sierra, contribute to differences in the protection of the press (*The Accommodation of Interests in Freedom of the Press and Protection of Reputation in the Constitutional Doctrine of the United States and Spain* [Ph.D. diss., Stanford University, 1998], abstracts in *Dissertation Abstracts International* 59 [1999]: 3946A).

The previous studies either dealt with defamation laws in one country or compared one jurisdiction with another. Also, they considered the impact of libel law on a country generally. These studies were important in demonstrating that libel laws and libel litigations by public officials and public figures could have a destabilizing effect on the governing process. However, there is not yet a study that specifically compares political defamation jurisprudence of several jurisdictions. Moreover, developments in the legal landscape, for example, of Australia and the United Kingdom suggest possible changes in their libel jurisprudence to be accounted for. The present study responds to the need of an extensive comparative study that examines the prevailing political defamation law of the United States, the ECHR, the United Kingdom and Australia. So, this study takes a different approach from the surveys and interviews by previous studies to examine defamation laws. Here, it takes multiple methods to compare and contrast authorities of those jurisdictions in a legal qualitative approach.

[2] See generally Matthew D. Bunker, *Critiquing Free Speech: First Amendment Theory and the Challenge of Interdisciplinarity* 1-17 (Lawrence Erlbaum Associates, 2001); see also Eugene L. Robert, Jr, *Free Speech, Free Press, Free Society,* in Peggie J. Hollingsworth, ed, *Unfettered Expression: Freedom in American Intellectual Life* 151-160 (University of Michigan Press, 2000), and see Alan Haworth, *Free Speech* at 24-32 (Routledge, 1998).

[3] John Milton, *Aeropagitica: A Speech for the Liberty of Unlicensed Printing to the Parliament of England.* Edited by Israel Gollancz (The Beacon Press 1951, original work 1644), 61.

[4] John Stuart Mill, *On Liberty*. Edited by David Spitz (W. W. Norton and Company, Inc. 1975, original work 1859), 18-20.

[5] *Abrams v United States*, 250 US 616 (1919).

[6] Id at 630 (Holmes, J., dissenting).

[7] *Whitney v California*, 274 US 357 (1927)(Brandeis, J., concurring).

[8] Id at 375-6 (Brandeis, J., concurring).

[9] Id at 375

[10] Zechariah Chafee, Jr., *Free Speech in the United States* 31 (Harvard University Press, 1941).

[11] Id.

[12] Id at 31.

[13] Id at 35.

[14] Kent Greenawalt, *Speech, Crime, and the Uses of Language* 18-19 (Oxford University Press, 1989).

[15] Id at 19.

[16] Id at 20.

[17] See Stanley Ingber, *The Marketplace of Ideas: Legitimizing Myth*, 1984 Duke L J 1 (Feb 1984).

[18] Laurence H. Tribe, *American Constitutional Law* § 12-1 at 786 (Foundation Press, 2d ed 1988); see also, Steven Shiffrin, *The First Amendment and Economic Regulation: Away from a General Theory of the First Amendment*, 78 Nw U L Rev 1212, 1218 (1983).

[19] C. Edwin Baker, *Scope of First Amendment Freedom of Speech*, 25 UCLA L Rev 964, 974-75 (1978); see also his *Human Liberty and Freedom of Speech* 12-22 (Oxford University Press, 1989).

[20] Id at 975.

[21] Cass R. Sunstein, *Democracy and the Problem of Free Speech* 19 (The Free Press, 1993).

[22] John Locke, *A Letter Concerning Toleration*. Edited by Mario Montuori (Martinus Nijhoff 1963, original work 1689), 79.

[23] Oliver Wendell Holmes, *The Path of the Law*, 10 Harv L Rev 447, 466 (1918).

[24] *American Communications Ass'n v Douds*, 339 US 382, 442 (1950)(Jackson, J., concurring and dissenting).

[25] Benjamin S. DuVal, Jr., *Free Communication of Ideas and the Quest for Truth: Toward a Teleological Approach to First Amendment Adjudication*, 41 Geo Wash L Rev 161, 190-191 (1972).

[26] *City of Houston, Texas v Hill*, 482 US 451, 472 (1987).

[27] Thomas Scanlon, Jr., *Freedom of Expression and Categories of Expression*, 40 U Pitt L Rev 519, 525 (1979), who commented on the open and free discussion:

Even if I dismiss what is said or shown to me as foolish and exaggerated, I am slightly different for having seen or heard it. This difference can be trivial but it can also be significant and have a significant effect on my later decisions. For example, being shown powerful photographs of the horrors of war, no matter what my initial reaction to them may be, can have the effect of heightening (or ultimately of dulling) my sense of human suffering involved, and this may later affect my opinions about foreign policy in ways I am hardly aware of.

[28] See Thomas Irwin Emerson, *The System of Freedom of Expression* 6-9 (Random House, 1970); see also his work, *Toward a General Theory of the First Amendment* (Random House, 1966).

[29] Thomas Irwin Emerson, *First Amendment Doctrine and the Burger Court*, 68 Cal L Rev 422, 423 (1980).

[30] Emerson, *Freedom of Expression* at 72 (cited in note 28).

[31] John Rawls, *A Theory of Justice* 34-35 (Harvard University Press, 1971).

[32] *Cohen v California*, 403 US 15, 26 (1971)(emphasis added). See also *First Nat'l Bank of Boston v Bellotti*, 435 US 765 (1978); *Consolidated Edison Co. v Public Serv Comm'n*, 447 US 530, 532 n 2 (1980), addressing the "role of the First Amendment in fostering individual self-expression."

[33] Thomas Scanlon, *A Theory of Free Expression*, 1 (2) Phil & Pub Aff 204 (1972); See also his *Categories of Expression* at 519 (cited in note 27).

[34] Scanlon, *Free Expression*, 204 (cited in note 33); see Martin Redish, *The Value of Free Speech*, 130 U Pa L Rev 591 (1982).

[35] *Procunier v Martinez*, 416 US 396, 427 (1974).

[36] *Bose Corp v Consumers Union*, 466 US 485, 503 (1984).

[37] See generally Frederick Schauer, *Free Speech: A Philosophical Enquiry* 47-58 (Cambridge University Press, 1982); see also Harry H. Wellington, *On Freedom of Expression*, 88 (6) Yale L J 1105, 1127-1135 (1979); and see Robert H. Bork, *Neutral Principles and some First Amendment Problems*, 47 Ind L J 1, 25 (1971).

[38] Rodney A. Smolla, *Smolla and Nimmer on Freedom of Speech* vol 1 at §§ 2:23-25 (Clark Boardman Callaghan, 1996). Also, Smolla's work is the authority that generally guided the discussion of free speech justifications in this chapter, see id § 2.

[39] Scanlon, *Free Expression*, 213-218 (cited in note 33); see also his *Categories of Expression*, 532-533 (cited in note 27).

[40] Vincent Blasi, *The Checking Value in First Amendment Theory*, ABF Res J 523, 550 (1977).

[41] Baker, *First Amendment Freedom* at 966 (cited in note 19).

[42] Robert Pullan, *Guilty Secrets: Free Speech and Defamation in Australia* 11 (Pascal, 1994).

[43] David M. Rabban, *Free Speech in Its Forgotten Years* 336 (Cambridge University Press, 1997).

[44] Vincent Blasi, *The Checking Value* at 531 (cited in note 40).

[45] John Locke, *The Second Treatise of Government.* Edited by J. W. Gough (Macmillan Co. 1956, original work 1689), ¶¶ 221-225.

[46] W. Rives and P. Fendall, eds, *Letters and Writings of James Madison, Fourth President of the United States* Vol 3 at 276 (Lippincott, 1865).

[47] Alexis de Tocqueville, *Democracy in America* 183 (David Campbell Publishers Ltd. 1994, original work 1835).

[48] Thomas M. Cooley, 2 *Constitutional Limitations* 886 (Little, Brown and Co., 8th ed 1927).

[49] See Alexander Meiklejohn, *Free Speech and Its Relation to Self-Government* (Harper, 1948).

[50] See Alexander Meiklejohn, *Political Freedom: The Constitutional Powers of the People* (Oxford University Press, 1965).

[51] Meiklejohn, *Free Speech and Its Relation* at 6 (cited in note 49).

[52] Meiklejohn, *Political Freedom* at 26-27 (cited in note 50).

[53] Id at 23.

[54] Alexander Meiklejohn, *The First Amendment Is an Absolute*, Sup Ct Rev 245, 257 (1961).

[55] See Meiklejohn, *Free Speech and Its Relation* at 88-89, 104 (cited in note 49).

[56] *Richmond Newspapers, Inc. v Virginia*, 448 US 555, 587 (1980)(Brennan, J., concurring).

[57] Bork, *Neutral Principles* at 1 (cited in noted 37). He also argued that protection of free speech should be interpreted as touching only speech that relates to political subjects rather than focusing on individual growth or satisfaction. He did not recognize individual self-fulfillment as satisfactory grounds for special protection of speech, even when related to political participation. Id at 28-29. For more on radical liberalism and free speech, see his *Slouching toward Gomorrah* 153 (ReganBooks, 1997).

[58] See Paul Chevigny, *More Speech: Dialogue Rights and Modern Liberty* 99-122 (Temple University Press, 1988).

[59] Schauer, *Free Speech* at 47-58 (cited in note 37). See Frederick Schauer, *The Cost of Communicative Tolerance*, in Raphael Cohen-Almagor, ed, *Liberal Democracy and the Limits of Tolerance* 28-42 (University of Michigan Press, 2000).

[60] Lee C. Bollinger, The Tolerant Society: Freedom of Speech and Extremist Speech in America (Oxford University Press, 1986).

[61] Also some jurists and scholars support the idea of toleration of free speech as a means for stability. See Justice Louis Brandeis, who commented that the framers of the United States' Constitution knew that "it is hazardous to discourage thought, hope and imagination; that fear breeds repression; that

repression breeds hate; that hate menaces stable government; that the path of safety lies in the opportunity to discuss freely supposed grievances and proposed remedies; and that the fitting remedy for evil counsels is good ones." *Whitney v California*, 274 US 357, 375-77 (1927). See also Professor Kent Greenawalt who argued that "[t]hose who are resentful because their interests are not accorded fair weight, and who may be doubly resentful because they have not even a chance to present those interests, may seek to attain by radical change in existing institutions what they have failed to get from the institutions themselves. Thus, liberty of expression, though often productive of divisiveness, may contribute to social stability." *Speech and Crime*, ABF Res J 647, 672-673 (1980). See also Rodney A. Smolla's view about the engendering value of tolerance: "If societies are not to explode from festering tensions, there must be valves through which the citizens may blow off steam. Openness fosters resiliency; peaceful protest displaces more violence than it triggers; free debate dissipates more hate than it stirs." *Free Speech in an Open Society* 13 (Alfred A. Knopf, Inc., 1992).

[62] Bollinger, *The Tolerant Society* at 197-200 (cited in note 60).

[63] James Fitzjames Stephen, *Liberty, Equality, Fraternity* ch 2 (Smith and Elder, 1874).

[64] Robert Paul Wolff, *A Critique of Pure Tolerance [by] Robert Paul Wolff, Barrington Moore, Jr. [and] Herbert Marcuse* 88 (Beacon Press, 1969).

[65] Geoffrey Marshall, *Press Freedom and Free Speech Theory*, Pub L 40, 47 (1983).

[66] See Gary L. Bauer, *Our Hopes, Our Dreams* 137-141 (Focus on the Family Publishing, 1996). Contrast Robert Boston, *Why the Religious Right Is Wrong* 189 (Prometheus Books, 1993).

[67] Thomas Storck, *A Case for Censorship*, New Oxford Rev 23 (May 1996).

[68] Id at 23-24.

[69] For more on the idea of toleration as opposed to the intolerable, see Alon Harel, *The Boundaries of Justifiable Tolerance*, in David Heyd, ed, Toleration 114-126 (Princeton University Press, 1996); see generally also David A. J. Richards, *Free Speech and the Politics of Identity* (Oxford University Press, 1999).

[70] See David Heyd, ed, *Toleration* 12-17 (Princeton University Press, 1996).

[71] See, for example, *Mills v Alabama*, 384 US 214, 218 (1966) ("Whatever differences may exist about interpretations of the First Amendment, there is practically universal agreement that a major purpose of that Amendment was to protect the free discussion of governmental affairs."); *Buckley v Valeo*, 424 US 1, 14 (1976) ("The First Amendment affords the broadest protection to such political expression ...."); *Herbert v Lando*, 441 US 153, 184-185 (1979) (Powell, J., concurring) (The First Amendment "bars the state from imposing upon its citizens an authoritative vision of truth. It forbids the state from interfering with the communicative processes through which its citizens

exercise and prepare to exercise their rights of self-government. And the Amendment shields those who would censure the state or expose its abuses.").

[72] Smolla, *Freedom of Speech* at § 2:36 (cited in note 38).

[73] Smolla, *Open Society* at 14-15 (cited in note 61).

[74] Smolla, *Freedom of Speech* at §§ 2:43-2:45 (cited in note 38).

[75] *Time, Inc. v Hill*, 385 US 374, 388 (1967).

[76] See Amitai Etzioni, *The Spirit of Community* (Touchstone, 1993); see also his *The Golden Rule* 28-32 (Basic Books, 1996).

[77] Joshua Cohen, *Freedom of Expression,* in David Heyd, ed, *Toleration* 173-225 (Princeton University Press). The analysis of Cohen is given an extensive consideration in this study because it brings together the basic interests for protecting speech. Also, his three considerations offer strong reasons for balancing free political speech against defamation of public figures.

[78] Id at 184. Cohen did not refute the values of free expression such as the discovery of the truth, individual self-expression, a well-functioning democracy, and a balance of social stability and social change. His aim was to establish firmly the importance of expression as related to certain fundamental interests.

[79] Id at 185.

[80] Id at 188.

[81] Id.

[82] On the costs of expression, Harry Kalven wrote, "Speech has *a price*. It is a liberal weakness to discount so heavily the price," cited from Harry Kalven's notes in the "Editor's Introduction" to *A Worthy Tradition: Freedom of Speech in America* xxii (Harper and Row, 1988).

[83] Cohen, *Freedom of Expression* at 178 (cited in note 77).

[84] Id at 192.

[85] Id at 194.

[86] Id at 213.

[87] Harry Kalven, Jr., *A Worthy Tradition* at 3 (cited in note 82).

[88] Id at 3-6.

[89] Steven Shiffrin, *Liberalism, Radicalism, and Legal Scholarship,* 30 UCLA L Rev 1103, 1197-1198 (1983).

[90] Kent Greenawalt, *Speech, Crime, and the Uses of Language* 14 (cited in note 14); for elaboration of his view that multiple rationales support the preferred position of free speech, see at 9-34. See also Emerson, *Freedom Expression* at 6-9 (cited in note 28).

[91] Tribe, *American Constitutional Law* §§ 12-1 at 789 (cited in note 18).

[92] Smolla, *Open Society* at 5 (cited in note 61).

[93] Id at 190-191.

[94] Political defamation concerns libel actions involving issues of political speech and the reputation of public figures. Chapters One and Two of this project have explained both issues.

[95] Thomas R. Lindlof, *Qualitative Communication Research Methods* 130 (Sage, 1995).

[96] Catherine Marshall and Gretchen B. Rossman, *Designing Qualitative Research* 78 (Sage, 3d ed 1999).

CHAPTER THREE

[1] John D. Stevens, Robert L. Bailey, Judith F. Krueger, and John M. Mollwitz, *Criminal Libel as Seditious Libel*, 45 Journalism Q 110, 110 (1966). For discussions of the history of the law of defamation, see generally Van Vechter Veeder, *The History and Theory of the Law of Defamation* (pts 1-2), 3 Colum L Rev 546 (1903), 4 Colum L Rev 33 (1904); Frank Carr, *The English Law of Defamation* (pts 1-2), 18 L Q Rev 255, 388 (1902); W. S. Holdsworth, *Defamation in the Sixteenth and Seventeenth Centuries* (pts 1-3), 40 L Q Rev 302, 397 (1924), 41 L Q Rev 13 (1925); Colin Rhys Lovell, *The "Reception" of Defamation by the Common Law*, 15 Vand L Rev 1051 (1962); Jerome Lawrence Merin, *Libel and the Supreme Court*, 11 Wm & Mary 371 (1969).

[2] For a discussion of forms of modern suppression of dissent, see generally Judith Schenck Koffler and Bennett L. Gershman, *The New Seditious Libel*, 69 Cornell L Rev 816 (1984).

[3] Statutes of the Realm, 3 Edw I, ch 34 (1275). A later statute in the reign of Richard II particularized the "great men of the realm": "Prelates, Dukes, Earls, Barons, and great men of the realm, and also of the Chancellor, Treasurer, Clerk of the Privy Seal, Steward of the King's House, Justices of the one bench or the other, and of other great officers of this realm." 2 Rich II, ch 5 (1378).

[4] J. R. Spencer, *Criminal Libel: A Skeleton in the Cupboard*, Crim L Rev 383, 384-387 (1977).

[5] Libel and Slander, 28 Halsbury's Laws of England ¶ 5 (Butterworths, 4th ed 1997).

[6] Clifton O. Lawhorne, *Defamation and Public Officials: The Evolving Law of Libel* 266 (Southern Illinois University Press, 1971); Geoffrey Robertson, *The Law Commission on Criminal Libel*, Pub L 208, 209 (Summer 1983).

[7] *De Libellis Famosis*, 5 Coke 125A (1606); see *Tollett v United States*, 485 F 2d 1087, 1098 n 27 (8th Cir 1973).

[8] James Paterson explained "breach of the peace" in his *Liberty of the Press, Speech and Public Worship* at 82 (Macmillan, 1880):

> The essence of seditious libel may be said to be its immediate tendency to stir up general discontent to the pitch of illegal courses, that is to say, to induce people to resort to illegal methods other than those provided by the Constitution, in order to redress the evils which press upon their minds ... Whenever a writing is so framed as to urge strongly the people, and especially the ignorant and turbulent portion

of the people, to take some shorter or illegal method, not at a future time, but at once, of attaining the end in view, then it may be said to be a seditious libel.

[9] Philip Hamburger, *The Development of the Law of Seditious Libel and the Control of the Press*, 37 Stan L Rev 661, 691(February 1985).

[10] *De Libellis Famosis*, 77 Eng Rep 250 [Star Chamber], 5 Coke 125A (1606). The Star Chamber, which decided this case, distinguished between libeling private citizens and officials. By doing so, Coke divided criminal libel into two categories. According to the court report:

Every libel ... is made either against a private man, or against a magistrate or public person. If it be against a private man it deserves a severe punishment, for although the libel ... tends ... to quarrels and breach of the peace ... and of great inconvenience: if it be against a magistrate, or other public person, it is a greater offence; for it concerns not only the breach of the peace, but also the scandal of Government; for what greater scandal of Government can there be than to have corrupt or wicked magistrates to be appointed and constituted by the King to govern his subjects under him? And greater imputation to the State cannot be, than to suffer such corrupt men to sit in the sacred seat of justice, or to have any meddling in or concerning the administration of justice. Id.

[11] Hamburger, *Development of Seditious Libel* at 694-696 (cited in note 9).

[12] Nathaniel B. Shurtleff, ed, *Records of the Governor and Company of the Massachusetts* vol 1 at 160-161 (William White Co., 1853). For early struggles for protection of free speech in New England, see generally Jane Kamensky, *Governing the Tongue: The Politics of Speech in Early New England* (Oxford University Press, 1997).

[13] Seditious libel was defined as "the intentional publication, without lawful excuse or justification, of written blame of any public man, or of the law, or of any institution established by law." See Zechariah Chafee, Jr., *Free Speech in the United States* 19, 500 (Harvard University Press, 1941). For a discussion of the elements of seditious libel, see Jeffrey K. Walker, *A Poisen in ye Commonwealthe: Seditious Libel in Hanoverian London*, 25 (3) Anglo-Am L Rev 341, 343-349 (1996).

[14] Defamation under the law of seditious libel dealt with criticism of the government as well as the governors. Records of such seditious libel cases can be found in Thomas B. Howell, comp, *A Complete Collection of State Trials and Proceedings for High Treason and Other Crimes and Misdemeanors* (Hansard, 1812)(hereinafter "State Trials"). For example, *Trial of Dover,*

Brewster and Brooks, [1663] 6 State Trials 539, 558 and 564. See also *Trial of the Seven Bishops*, [1688] 12 State Trials 183, 428.

[15] In Baxter's case, the King's Bench said that allusions to persons by innuendo or suggestion had to be such that "no other persons could be reasonably intended," and the jury found that Baxter's innuendo referred to "the English bishops." See *Proceedings against Mr. Baxter*, [1685] 11 State Trials at 502.

[16] *Trial of Dover, Brewster and Brooks*, 6 State Trials at 563.

[17] *Trial of Sir Samuel Barnardiston*, [1684] 9 State Trials 1333, 1334-1335.

[18] Id at 1349.

[19] Id at 1356.

[20] *Seven Bishops' Trial*, 12 State Trials 183 at 239 (1688).

[21] Id at 425-427.

[22] This absolute privilege exists today in British Parliament, and in the United States Congress and other government bodies. For a brief discussion of this special privilege, see Geoffrey Marshall, *Press Freedom and Free Speech Theory*, Pub L 40, 41 (1983).

[23] See Parry-Giles Trevor, *Parliament, Puritans, and Protestors: The Ideological Development of the British Commitment to "Free Speech,"* 31 Free Speech Yearbook 16, 29-34 (1993).

[24] For account of the decline in seditious libel prosecutions in early America, see Larry D. Eldridge, *A Distant Heritage: The Growth of Free Speech in Early America* 91-131 (New York University Press, 1994).

[25] *Trial of John Tutchin*, 14 State Trials 1095, 1097 (1704).

[26] *Queen v Tutchin*, 90 Eng Rep 1133 (1704).

[27] Id at 1133-1134.

[28] 14 State Trials at 1195.

[29] Fredrick S. Siebert, *Freedom of the Press in England* 338 (University of Illinois Press, 1965).

[30] John H. Plumb, *The Origins of Political Stability in England, 1675-1725* at 170-173 (Houghton Mifflin, 1967).

[31] James Fitzjames Stephen, *A History of the Criminal Law of England* 300 (London, 1883); and see, Siebert, *Freedom of the Press in England* at 270 (cited in note 29).

[32] Clyde Augustus Duniway, *The Development of Freedom of the Press in Massachusetts* 101-102 (Longmans, Green & Co., 1906).

[33] Harold L. Nelson, *Seditious Libel in Colonial America*, 3 Am J Legal Hist 160, 170 (1959).

[34] *Attorney General v John Peter Zenger*, 17 State Trials 675, 710 (1735).

[35] William O. Douglas, *The Right of the People* 38 (Doubleday & Co. Inc., 1958).

[36] Josiah Quincy, Jr., ed, *Reports of Cases Argued and Adjudged in the Superior Court of Judicature of the Province of Massachusetts Bay between 1761 and 1772* at 266-267 (Little, Brown & Co., 1865).

[37] William Blackstone argued that "the tendency of these libels is the breach of the peace, by stirring up the objects of them to revenge, and perhaps to bloodshed." He did not object to inadmissibility of truth as a defense in libel cases. While he maintained the importance of freedom of the press, he said it is restricted to "laying on previous restraints upon publications, and not in freedom from censure for criminal matters when published." See his *Commentaries on the Laws of England* vol 2 at 150-152 (London, 1765-1769; reprint Chicago 1873).

[38] Quincy, *Reports* at 309 (cited in note 36).

[39] *King v John Wilkes*, 19 State Trials 982 (1763).

[40] Donald Thomas, ed., *State Trials: Treason and Libel* 165-166 (Routledge and K. Paul, 1972).

[41] George Rudé, *Hanoverian London: 1714-1808* at 219 (University of California, 1971).

[42] Siebert, *Press in England* at 361-362 (cited in note 29).

[43] 13 Halsbury's Statutes of England 1120 (1949)(reproducing *The Libel Act 1792*, 32 Geo 3 ch 60).

[44] 32 Geo 3 ch 60, in 37 The Statutes at Large at 627-628 (Archdeacon, n.d.); see Loren Reid, *Charles James Fox: A Man for the People* 308-321 (University of Missouri Press, 1969).

[45] See Reid, *Charles James Fox* at 275 (cited in note 44).

[46] For detailed account of Oswald's life, see Towne Wheeler, *The Maryland Press [1777-1790]* at 19-36 (Maryland Historical Society, 1938); see also Ward L. Miner, *William Goddard: Newspaperman* 166-174 (Duke University Press, 1962).

[47] Wilkes [pseud], *Independent Gazetteer* (Oct 19, 1782).

[48] Junius Wilkes [pseud], *Independent Gazetteer* (Nov 9, 1782).

[49] For detailed account and analysis of the struggles for freedom of speech, see generally Robert Hargreaves, *The First Freedom: A History of Free Speech* (Sutton, 2002). See Michael Kent Curtis, *Free Speech, "the People's Darling Privilege": Struggles for Freedom of Expression in American History* 52-104, 216-383 (Duke University Press, 2000).

[50] For explanation of the Federalists' reasons for passing the Sedition Act of 1798, see Leonard W. Levy, *Emergence of a Free Press* 298-301 (Oxford University Press, 1985).

[51] 1 Stat 596 (1798).

[52] Norman L. Rosenberg, *Protecting the Best Men: An Interpretive History of the Law of Libel* 86 (University of North Carolina Press, 1986), citing Alexander Addison, *Liberty of Speech and of Press: A Charge to the Grand Juries of the County Courts of the Fifth Circuit of the State of Pennsylvania* 20 (Washington, Pa., 1798).

[53] 1 Stat 596 (1798).

[54] For an account of the act's enforcement against Jeffersonians, see James Morton Smith, *Freedom's Fetters: The Alien and Sedition Laws and American Civil Liberties* 159-217 (Cornell University Press, 1966). See Levy, *Emergence of a Free Press* at 297-300 (cited in note 50); see also Michael T. Gibson, *Freedom of Expression from 1791 to 1917*, 55 (3) Fordham L Rev 263, 273 (1986).

[55] Albert Jeremiah Beveridge, *The Life of John Marshall* vol 3 at 40-42, 48-49 (Houghton Mifflin, 1919).

[56] Leonard W. Levy, *Freedom of Speech and Press in Early American History: Legacy of Suppression* xxii, 13-15 (Harper & Row, Harper Torchbook ed 1963).

[57] Tunis Wortman, *A Treatise concerning Political Inquiry and the Liberty of the Press* 260 (1800, Da Capo Press, 1970); see also George Hay, *An Essay on the Liberty of the Press* 23 (Philadelphia, 1799); and see James Madison, *Report on the Virginia Resolutions*, 4 The Debates in Several State Conventions on the Adoption of the Federal Constitution ... and Other Illustrations of the Constitution. Edited by Jonathan Eliot (Lippincott, 2d ed 1937), 573.

[58] See generally Akhil Reed Amar, *The Bill of Rights: Creation and Reconstruction* (Yale University Press, 1998).

[59] Spencer, *Criminal Libel* at 465 (cited in note 4).

[60] For example, New York law of 1805 allowed jurors to determine both the law and the fact, and admitted truth and non-malice in criminal libel defense. The law became the model for most libel provisions in the nineteenth century. It provided:

> That in every prosecution for writing or publishing any libel, it shall be lawful for the defendant, upon the trial of the cause, to give in evidence in his defense, the truth of the matter contained in the publication charged as libelous: Provided always, that such evidence shall not be a justification, unless on the trial it shall be further made satisfactorily to appear, that the matter charged as libelous, was published with good motives and for justifiable ends. *Crosswell v People*, 3 Reports of Cases Adjudged in the Supreme Court of Judicature of the State of New York 337, 412 (William Johnson, ed, E. F. Backus 1834-1836), quoting the Act of April 6, 1805, Sess 28 ch 90; see *Journal of the Senate of the State of New York [1804]* at 10 (Albany, 1805).

[61] Clifton O. Lawhorne noted only three criminal libel prosecutions between 1812 and 1838: *Commonwealth v Child*, 30 Mass 198 (1832); *Commonwealth v Snelling*, 32 Mass 321 (1834); *State v Burnham*, 31 Am Dec [NH] 217 (1838); see his *Newspapermen v Public Officials: The Evolving Law of Libel* 151 (Ph.D. diss., Southern Illinois University at Carbondale, 1968).

[62] See Rosenberg, *Protecting the Best Men* 120-129 (cited in note 52).

[63] United States v Hudson and Goodwin, 7 Cr [US] 32, 34 (1812).

[64] Rosenberg, *Protecting the Best Men* 121-129 (cited in note 52), citing libel decisions such as *Lewis v Few*, 5 Johns Rep 1 (NY 1809) and *Root v King*, 4 Wend 113 (NY 1829).

[65] Rosenberg, *Protecting the Best Men* at 159 (cited in note 52), quoting *Critical Notice: A Treatise on the Law of Slander and Libel*, 2 Am L Mag 247, 255 (1843-1844).

[66] Public Acts Passed by the General Assembly of the State of Connecticut, May Sess at 99 (Hartford, 1855).

[67] Hotchkiss v Porter, 30 Conn 414, 420-421 (1862).

[68] *Negley v Farrow*, 60 Md 158, 170 (1882).

[69] Great Britain, Libel Act 1843 § 6. See *R. v Perryman* (1892) in 115 Cent Crim Ct Sess Papers 358, 378 where the jury found that an editor's allegation that a solicitor was party to a major company fraud was true, but he was convicted of criminal libel because it was not in the public interest that this truth be published.

[70] *R v Wicks*, 1 All ER 384 (1936).

[71] *De Libellis Famosis*, 77 ER 250 (1606). See *R. v Labouchère*, 12 QBD 320, 324 (1884), Justice Coleridge gave a reasoning that the libel must have been published with intent to provoke a breach of the peace by the deceased's relations.

[72] Libel Act 1843 §§ 4-5 (cited in note 69).

[73] 40 Stat ch 75 at 553.

[74] *Schenck v United States*, 249 US 47, 52 (1919).

[75] *Abrams v United States*, 250 US 616, 630 (1919), Holmes, J., dissenting.

[76] *Gitlow v New York*, 268 US 652, 666 (1925). But, in a footnote, the Court quickly added that whereas freedom of speech and of press have constitutional protection, the Constitution does not confer absolute freedom of speech and of the press. Id.

[77] *Near v Minnesota*, 283 US 697 (1931).

[78] *Time, Inc v Hill*, 388 US 374, 388 (1967). Though the issue before the Court was on invasion of privacy, the Court threw light on freedom of discussion and matters of public interest.

[79] *Garrison v Louisiana*, 379 US 64 (1964); see John Stevens, Robert L. Bailey, Judith F. Krueger and John M. Mollwitz, *Criminal Libel as Seditious Libel [1916-65]*, 45 Jrnl Q 110, 110-113 (1966).

[80] *Garrison*, 379 US at 77-79.

[81] Id at 80.

[82] *Beauharnais v Illinois*, 343 US 250, 254-257 (1952).

[83] Spencer, *Criminal Libel* at 389 (cited in note 4)

[84] Great Britain, Defamation Act 1952 § 17(2).

[85] See generally *Schenck v United States*, 249 US 47 (1919), *Near v Minnesota*, 283 US 697 (1931), *Bridges v California*, 314 US 252 (1941). See also generally *City of Chicago v Tribune Co.*, 307 Ill 595 (1923).

[86] *New York Times v Sullivan*, 376 US 254 (1964).

[87] See discussions of David A. Strauss, *Freedom of Speech and the Common Law Constitution*, in Lee C. Bollinger and Geoffrey R. Stone, ed, *Eternally Vigilant: Free Speech in the Modern Era* 32-59 (University of Chicago Press, 2002). See also Kermit L. Hall, *Cultural History and the First Amendment: New York Times v Sullivan and Its Times*, in Sandra F. VanBurkleo, Kermit L. Hall and Robert J. Kaczorowski, eds, *Constitutionalism and American Culture: Writing the New Constitutional History* 267-306 (University Press of Kansas, 2002).

[88] Id at 279-280.

[89] Anthony Lewis, *New York Times v Sullivan Reconsidered: Time to Return to "The Central Meaning of the First Amendment,"* 83 Colum L Rev 603, 622 (1983).

[90] *New York Times*, 376 US at 276.

[91] *New York Times*, 376 US at 285-286.

[92] *St. Amant v Thompson*, 390 US 727, 731 (1968).

[93] Curtis Publishing Co. v Butts, and *Associated Press v Walker*, 388 US 130 (1967).

[94] *Gertz v Robert Welch, Inc.*, 418 US 323 (1974).

[95] Id at 347-349.

[96] Law Commission [Great Britain], Report on Criminal Libel, 1985, Cmnd 9618, L Com No 149 ¶ 2.3.

[97] *Gleaves v Deakin*, AC 477 (1980); 2 All ER 497 (HL 1979).

[98] Id at AC 483.

[99] See Defamation Act 1952 § 5, the civil defendant is entitled to win if he can prove the truth of the serious allegations, but not the minor ones; see also, Report on Criminal Libel ¶ 4.2 (cited in note 96): Although Section 6 of the Libel Act 1843 provides a defense of the truth of the publication in criminal proceedings, the truth of the words complained of is a complete defense to a civil action, while in criminal proceedings the defendant must prove not only that the defamatory matter is true, but also that its publication was for the public benefit. A person can be convicted for telling the truth in criminal libel proceedings unless he can prove publication for the public benefit. A defendant may be convicted even though he or she published what he or she honestly and reasonably believed to be true. Under the Libel Act 1843 § 5, the defendant who was convicted was subject to a maximum of 12 months' imprisonment, in cases where publication is made with knowledge of the falsity of the defamatory matter, two years' imprisonment.

[100] J. R. Spencer, *Criminal Libel: The Law Commission's Working Paper*, Crim L Rev 525 (1983).

[101] Report on Criminal Libel, L Com No 149 ¶ 1.1 (cited in note 96).

[102] Id.

[103] Id ¶ 7.1.

[104] Id ¶ 1.1.

[105] Id ¶ 7.9 .

[106] Id ¶ 7.13.

[107] Id ¶¶ 7.28, 7.53, 7.61.

[108] Id ¶ 7.64. The defense of absolute privilege is of limited scope but confers complete protection with respect to statements made in the course of Parliamentary proceedings; all reports, papers, votes and proceedings published by or under the authority of either Houses of Parliament; statements made in the course of judicial and quasi-judicial proceedings; statements made by one officer of State to another in the course of duty; which are fair and accurate reports in newspapers of judicial proceedings in the United Kingdom if published contemporaneously. The Law Commission was cautious not to recommend definition of the situations in which absolute privilege may be claimed.

[109] Id ¶ 7.65. Qualified privilege is available in a wider range of situations than absolute privilege. For example, statements made in the performance of a legal, social or moral duty to a person who has a corresponding duty or interest to receive them, statements made in the protection of a common interest to a person sharing the same interest, fair and accurate reports of judicial or Parliamentary proceedings.

[110] See Thomas Emerson's idea of democracy, participation and self-fulfillment, in his *System of Freedom of Expression* (Random House, 1970).

[111] S. Kentridge, *Freedom of Speech: Is it the Primary Right?* 45 Intl & Comp L Q 253, 264 (April 1996).

[112] Report on Criminal Libel ¶ 7.11 (cited in note 96). "Falsity" in the new offense is limited as to "communicate false information" expressly or by implication.

[113] *Derbyshire County Council v Times Newspapers Ltd.*, 1 All ER 1011 (1993).

[114] Id at 1013.

[115] Id at 1019.

[116] Id at 1017.

[117] *City of Chicago v Tribune Co.*, 307 Ill 595 (1923).

[118] *Derbyshire*, 1 All ER at 1018.

[119] Further liberalizing development in English libel law is discussed below under the European Convention on Human Rights.

[120] 3 All ER 961 (1998).

[121] Id at 994-995.

[122] Id at 1006.

[123] Libel and Slander, 28 Halsbury Laws of England ¶ 109 (cited in note 5).

[124] Alexander Meiklejohn, *Political Freedom: The Constitutional Powers of the People* (Oxford University Press, 1965).

[125] *Reynolds*, 3 All ER at 1006.

[126] 472 US 749 (1985).

[127] Id at 765.

[128] *Reynolds*, 3 All ER at 995. Status refers to the degree to which information on a matter of public concern may (because of its character and known provenance) command respect…. The higher the status of a report, the more likely it is to meet the circumstantial test. Conversely, unverified information from unidentified and unofficial sources may have little or no status, and where defamatory statements of fact are to be published to the widest audience on the strength of such sources, the publisher undertakes a heavy burden in showing that the publication is "fairly warranted by any responsible occasion of exigency."

[129] 388 US 130 (1967).

[130] Id at 155-158.

[131] *Reynolds*, 3 All ER at 1006.

[132] Id.

[133] Id.

[134] A. H. Robertson, *Human Rights in Europe* 3 (Manchester University Press, 1977).

[135] Id at 5 nn 7-8. The sixteen delegates were from Austria, Belgium, Britain, Denmark, Ireland, France, Germany, Greece, Italy, Liechtenstein, Luxembourg, Netherlands, Norway, Saar, Sweden, and Switzerland. The ten observers consisted of Bulgaria, Canada, Czechoslovakia, Finland, Hungary, Poland, Roumania, Spain, the United States, and Yugoslavia.

[136] Council of Europe, *Collected Edition of the Travaux Préparatoires* vol 1 at xxii (The Hague, Netherlands 1975).

[137] Id at xxiv.

[138] The eight countries that ratified the European Convention in September 1953 were Denmark, the Federal Republic of Germany, Iceland, Ireland, Luxembourg, Norway, Sweden, and the United Kingdom.

[139] P.-H. Teitgen, *Introduction to the European Convention on Human Rights*, in R. St. J. Macdonald, F. Matscher and H. Petzold, eds, *The European System for the Protection of Human Rights* 3, 3-14 (Martinus Nijhoff, 1993).

[140] *Speech by the Secretary General at the Commemorative Ceremony for the 50th Anniversary of the European Convention on Human Rights*. Rome: 4 November 2000.

[141] Paul Mahoney, *Principles of Judicial Review As developed by the European Court of Human Rights: Their Relevance in a National Context*, in Lammy Betten, ed, *The Human Rights Act 1998 What it means: The Incorporation of the European Convention on Human Rights into the Legal Order of the United Kingdom*, 65, 65-66 (Kluwer Law International, 1999)[Paul Mahoney is deputy registrar of the European Court of Human Rights]; see his *Universality versus Subsidiarity in Free Speech Cases*, 1997

Eur HR L Rep 364, 368-69, where he commented that the second level of protection aims at defending individuals and groups against excesses of majoritarian rule in a democracy.
[142] Donald W. Jackson, *The United Kingdom confronts the European Convention on Human Rights* 12 (University Press of Florida, 1997).
[143] Mahoney, *Principles of Judicial Review* at 66 (cited in note 141).
[144] *Feldbrugge v Netherlands*, 99 EHRR (Series A) ¶ 24 [29 May 1986]; for other comments on the evolutive interpretation of European Court of Human Rights, see Mahoney, *Principles of Judicial Review* at 73-78 (cited in note 141); see also his *Marvelous Richness of Diversity or Invidious Cultural Relativism*, 19 HR L J 1, 2 (April 30, 1998). Also see Jackson, *European Convention on Human Rights* at 29 (cited in note 142) for an explanation of the liberal approach of the Court. He wrote that the European Court of Human Rights follows an evolutive style of interpretation by interpreting the provisions of the Europe Convention on Human Rights in light of current conditions and circumstances. Jackson cited Judge Matscher of the Court, for example, who wrote an article in 1993 on interpreting the European Court of Human Rights as an evolutive or dynamic method of interpretation as contrasted with a static or historical method (Id at 30); and see F. Matscher, *Methods of Interpretation of the Convention*, in R. St. J. Macdonald, F. Matscher, and H. Petzold, eds, *The European System for the Protection of Human Rights* 63, 68 (Martinus Nijhoff, 1993): "This means that the concepts used in the Convention are to be understood in the context of the democratic society of today, and not in that of the forty years ago when the Convention was drafted." Matscher also described the Court's style as an "autonomous interpretation," one that transcends a meaning peculiar to a particular state-member and seeks a general definition and understanding (Id at 70).
[145] Article 10 of the European Convention states that (1) Everyone has the right to freedom of expression. The right shall include freedom to hold opinions and to receive and impart information and ideas without interference by public authority and regardless of frontiers. This Article shall not prevent States from requiring the licensing of broadcasting, television or cinema enterprises. (2) The exercise of these freedoms, since it carries with it duties and responsibilities, may be subject to such formalities, conditions, restrictions or penalties as are prescribed by law and are necessary in a democratic society, in the interests of national security, territorial integrity or public safety, for the prevention of disorder or crime, for the protection of health or morals, for the protection of the reputation or rights of others, for preventing the disclosure of information received in confidence, or for maintaining the authority and impartiality of the judiciary.
[146] *Handyside v United Kingdom*, 1 EHRR 737 (1976). For discussion of European Court of Human Rights' doctrines of "margin of appreciation," "principle of proportionality and the balancing of interests," and the "doctrine

of precedent and incremental decisionmaking" see the collection of articles under *Doctrine of the Margin of Appreciation under the European Convention on Human Rights: Its Legitimacy in Theory and Application in Practice*, 19 HR L J 1-36 (April 30, 1998); see also Mahoney, *Principles of Judicial Review* at 78-85 (cited in note 141).

[147] See *Handyside v The United Kingdom*, 1 EHRR 737; *Lingens v Austria*, 8 EHRR 407 (1986).

[148] *Lingens v Austria*, 8 EHRR at ¶ 42.

[149] *Castells v Spain*, 14 EHRR 445 (1992).

[150] *United Communist Party of Turkey and Others v Turkey*, 26 EHRR 121 ¶ 45 (1998).

[151] *Reynolds v Times Newspapers*, 4 All ER 609, 625 (HL 1999). See also the Appeals Court decision in *Reynolds*, 3 All ER 961 (1998).

[152] Paul Mitchell, *Malice in Defamation*, 114 L Q Rev 639, 664 (1998).

[153] Jackson, *European Convention on Human Rights* at ix [preface](cited in note 142).

[154] Id. See Maurice Sunken, *The Incidence and Effect of Judicial Review Procedures against Central Government in the United Kingdom*, in D. Jackson and N. Tate, eds, *Comparative Judicial Review and Public Policy* 143, 145 (Greenwood Press, 1992); and see Kenneth C. Davis, *Discretionary Justice: A Preliminary Inquiry* 55 (University of Illinois Press, 1971).

[155] *Chief Constable of the North Wales Police v Evans*, 3 All ER 141, 173-74 (1982).

[156] R. Bernhardt, *The Convention and Domestic Law*, in R. St. J. Macdonald, F. Matscher, and H. Petzold, eds, *The European System for the Protection of Human Rights* 25-40 (Martinus Nijhoff, 1993).

[157] Jackson, *European Convention on Human Rights* at 9 (cited in note 142). For more discussion of the impact of the libel jurisprudence of the European Court of Human Rights on member-states, see generally Les P. Carnegie, *Privacy and the Press: The Impact of Incorporating the European Convention of Human Rights in the United Kingdom*, 9 Duke J Comp & Intl L 311 (1998); Sandra Coliver, *Defamation Jurisprudence of the European Court of Human Rights*, 13 J Media L & Prac 250 (1992); Dirk Voorhoof, *Defamation and Libel Law in Europe -- The Framework of Article 10 of the European Convention on Human Rights*, 13 J Media L & Prac 254 (1992).

[158] Editorial, Eur HR L Rev 1 (Launch Issue 1995). On how some English judges have creatively used the European Convention, see Michael Beloff, *What does It All mean? Interpreting the Human Rights Act 1998*, in Lammy Betten, ed, *The Human Rights Act 1998 What It means* 11, 24 (Kluwer Law International, 1999).

[159] *Derbyshire*, 1 All ER at 1021. About Lord Keith of Kinkel's view that there was no difference between English common law relating to freedom of speech and the provisions of Art. 10 of the Convention, see *Ming Pao*, AC 957 (1994); In *R. v Central Independent TV plc*, 3 All ER 641, 651-2 (1994), per Lord Hoffman.

[160] John Gardner, *Freedom of Expression*, in C. McCrudden and G. Chambers, eds, *Individual Rights and the Law in Britain* 209 (Clarendon Press, 1994).

[161] Lammy Betten, ed, *The Human Rights Act 1998 What It Means: The Incorporation of the European Convention on Human Rights into the Legal Order of the United Kingdom* 2 (Kluwer Law International, 1999). See Les P. Carnegie, *Privacy and the Press: The Impact of Incorporating the European Convention on Human Rights in the United Kingdom*, 9 Duke J Comp & Intl L 311 (1998).

[162] Betten, *Human Rights Act 1998* at 2 (cited in note 161). Clause 3 of the Human Rights Bill (HL) provides that primary and subordinate legislation, whenever enacted, must as far as possible be read and given effect in a way which is compatible with the Convention rights. It also provides that this does not affect the validity, continuing operation or enforcement of any incompatible primary legislation, or any incompatible subordinate legislation if primary legislation prevents the removal of the incompatibility.

Clause 7 provides that a person who claims that a public authority has acted (or proposes to act) in a way which is unlawful, because incompatible with a Convention right, may bring proceedings against that authority under the Bill, or may rely on the Convention rights in any legal proceedings. Such a person may only bring proceedings or rely on the Convention rights if he is (or would be) a victim of the unlawful act.

[163] Accompanying Government White Paper, 1997, Cmnd 3782, at 10 ¶ 2.7.

[164] For more benefits of United Kingdom's incorporation of the Convention, see Accompanying Government White Paper, 1997, Cmnd 3782, at 7-8; see also Robert Blackburn, *Towards a Constitutional Bill of Rights for the United Kingdom* 360-361 (Pinter, 1999).

[165] *Handyside v United Kingdom*, 1 EHRR 737 (1976). The margin of appreciation doctrine explains the Convention legal order of allowing states certain freedom of evaluation subject to supervision at ECHR. The margin of appreciation has been used, for example, in applying the principle of proportionality to restrictions upon non-absolute rights. See Michael J. Beloff, *What Does it All Mean*, in Lammy Betten, ed, *The Human Rights Act: What it Means* 11, 46-47 (Kluwer Law International, 1999).

[166] Human Rights Act 2 (1)(a) states: A court or tribunal determining a question which has arisen in connection with a Convention right must take into account any judgment, decision, declaration or advisory opinion of the European Court of Human Rights.

[167] HL Deb, 18 November 1997, cols 514, 515.

[168] HL Deb, 19 January 1998, cols 1270, 1271.

[169] *Reynolds*, 4 All ER at 621-622.

[170] See *Handyside*, 1 EHRR ¶ 48.

[171] See Frederick Schauer, *Free Speech: A Philosophical Enquiry* 86 (Cambridge University Press, 1982).

[172] Mahoney, *Principles of Judicial Review* at 65-66 (cited in note 141).

[173] *New York Times*, 376 US at 270; *Lingens*, 8 EHRR at 418.

[174] See *Lingens*, 8 EHRR at 418; compare *New York Times*, 376 US at 279-280.

[175] See Mahoney, *Marvelous Richness of Diversity* at 3 (cited in note 144).

[176] Jackson, *European Convention on Human Rights* at 9 (cited in note 138).

[177] Patrick Parkinson, *Tradition and Change in Australian Law* 125 (The Law Book Co. Ltd., 1994).

[178] Austl Const Acts, 63-64 Vict, ch 12 (1900).

[179] For insights into debates before the referendum, see *The Republic and the States Papers delivered at a TC Beirne Law School Symposium held at the Heritage Hotel, Brisbane on 11 June 1998*, 20 [2] U Q L J 54 (1999).

[180] Parkinson, *Tradition and Change* at 168-171 (cited in note 177).

[181] Id at 143.

[182] See Robert McKewen and Philip Lewis, *Gatley on Libel and Slander* 2 (7th ed 1977).

[183] For information on the *Judiciary Act 1903* establishing the High Court of Australia and its jurisdiction, see Parkinson, *Tradition and Change* at 186-188 (cited in note 177). For origin of the United States doctrine of judicial review, see *Marbury v Madison*, 5 US 137 (1803). The doctrine establishes United States Supreme Court as the final arbiter of the law.

[184] Royal Commission on the Press, Final Report, 1977, at 183.

[185] *James v Commonwealth*, 55 CLR 1, 56 (1936).

[186] 1 Stat Art I, at 21.

[187] David Hunt, *Why No First Amendment? The Role of the Press in Relationship to Justice*, 54 (8) AL J 458 (August 1980).

[188] Law Reform Commission of Australia, *Unfair Publication* 19-22 (1979).

[189] Michael Newcity, *The Sociology of Defamation in Australia and the United States*, 26 Tex Intl L J 1, 4 (1991).

[190] Rodney A. Smolla, *Balancing Freedom of Expression and Protection of Reputation under the Charter*, in David Schneiderman, ed, *Freedom of Expression and the Charter* at 277 (Thomson Professional Pub., 1991). For an evaluation of the public-private distinction, see Matthew D. Bunker, *Critiquing Free Speech: First Amendment Theory and the Challenge of Interdisciplinarity* 127-156 (Lawrence Erlbaum Associates, 2001).

[191] John G. Fleming, *The Law of Torts* 539 (The Law Book Co. Ltd., 8th ed 1992).

[192] For detail discussion of the libel defenses in Australia, see generally id at 553-593.

[193] Mark Armstrong, Michael Blakeney and Ray Watterson, *Media Law in Australia* 45 (Oxford University Press, 1983). The authors pointed out that one

English court has characterized the defense of fair comment as "one of the essential elements that go to make up our freedom of speech." Id at 44, quoting *Slim v Daily Telegraph*, 2 QB 167, 170 (CA 1968).

[194] It is worth noting that the Restatement (Second) of Torts has deleted fair comment from its list of defamation defenses. See Restatement (Second) of Torts § 566 comment c, and note after §§ 606-10 (1977). See also Rodney Smolla, *Law of Defamation* § 6.02 [4][a] (Clark Boardman Co., 1986).

[195] *Bjelke-Petersen v Burns*, 2 QR 129 (1988).

[196] *Porter v Mercury Newspaper*, Tas St R 279, 283-286 (1964).

[197] *Comalco v ABC*, 64 ACTR 1 (1985).

[198] *Thomas v Bradbury*, 2 KB 627 (1906); followed in *Fackle v Herald Ltd.*, VLR 56, 72 (1925).

[199] T. Barton Carter, et al, *Mass Communication Law in a Nutshell* 71 (West Publishing Co., 4th ed 1994).

[200] Id at 72.

[201] *Milkovich v Lorain Journal*, 497 US 1, 11-21 (1990).

[202] See *Adam v Ward* (1917) AC 309, 334, per Lord Atkinson; but under the Codes, qualified privilege is conditioned by good faith, see Criminal Code 1899 § 377 (Queensl); Criminal Code 1913 § 357 (W Austl); Defamation Act 1957 § 16[2] (Tas). The burden of proof is on the plaintiff: Queensl Stat § 378; W Austl § 358; Tas § 18.

[203] *Hughes v Western Australian Newspapers*, 43 WALR 12, 13-14 (1940); *Restatement* (Second) of Torts § 611 (1977); *Medico v Time, Inc.*, 643 F 2d 134, 137-143 (3d Cir 1981).

[204] "Code states" refers to a group of Australian states that follow the civil and criminal defamation proceedings provided in Queensland Defamation Law of 1889 or its amended version.

[205] The Queensland Code provisions on defamation were adopted in substantially identical form in Tasmania, see Defamation Act 1895 (Tas); as amended see Defamation Act 1957 (Tas).

[206] It became the Criminal Code, 1913, ch 35 (W Austl).

[207] Defamation Act of Queensland, 1889, 53 Vict No 12; see also Criminal Code Act, 1899, ch 25, §§ 365-389.

[208] See Defamation Act 1958 (NSW).

[209] Edward I. Sykes, *Some Aspects of Queensland Defamation Law*, 1951 U Q L J 19, 20-22.

[210] Queensl, § 377; W Austl, § 357; Tas, § 16.

[211] Sykes, *Queensland Defamation Law* 22 (cited in note 209).

[212] Anthony Smith, *Publish and Be Damned*, 61 L Inst J 914, 917 (1987).

[213] See *Chapman v Ellesmere*, 2 KB 43 (1932); *Morosi v Mirror Newspapers Ltd.*, 2 NSWLR 749 (1977).

[214] New South Wales Law Reform Commission, Working Paper on Defamation (1968).

[215] New South Wales Reform Commission, Defamation and Freedom of the Press, Report No 11 (1971).

[216] Defamation Act 1974 § 22 (NSW), read: (1) Where in respect of any matter published to any person -- (a) the recipient has an apparent interest in having information on some subject; (b) the matter is published to the recipient in the course of giving him information on that subject; and (c) the conduct of the publisher in publishing that matter is reasonable in the circumstances, there is a defense of qualified privilege.

[217] Under the Codes, a defamatory imputation is defined as "any imputation concerning any person, or any member of his family, whether living or dead, by which the reputation of that person is likely to be injured, or by which he is likely to be injured in his profession or trade, or by which other persons are likely to be induced to shame, avoid or ridicule or despise him": Criminal Code 1899 § 366 (Queensl); Defamation Act 1957 § 5 (Tas); Criminal Code 1913 § 346 (W Austl).

[218] Sally Walker, *The Law of Journalism in Australia* 137 (Law Book Co., 1989).

[219] For more information on the application of the statutory qualified privilege under *Defamation Act 1974* § 22 (NSW), see id at 192-194.

[220] South Australia Law Reform Committee, 1972, Rep No. 15.

[221] Law Reform Committee of Western Australia, Working Paper on Newspaper Libel and Registration Act 1884-1957, July 1969, Proj No 8 (pt 1).

[222] Western Australia Law Reform Commission Report, Defamation: Privileged Reports, July 1972.

[223] Western Australia Law Reform Commission Report, *Defamation*, 1979, Proj No 18.

[224] Australian Constitutional Convention, Minutes of Proceedings and Official Record of Debates of the Australia Constitutional Convention 17 (Oct 23, 1976).

[225] Australian Law Reform Commission [ALRC], Discussion Paper 1: Defamation -- Options for Reform, 1977.

[226] ALRC, Unfair Publication: Defamation and Privacy, 1979, Rep No 11.

[227] Id pt 2 ¶¶ 42-47.

[228] Id ch 13.

[229] Parkinson, *Tradition and Change* at 187 (cited in note 177). For a discussion of the court system in the Australian federation, see id ch 7.

[230] Peter Handford, *Defamation and the Conflict of Laws in Australia,* 32 (2) Intl & Comp L Q 452, 474-475 (April 1983).

[231] Though the Australian Law Reform Commission was unsuccessful in attaining uniformity of defamation law, its objective was realized in the implied constitutional mechanism developed in 1992.

[232] For a study of the differences in the defamation laws of the various States and Territories of Australia, see Handford, *Defamation and the Conflict of Laws in Australia* at 454-475 (cited in note 230); see also Fleming, *The Law of Torts* at 524-525 (cited in note 191). Australian defamation law was largely

statutory in nature. Of the eight states and federal territories into which
Australia is divided, defamation law was statutorily codified in the states of
Queensland, Tasmania, Western Australia, and New South Wales. In the States
of Victoria and South Australia and the two federal territories (the Australian
Capital Territory and the Northern Territory), the common law prevailed.
    [233] (1977) 16 ACTR 35 [ACT S Ct]. For a similar incident where the
same publication is defamatory in some States but not in others, see *Gorton v
Australian Broadcasting Commission* (1974) 22 FLR 181.
    [234] *Renouf*, 16 ACTR at 59.
    [235] For aspects of United States' free speech principles that may apply in
Australia, see generally Michael R. Chesterman, *Freedom of Speech in
Australian Law: A Delicate Plant?* 15-153 (Ashgate, 2000).
    [236] Fleming, *Law of Torts* at 570 (cited in note 191), citing, for example,
(U.K) Press Council, *Reforming the Law of Defamation* (1973); *Faulks* §§ 211-
215.
    [237] Australian Law Reform Commission, Unfair Publication: Defamation
and Privacy, 1979, Rep No 11 at 247.
    [238] See, for example, Robert Pullan, *Guilty Secrets: Free Speech in
Australia* 18-19, 212 (Methuen Australia Pty, 1984); see also Graham Fricke,
Libel, Lampoons and Litigants 19-97 (Hutchinson Publishing Group Pty Ltd,
1984).
    [239] 177 CLR 106 (1992).
    [240] 177 CLR 1 (1992).
    [241] *Theophanous v The Herald and Weekly Times Ltd.*, 182 CLR 104
(1994).
    [242] Id at 134.
    [243] Id.
    [244] Id at 211.
    [245] Id at 124.
    [246] Id 141.
    [247] Id at 140.
    [248] Id.
    [249] 189 CLR 520 (1997).
    [250] Id at 559.
    [251] Id at 560.
    [252] Id at 567.
    [253] Id at 562.
    [254] Id at 569-571.
    [255] Id at 571.
    [256] Id at 574.
    [257] See *Theophanous*, 182 CLR at 130.
    [258] *Lange*, 189 CLR at 559-561.
    [259] *Lingens*, 8 EHRR at 417.

[260] *Lange*, 189 CLR at 567-569.
[261] *Lingens*, 8 EHRR at 418.
[262] Id at 419.
[263] *Lange*, 189 CLR at 572.
[264] *Lingens*, 8 EHRR at 419.

CHAPTER FOUR

[1] A legal analogy looks for key "facts and the reasoning of the controlling authority" to establish "meaningful and significant relationship[s]" in the cases (David S. Romantz and Kathleen Elliott Vinson, *Legal Analysis* 34 [Carolina Academic Press, 1998]), for courts follow precedents in their rulings where claims addressed either have similar facts and issues or share common characteristics (Id at 35). This analogical task requires identifying the "critical facts" of the controlling authority and synthesizing cases. According to Romantz and Vinson, "Critical facts are facts from the controlling precedent that the court found dispositive when it resolved a legal dispute" (Id at 36). To identify critical facts this study examined the reasoning of the key cases, because the "reasoning of the case shows which facts are significant or dispositive" (Id at 37). Because an argument should compare facts, a detailed analysis must examine all critical facts in the court's reasoning in every case. One technique to do this is case synthesis. The case synthesis allows the legal researcher to analyze several cases about a particular issue at once and can "incorporate an entire body of law in a concise and comprehensive analysis" (Id at 39). It requires a careful look at opinions that are relevant to political defamation, and identifying "the critical facts, holdings, reasoning, and any rules articulated" (Id at 40). It also checks for a "common denominator, or thread among the critical facts of the different opinions ... in order to blend all the holdings of the applicable authority" (Id). In this the analogical analysis allows comparison of the four regimes around each jurisprudential common denominator, "instead of organizing the analysis around individual cases" (Id). Thus, the case synthesis integrates several cases to find a common denominator among the precedents for a workable comparison. Conjoining the analogical analysis is a qualitative content analysis of the cases. This unobtrusive measure was useful and convenient for obtaining valuable information about the development of legal understandings in the different regimes. Court cases were analyzed for the comparative analysis in this inquiry. The categories of analysis consisted of the issue, identity, interest, rationale and doctrinal approach. Also, the study coded the cases according to these categories. The categories were more "ideational" (Thomas R. Lindlof, *Qualitative Communication Research Methods* 220 [Sage, 1995]), characterizing the theoretical concepts and legal practices. The category generation reveals patterns and meanings that note convergence and divergence of the various jurisprudences. The coding categories were based on free speech theory; however, "the notion of calculating intercoder agreement as found in formal

content analysis does not apply in qualitative content coding" (Id at 221). For, the "purposes of qualitative coding are to tag segments of interest and to look for ways to categorize action ... that will lead toward inductive proposition" (Id). The qualitative analysis deals with the "latent content of the message for meaning holistically in their contexts" (Carolyn A. Stroman and Kenneth E. Jones, *The Analysis of Television Content*, in Joy Keiko Asamen and Gordon L. Berry, eds, *Research Paradigms, Television, and Social Behavior* 275 [Sage, 1998]). Here, the cases of study were important for conceptual development and inference, for evaluating their usefulness and centrality to understanding political defamation, and for searching for critical explanations and interpretation of the data.

[2] 376 US 254 (1964).

[3] 418 US 323 (1974).

[4] 472 US 749 (1985).

[5] 8 EHRR 407 (1986).

[6] 14 EHRR 445 (1992).

[7] 29 EHRR 125 (1999).

[8] 1 All ER 1011 (1993).

[9] 3 All ER 961 (CA 1998).

[10] 4 All ER 609 (HL 1999).

[11] 117 CLR 106 (1992).

[12] 182 CLR 104 (1994).

[13] 189 CLR 579 (1997).

[14] 376 US 254.

[15] 347 US 483 (1955).

[16] See, for example, Anthony Lewis, *Make No Law* 5-7 (Random House, 1991).

[17] *New York Times* 25 (March 29, 1960); the Supreme Court attached a copy of the advertisement as an appendix to its opinion, see *New York Times v Sullivan*, 376 US at 292 (1964).

[18] *New York Times*, 376 US at 257-259.

[19] For an analysis of the inaccuracies in the ad, see Rodney A. Smolla, 2 *Smolla and Nimmer on Freedom of Speech* § 23:2 nn 4 and 9 (Clark Boardman Callaghan, 1996).

[20] Id.

[21] *New York Times Co. v Sullivan*, 273 Ala 656, 144 So 2d 25 (1962).

[22] Id, 144 So 2d at 37.

[23] Id at 39.

[24] Though Justices Black, Douglas and Goldberg agreed with the majority opinion, their concurring opinions sought absolute immunity from political libel actions.

[25] 78 Kan 711 (1908).

[26] For a discussion of how the United States Supreme Court formulated the new constitutional rule from existing common law privileges, see Joel D. Eaton, *The American Law of Defamation through Gertz v Robert Welch, Inc. and Beyond: An Analytical Primer*, 61(7) Va L Rev 1349, 1366-1367 (1975); see also *New York Times*, 376 US at 292 n 30:

> [R]ecovery is precluded in this case by the doctrine of fair comment. Since the Fourteenth Amendment requires recognition of the conditional privilege for the misstatement of fact, it follows that a defense of fair comment must be afforded for honest expression of opinion based upon privileged, as well as true, statement of fact. Both defenses are of course defeasible if the public official proves actual malice, as was not done here.

[27] *New York Times*, 376 US at 279-280.

[28] See Justice Brennan's opinion in *Roth v United States*, 354 US 476, 484 (1957), that the First Amendment "was fashioned to assure unfettered interchange of ideas for the bringing about of political and social changes desired by the people."

[29] Id at 275, 282, quoting James Madison, 4 *Annals of Congress* 934 (1794).

[30] Id at 269, citing *Stromberg v California*, 283 US 359, 369 (1931).

[31] *New York Times*, 376 US at 270, citing *Terminiello v Chicago*, 337 US 1, 4 (1949); *DeJonge v Oregon*, 299 US 353, 365 (1937). Justice Brennan's opinion indirectly endorsed Alexander Meiklejohn's view of political speech:

> Public discussions of public issues, together with the spreading of information and opinion bearing on those issues, must have a freedom unabridged by our agents. Though they govern us, we, in a deeper sense, govern them. Over our governing, they have no power. Over their governing we have sovereign power. Alexander Meiklejohn, *The First Amendment Is an Absolute*, 1961 S Ct Rev 245, 257. Meiklejohn's argument was that speech concerning the political process must have absolute protection under the First Amendment.

[32] *New York Times*, 376 US at 271-272.

[33] Id at 279.

[34] Id at 273.

[35] Id; see Harry Kalven, Jr., *The New York Times Case: A Note on "The Central Meaning of the First Amendment,"* 1964 S Ct Rev 191.

[36] *New York Times*, 376 US at 279-280.

[37] Id at 285-286.

[38] Id at 286-288.

[39] Id at 288-291.

[40] Id at 292, citing *City of Chicago v Tribune Co*, 307 Ill 595, 601, 139 NE 86, 88 (1923).

[41] Harry Kalven, Jr., *A Worthy Tradition* at xxii [preface](1988).

[42] See Justice Brennan's opinion, *Garrison v Louisiana*, 379 U.S. 64, 75 (1964).

[43] *Garrison*, 379 US at 78-79.

[44] 390 US 727 (1968).

[45] Id at 731.

[46] *New York Times*, 376 US at 293-295 (*per* Black, J), at 298 and 304 (*per* Douglas and Goldberg, JJ), citing *Barr v Matteo*, 360 US 564, 571 (1959), *Wood v Georgia*, 370 US 375, 389 (1962); see comments of Joel Eaton, *The American Law of Defamation* at 1369 (cited in note 26), citing those tests established in *Schenk v United States*, 249 US 47, 52 (1919); *Konigsberg v State Bar of California*, 366 US 36, 50-51 (1961).

[47] *New York Times*, 376 US at 283 n 23.

[48] 388 US 130 (1967).

[49] 388 US 130 (1967).

[50] Id at 154.

[51] Id at 162, 164 (Warren, CJ).

[52] 418 US 323 (1974).

[53] Id at 326.

[54] Id.

[55] Id at 323.

[56] Id at 341.

[57] Id at 343-345.

[58] Id at 351-352.

[59] Id at 342-343.

[60] Id at 345-348. States have the option to develop for themselves the standard of liability claim by private plaintiffs, but most states have chosen the proof of "negligence." See Smolla, *Freedom of Speech*, § 23:4 n 33 (cited in note 19).

[61] Id.

[62] Id at 344.

[63] Id at 344 n 9.

[64] Id at 345.

[65] Id at 345. See id at 352. The notoriety or fame of unlimited public figures may be inferred from their voluntary exposure to increased risk of injury, and so become public figures for all purposes and in all contexts. For a critical view against modern application of the *Gertz* rule to celebrities when they are neither pervasively involved in public matters nor sufficiently connected to those affairs, see James C. Mitchell, *The Accidental Purist:*

Reclaiming the Gertz All-Purpose Public figure doctrine in the Age of "Celebrity Journalism," 22 Loy L A Ent L Rev 559 (2002).

[66] Id at 351-352.

[67] Id at 345.

[68] Id at 351.

[69] Id at 352.

[70] Id at 349. The Court allows states to use their discretion in setting the liability requirement as regards compensatory damages for private figure plaintiffs.

[71] Id at 345.

[72] Id at 345-346.

[73] *Hutchinson v Proxmire*, 443 US 111, 133 n 16 (1979), the Court declared that it had never ruled whether the *New York Times* standard could apply to suits by private parties against nonmedia defendants; see also *Babbitt v United Farms Workers*, 442 US 289, 309 n 16 (1979).

[74] 472 US 749 (1985).

[75] In *Gertz*, 418 US 323 (1974), the Court prohibited any award of "presumed" or "punitive" damages in the absence of actual malice in cases involving media defendants.

[76] *Greenmoss v Dun & Bradstreet*, 143 Vt 66, 73-74, 146 A 2d 414, 418 (1983).

[77] Id at 75, 146 A 2d at 418.

[78] Id at 763.

[79] *Dun & Bradstreet, Inc. v Greenmoss Builders, Inc.*, 472 US 749 (1985).

[80] Id at 758-759, citing *First National Bank of Boston v Bellotti*, 435 US 765, 776 (1978); *Thornhill v Alabama*, 310 US 88, 101 (1940); *Connick v Myers*, 461 US 138, 145 (1983); *Roth v United States*, 354 US 476, 484 (1957); *New York Times Co. v Sullivan*, 376 US 254, 269 (1964); *Garrison v Louisiana*, 379 US 64, 74-75 (1964); *NAACP v Claiborne Hardware Co.*, 458 US 886, 913 (1982); *Carey v Brown*, 447 US 455, 467 (1980).

[81] *Dun & Bradstreet*, 472 US at 759, referring to *Connick v Myers*, 461 US 138, 146-147 (1983).

[82] *Dun & Bradstreet*, 472 US at 760, quoting William Prosser, *Law of Torts* § 112 at 765 (4th ed, 1971); also cited *Rowe v Metz*, 195 Colo 424, 425-426, 579 P 2d 83, 84 (1978), and Note, *Developments in the Law -- Defamation*, 69 Harv L Rev 875, 891-892 (1956).

[83] *Dun & Bradstreet*, 472 US at 760-761, citing Restatement of Torts § 568, comment b at 162 (1938).

[84] Id at 761.

[85] Id. Justice Powell, in a footnote, criticized the dissenting opinion of Justice Brennan as a balancing test based on misinterpretation. He noted that the dissent risked the "protection of all libels -- no matter how attenuated their constitutional interest." Supposing "the dissent were the law, a woman of impeccable character who was branded a 'whore' by a jealous neighbor would have no effective recourse unless she could prove 'actual malice' by clear and

convincing evidence." As it seems more demanding than the sense of *New York Times*, so the "dissent would, in effect, constitutionalize the entire common law of libel." Id at 761 n 7.

[86] Id at 761, citing *Connick v Myers*, 461 US at 147-148.

[87] *Dun & Bradstreet*, 472 US at 762.

[88] Id, citing *Central Hudson Gas & Elec. Corp v Public Service Comm'n of New York*, 447 US 557, 561 (1980).

[89] *Dun & Bradstreet*, 472 US at 762, quoting *Virginia Pharmacy Bd. v Virginia Citizens Consumer Council, Inc.*, 425 US 748, 764 (1976).

[90] *Dun & Bradstreet*, 472 US at 762.

[91] See *Philadelphia Newspapers, Inc. v Hepps*, 475 US 767 (1986).

[92] See *Milkovich v Lorain Journal Co.*, 497 US 1 (1990).

[93] Article 10 of European Convention for the Protection of Human Rights provides that: (1) Everyone has the right to freedom of expression. This right shall include freedom to hold opinions and to receive and impart information and ideas without interference by public authority and regardless of frontiers. This article shall not prevent States from requiring the licensing of broadcasting, television or cinema enterprises. (2) The exercise of these freedoms, since it carries with it duties and responsibilities, may be subject to such formalities, conditions, restrictions or penalties as are prescribed by law and are necessary in a democratic society, in the interests of national security, territorial integrity or public safety, for the prevention of disorder or crime, for the protection of health or morals, for the protection of reputation or rights of others, for preventing the disclosure of information received in confidence, or for maintaining the authority and impartiality of the judiciary.

[94] J. G. Merrills, *The Development of International Law by the European Court of Human Rights* 122 (Manchester University Press, 1988).

[95] Mark Janis, Richard Kay, & Anthony Bradley, *European Human Rights Law* 157 (Clarendon Press, 1995).

[96] See, for example, *Lingens*, 8 EHRR 407, 416-417 ¶ 35 (1986), citing *Barthold v Germany*, 7 EHRR 383, ¶ 43 (1985); see also D. J. Harris, M. O'Boyle, and C. Warbrick, *The European Convention on Human Rights* 377 (Butterworths, 1995).

[97] *Barthold*, 7 EHRR 383, ¶ 55; *Lingens*, 8 EHRR 418 ¶ 39.

[98] *Handyside v United Kingdom*, 1 EHRR 737, ¶¶ 18-49 (1979-1980).

[99] See *Vogt v Germany*, 21 EHRR 202, 235 (1996); *James v United Kingdom*, 8 EHRR 123, 142 (1986).

[100] *Observer and Guardian v United Kingdom*, 14 EHRR 153, ¶ 59 (1991).

[101] *Handyside*, 1 EHRR at 754 ¶ 49.

[102] Id.

[103] Article 10(2) of the European Convention states: The exercise of these freedoms, since it carries with it duties and responsibilities, may be subject to such formalities, conditions, restrictions or penalties as are prescribed by law

and are necessary in a democratic society, in the interests of national security, territorial integrity or public safety, for the prevention of disorder or crime, for the protection of health or morals, for the protection of reputation or rights of others, for preventing the disclosure of information received in confidence, or for maintaining the authority and impartiality of the judiciary.

[104] 8 EHRR 407 (1986).

[105] Id at 418 ¶ 41.

[106] Id.

[107] Id at 418-419 ¶ 42.

[108] Id at 419 ¶ 42.

[109] Id.

[110] Id at 420 ¶ 46. The Court repeated the distinction between facts and value judgments in *De Haes v Belgium*, 25 EHRR 1, 54 ¶ 42 (1998).

[111] *Lingens*, 8 EHRR at 421 ¶¶ 46-47. This idea of publication of opinion in good faith is similar to common law fair comment privilege vis-à-vis political speech. See Restatement (Second) of Torts § 566 cmt a (1977).

[112] 14 EHRR 445 (1992).

[113] Article 161 of Spain's Criminal Code imposed "long-term prison sentences" on persons who "seriously insult, falsely accuse or threaten the government," while Article 162 imposed a lesser sentence in respect of accusations or insults which were not "serious." Also, the Criminal Code did not recognize truth as a defense to either charge. Castells was convicted under Article 162, and sentenced to a one-year prison term.

[114] Id at ¶¶ 36, 48.

[115] Id.

[116] See id at 476 ¶¶ 43, 46.

[117] Id at 476 ¶ 43.

[118] Id at ¶ 46.

[119] Id. For a similar holding, see *Thorgeir Thorgeirson v Iceland*, 14 EHRR 843 (1992), the Court found that a conviction of a citizen and writer who wrote articles highly critical of alleged police brutality was an interference by a public authority not necessary in a democratic society; see also *Grigoriades v Greece*, 27 EHRR 464 (1997), the Court held that Article 10 applies to military personnel. As a result, a letter of a conscripted army officer, that contained general and lengthy discourse critical of army life and the army as an institution, did not warrant conviction in a democratic society; for the Court's principle of making distinctions in the status of plaintiffs and the nature of information, see, for example, *Oberschlick v Austria* [No 2], 25 EHRR 357 (1997), wherein the Court said that the conviction of a journalist for insulting a politician was unjustified; see also *De Haes and Gijsels v Belgium*, 25 EHRR 1 (1998), the European Court gave special protection of political expression. Though political speech is not absolute, the Court held that it covers information and ideas on all matters of public interest, including those relating to the functioning of the judiciary. The comment in public might have

offended the four Belgian judges but it was proportional to the stir and indignation caused by the matters alleged in the journalists' articles. Id at ¶ 48.

[120] *Castells*, 14 EHRR ¶ 46.

[121] *Bladet Tromso and Stensaas v Norway*, 29 EHRR 125 (1999).

[122] Id at 164 ¶ 51.

[123] Under Article 253 of the Penal Code (Norwegian defamation law), "When evidence of the truth of an allegation is admissible and such evidence has not been produced, the aggrieved person may demand that the allegation be declared null and void unless otherwise provided by statute."

[124] The test requires the Court to decide whether any restriction on free expression corresponded to a "pressing social need," whether it was proportionate to the legitimate interest pursued and whether the reasons given by the national authorities to justify it are relevant and sufficient. Id at 166-167 ¶ 58, citing *The Sunday Times v United Kingdom* [No 1], 2 EHRR 245, ¶ 62 (1979).

[125] *Bladet Tromso*, 29 EHRR at 168 ¶¶ 62-63.

[126] Id at 169 ¶ 63.

[127] Id at 169 ¶ 65, citing *Goodwin v United Kingdom*, 22 EHRR 123 ¶¶ 31 and 39.

[128] *Bladet Tromso*, 29 EHRR at 169 ¶ 64, citing *Jersild v Denmark*, 19 EHRR 1, ¶ 35 (1995).

[129] *Bladet Tromso*, 29 EHRR at 170 ¶ 66.

[130] Id at 170 ¶ 67.

[131] Id.

[132] Id at 170-171 ¶ 67.

[133] Id at 171 ¶ 68.

[134] Id at 172 ¶ 72. This view of the Court regarding fair and accurate account of public action or proceeding is similar to "fair reportage" privilege. See Restatement (Second) of Torts ¶ 611 (1977).

[135] *Bladet Tromso*, 29 EHRR at 172 ¶ 73.

[136] Libel and Slander, 28 Halsbury's Laws of England ¶ 109 (Butterworths, 4th ed 1997); see id ¶¶ 128-130.

[137] See *Adam v Ward*, [1971] AC 309, 334, *per* Lord Atkinson; see also *Toogood v Spyring*, 149 ER 1044, 1049-1050 (1834), the first to offer the qualified privilege test, that common law recognized the defense in circumstances which are to "the common convenience and welfare of society."

[138] *Hector v Attorney-General of Antigua*, 2 AC 312, 318 (PC 1990). Similar to the reasoning in the *New York Times v Sullivan* case, the *Hector* court held, if an editor hears highly discreditable information about a prominent politician, the public ought to know if it is true. Because this should not imperil the press' function, Lord Bridge of the Privy Council commented that open criticism of those who hold office in government must be permitted in a free and democratic society. He added that "[a]ny attempt to stifle or fetter

such criticism amounts to political censorship of the most insidious and objectionable kind." Id.

[139] 28 Halsbury's Laws of England ¶ 3 (cited in note 136).

[140] *Derbyshire County Council v Times Newspapers Ltd.,* 1 All ER 1011 (1993).

[141] Id at 1013.

[142] 1 QB 94, 63 LT 805 (1891); for the House of Lords' analysis of that case, see *Derbyshire*, 1 All ER at 1014-1016.

[143] 2 All ER 6, 2 QB 169 (1972); for the House of Lords' discussion of that case, see *Derbyshire*, 1 All ER at 1016-1017.

[144] *Derbyshire*, 1 All ER at 1021.

[145] Id. Lord Keith failed to note that in *Associated Newspapers Group v Wade*, 1 WLR 697, 708 (1979) Lord Dening said that it was a "fundamental principle of our law that the press shall be free." "In this respect," Denning wrote, "our law corresponds with Art. 10 [1] of the European Convention." Also Lord Keith overlooked the fact that in 1980, Lord Scarman, writing for the House of Lords in *Attorney General v British Broadcasting Corporation*, 3 All ER 161, 177-178 (1980), had recognized the ruling of ECHR in *The Sunday Times v United Kingdom*, 2 All ER 245 (1979), a contempt of court case that recognized the international obligation, noting that the traditional discretionary powers of British courts allowed for the influence of Article 10 of the ECHR.

[146] *Derbyshire*, 1 All ER at 1018, citing *New York Times v Sullivan*, 376 US 254, 277 (1964).

[147] *Derbyshire*, 1 All ER at 1018, citing *City of Chicago v Tribune Co*, 307 Ill 595, 606-608 (1923).

[148] *Derbyshire,* 1 All ER at 1018.

[149] Id at 1013.

[150] Id at 1019.

[151] Id at 1017.

[152] Id at 1018.

[153] 3 All ER 961 (CA 1998).

[154] Id at 989.

[155] Id at 994-995. Concerning malice, the court maintained the precedent that a heavy burden rests on the plaintiff. Id at 995, citing Lord Diplock in *Horrocks v Lowe* [1974] 1 All ER 662, [1975] AC 135.

[156] *Reynolds* [CA], 3 All ER at 1004; compare earlier decisions, for example, *Blackshaw v Lord*, 2 All ER 311, 327 (1983), *per* Stephenson, LJ.

[157] 189 CLR 520 (1997).

[158] The reasonableness test in *Lange* allowed defendants to plead extended qualified privilege when the defamatory material concerns communication of political matters to the public.

[159] *Reynolds* [CA], 3 All ER at 1006.

[160] Id.

[161] Id at 995. Status refers to the degree to which information on a matter of public concern may (because of its character and known provenance)

command respect .... The higher the status of a report, the more likely it is to meet the circumstantial test. Conversely, unverified information from unidentified and unofficial sources may have little or no status, and where defamatory statements of fact are to be published to the widest audience on the strength of such sources, the publisher undertakes a heavy burden in showing that the publication is "fairly warranted by any responsible occasion of exigency."

[162] Id. See also at id at 1004, the Appeal Court argued:

> Assuming in each case that a statement is defamatory and factually false although honestly believed to be true, it is one thing to publish a statement taken from a government press release, or the report of a public company chairman, or the speech of a university vice-chancellor, and quite another to publish the statement of a political opponent, or a business competitor or a disgruntled ex-employee; it is one thing to publish a statement which the person defamed has been given the opportunity to rebut, and quite another to publish a statement without any recourse to the person defamed where such recourse was possible; it is one thing to publish a statement which has been so far as possible checked, and quite another to publish it without such verification as was possible and as the significance of the statement called for.

[163] Id at 1004-1005.

[164] Id at 1006.

[165] Id.

[166] See id at 910, but the test would apply in an action by a politician as well as a commercial organization, for the privileged occasion in England may arise outside the context of government and political matters; however, see also *Lange v Australian Broadcasting Corporation*, (1997) 189 CLR 520, the test of reasonableness applied to government or political matters.

[167] See Eric Barendt et al, *Libel and the Media: The Chilling Effect* 191-192 (Clarendon Press, 1997).

[168] *Reynolds v Times Newspapers*, 3 All ER 961, 965-972 (CA 1998).

[169] *Reynolds v Times Newspapers*, 4 All ER 609 (HL 1999).

[170] Id.

[171] Id at 614-620.

[172] Id at 622 and 625.

[173] Id at 622. Here Lord Nicholls used the European Convention requirement of Article 10 and the jurisprudence of the ECHR concerning political speech. But what seemed to be his anticipation of the Human Rights Act 1998 did not reach that standard. His conclusion was not as media-friendly as the ECHR is in relation to free press and political speech.

[174] Id at 625.

[175] Id at 626.

[176] Id at 623 and 626.

[177] Id at 619.

[178] Id at 643, *per* Lord Cooke [concurring]; see also id at 621-622, 625. But, the ECHR jurisprudence is noted for upholding the pre-eminent role of political speech in a democratic society. So, if the purpose of the Human Rights Act is to give legal recognition and further effect to the European Convention in United Kingdom law while the ECHR continues to give the final ruling on the application of the articles of the Convention, it behooves the United Kingdom Court to be strongly persuaded by the ECHR jurisprudence on political speech. See also Robert Blackburn, *Towards a Constitutional Bill of Rights* at xxxv [introduction](Pinter, 1999).

[179] *Reynolds* [HL], 4 All ER at 626.

[180] Id at 628.

[181] Id at 628-629.

[182] Id at 629-635, citing, for example, *Goodwin v UK*, 22 EHRR 123, 143 ¶ 39 (1996), *Castells v Spain*, 14 EHRR 445, 476 ¶ 43 (1992), *De Haes v Belgium*, 25 EHRR 1 (1997), *Lingens v Austria*, 8 EHRR 407, 419 ¶ 42 (1986), *Oberschlick v Austria*, 19 EHRR 389, 422 ¶ 59 (1991), and *Sunday Times v UK [No 2]*, 14 EHRR 229, 242 ¶ 51 (1991).

[183] *Reynolds* [HL], 4 All ER at 653.

[184] Id at 653-654.

[185] 28 *Halsbury's Laws of England* ¶ 82 (cited in note 136). As to details of the law of libel and its defenses see id ¶¶ 82-109.

[186] 28 Halsbury's Laws of England ¶ 109 (cited in note 136); see id ¶¶ 128-130.

[187] *Uren v John Fairfax & Sons Ltd.*, 117 CLR 118 at 150 (1966) *per* Windeyer, J.

[188] 117 CLR 1 (1992).

[189] 117 CLR 106 (1992)("ACTV"). The case involved the Commonwealth *Political Broadcasts and Political Disclosures Act 1991*, which regulated political advertising in order to reduce the impact of a candidate's wealth on the outcome of the electoral process. The majority decision in ACTV, greatly influenced by the First Amendment jurisprudence of the United States Supreme Court, acknowledged the full implication of the guarantee of freedom of communication about political matters.

[190] Industrial Relations Act 1988 § 299(1)(d) provided: "A person shall not ... by writing or speech use words calculated ... to bring a member of the Commission or the Commission into disrepute."

[191] *Nationwide News*, 177 CLR 34 (Mason, CJ); see id at 91 (Dawson, J); see also id at 104 (McHugh, J).

[192] In ACTV, 117 CLR 106 (1992), all the Justices but Justice Dawson recognized the existence of the implied freedom of political speech.

[193] *Nationwide News*, 117 CLR at 69.

[194] Id at 47.

[195] For circumstances for the legitimate curtailment of free political speech, see *Nationwide News*, 177 CLR at 51(Brennan, J), id at 77 (Dean and Toohey, JJ); see also ACTV, 177 CLR at 150 (Brennan, J), id at 236 (McHugh, J).

[196] *Nationwide News*, (1992) 177 CLR at 48.

[197] Id at 47; see also ACTV, 177 CLR at 149 (Brennan, J).

[198] *Nationwide News*, 177 CLR at 50 (Brennan, J).

[199] Id at 73 (Dean and Toohey, JJ).

[200] ACTV, 177 CLR at 138, 141 (Mason, J).

[201] Id at 212 (Gaudron, J); see also id at 227-233 (McHugh, J).

[202] 182 CLR 104 (1994).

[203] 182 CLR 211 (1994). Stephens and other five plaintiffs brought a defamation action before the Supreme Court of Western Australia. The plaintiffs were members of the Legislative Council of Western Australia (the upper house of the State Parliament) and members of one of its standing committees. The Weekly Times Ltd published three articles claiming that the plaintiffs had gone on an "overseas junket of mammoth proportions" at Parliament's expense without the knowledge of Parliament. The plaintiffs contended that the articles contained defamatory imputations that they had participated in unauthorized use of public funds, had dishonestly procured the use of public moneys for an improper purpose, had dishonestly concealed from Parliament the expenditure of public moneys and acted in breach of their obligations as members of the Legislative Council not to deceive the Council. In a ruling that favored the defendant, the majority of the High Court of Australia decided that the fundamental premise of the structure of the Constitution, and in particular of the electoral process, affords citizens the continuous ability to make informed judgments on matters of political significance. According to the majority, the freedom of communication implied in the Federal Constitution, and also necessarily implied in the Western Australian Constitution, extended also to public discussion of the performance, conduct and fitness for office of members of the State legislature. This involves the capacity at all times for free and unlimited public discussion, for the implied freedom protects political discussion of matters relating to all levels of government.

[204] *Theophanous*, 182 CLR at 118.

[205] Justice Deane joined the plurality opinion of Chief Justice Mason. However, Deane preferred an interpretation of the implied freedom of communication that absolutely prohibited defamation actions by politicians as regards political discussion. See id at 163-188 (per Deane, J).

[206] *Nationwide News*, 177 CLR 1 (1992).

[207] ACTV, 177 CLR 106 (1992).

[208] *Theophanous*, 182 CLR at 122-123, 140. About the extent of freedom of discussion, the majority stated:

> The concept also includes discussion of the political views and public conduct of persons who are engaged in activities that have become the subject of political debate, e.g., trade union leaders, Aboriginal political leaders, political and economic commentators. Indeed, in our view, the concept is not exhausted by political publications and addresses which are calculated to influence choices. Id at 124.

[209] Id at 124-125.

[210] Id at 125.

[211] Id at 126.

[212] Id at 130.

[213] Id at 123.

[214] Id at 137, 141, citing *City of Chicago v Tribune Co.*, 139 NE 86, 90 (Ill, 1923); *New York Times Co. v Sullivan*, 376 US 254 (1964); and *Derbyshire County Council v Times Newspapers Ltd.*, [1993] AC 534, 547-458.

[215] *Theophanous*, 182 CLR at 137.

[216] 189 CLR 520 (1997). With this case, the High Court concurrently heard a demurrer in *Levy v Victoria*, 189 CLR 579 (1997).

[217] *Lange*, 189 CLR at 551.

[218] Ian Loveland, *Taking the Constitution out of the Common Law: Political Libels and Freedom of Communication in Australia*, 21 Liverpool L Rev 17, 25 (1999); see comments of Sally Walker, *Lange v ABC: The High Court Rethinks the "Constitutionalization" of Defamation Law*, 6 Torts L J 9, 14 (1998).

[219] *Lange*, 189 CLR at 576.

[220] Id at 558.

[221] Id at 559.

[222] Id at 558-559.

[223] Id at 560.

[224] Id at 575.

[225] Id at 562.

[226] Id at 576-577.

[227] Id at 566.

[228] Id at 561.

[229] Id at 565-566, citing *Toogood v Spyring* (1834) 1 CM & R 18 at 193, 149 ER 1044 at 1050; *Jumbunna Coal Mine NL v Victorian Coal Miners' Association*, 6 CLR 309 (1908); *Australian National Airways Pty. Ltd. v The Commonwealth*, 71 CLR 29 at 81 (1945).

[230] *Lange*, 189 CLR at 561.

[231] Id at 567, see also id at 561-562, citing *Cunliffe v The Commonwealth*, 182 CLR 272 at 300, 324, 337, 339, 387-388 (1994) to explain that "there is

little difference between the test of 'reasonably appropriate and adapted' and the test of proportionality," again citing *Cunliffe* at 377 and 396.

[232] *Lange*, 189 CLR at 568.

[233] Section 22 (1) of the *Defamation Act 1974* (NSW) provides:

> Where, in respect of matter published to any person: (a) the recipient has an interest or apparent interest in having information on some subject; (b) the matter is published to the recipient in the course of giving to him information on that subject; and (c) the conduct of the publisher in publishing that matter is reasonable in the circumstances, there is a defense of qualified privilege for that publication.

[234] Id at 569-70, citing *Stephens* (1994) 182 CLR 211 at 242-251.

[235] *Lange*, 189 CLR at 572.

[236] Id at 569.

[237] Id at 570.

[238] Id at 570-571.

[239] Id at 571.

[240] Id.

[241] Id.

[242] Id at 572.

[243] Id.

[244] Id at 572-573.

[245] Id at 573.

[246] Id.

[247] Id.

[248] Id.

[249] Id.

[250] Id at 574, citing *Stephens* (1994) 182 CLR 211 at 252-253.

[251] *Lange*, 189 CLR at 574.

[252] Id.

[253] Id.

[254] Id.

[255] For an elaboration on the remarks made of *Lange*, see F. A. Trindade, *Defamation in the Course of Political Discussion -- The New Common Law Defense*, 114 L Q Rev 1, 7-8 (January 1998).

[256] *Gertz*, 418 US at 344.

[257] *New York Times*, 376 US at 270.

[258] A heightened scrutiny approach is one of the doctrinal methods that the courts used to balance free speech and personal reputation. Free speech jurisprudence follows three dominant and broad organizing approaches, namely "absolutism," "ad hoc balancing," and "heightened scrutiny." Discussions of the three free speech methods are taken from Rodney A. Smolla, *Smolla and*

Nimmer on Freedom of Speech vol 1 at §§2:10-12, 2:47-63 (Clark Boardman Callaghan, 1996); see also Jeremy Cohen and Timothy Gleason, *Social Research in Communication and Law* 61-65 (Sage, 1990).

Absolutism referred to the method of resolving free speech problems that gave unconditional (absolute) protection of speech against any restriction by government. For instance, Justice William O. Douglas, one of the advocates of this view, wrote in a 1973 concurring opinion, "The ban of 'no' law that abridges freedom of the press is in my view total and complete" (*Columbia Broadcasting Sys., Inc. v Democratic Nat'l Comm*, 412 US 94, 156 [1973][Douglas, J., concurring]). However, legal defenders of absolutism modify their absolutist stance and give exceptions when the time, place, and manner of the expression demand reasonable government intervention. For the principles relating "time, place, and manner" regulations see, for example, *Regan v Time, Inc.*, 468 US 641, 648 (1984)("In order to be constitutional, a time, place, and manner regulation must meet three requirements. First, it 'may not be based upon either the content or subject matter of speech' ... Second, it must 'serve a significant governmental interest' ... And third, it must 'leave open ample alternative channels for communication of the information.'"). Another exception is the expression and conduct distinction that Justice Hugo Black followed. But this approach is defeated by such inconsistencies in the approach (see Robert Bork, *Neutral Principles and Some First Amendment Problems*, 47 Ind L J 1 [1971]). As Smolla mentioned, it is not enough to maintain that speech is absolutely protected, but not conduct, because all speech is conduct (Rodney Smolla, *Free Speech in an Open Society* 26 [Alfred Knopf, Inc., 1992]). Thus, the absolutist method has never been the approach of the Supreme Court of the United States (see, for example, *Nebraska Press Ass'n v Stuart*, 427 US 539, 709 [1976]; *Terminiello v Chicago*, 337 US 1, 4 [1949]; *Near v Minnesota*, 283 US 697, 708 [1931]; *Gitlow v New York* 268 US 652, 666 [1925]; *Seattle Times Co. v Rhinehart*, 467 US 20, 31 [1984], the Court said that "even though the broad sweep of the First Amendment seems to prohibit all restraints on free expression, this Court has observed that 'freedom of speech ... does not comprehend the right to speak on any subject at any time.'").

The other extreme of the absolutist position is the "ad hoc balancing" method. Here, when freedom of speech is in conflict with other competing interests, the value of the speech is balanced against the importance of the competing interest in a specific case. Because the approach of weighing competing interests can be generally applied in every free speech conflict, it has appealed to several United States Supreme Court justices (see Pierre Schlag, *An attack on Categorical Approaches to Freedom of Speech*, 30 UCLA L Rev 671 [1983]; Professor Schlag defended the *ad hoc* balancing approach and wrote that the approach "refuses to provide [the court with] ready-made apologies" [Id at 737-738]). It is recognized in both common law and constitutional law decisions. However, it does not give a fixed doctrinal rule and may thus threaten free speech, for it can deter people from entering the marketplace of ideas. As the Supreme Court related in light of freedom of the press and protection of reporter's sources, the *ad hoc* balancing is not certain since "[u]nder the case-by-case method of developing rules, it will be difficult for potential informants and reporters to predict whether testimony will be compelled since the decision will turn on the judge's ad hoc assessment in different fact settings of 'importance' or 'relevance' in relation to the free press interest. A 'general' deterrent effect is likely to result" (see *Branzburg v Hayes*, 408 US 665, 703 n 39 (1972).

The third method in free speech jurisprudence is heightened scrutiny or the preferred position balancing. It gives slightly less protection to free speech than absolutism, yet it is much more protective of free speech than ad hoc balancing. It is the principal approach in contemporary First Amendment jurisprudence, and it balances free speech interest against other interests. So it places a heavy burden on government whenever a governmental action is challenged as a violation of free speech protection, and it makes it very difficult for public figures to win a defamation suit.

[259] *New York Times v Sullivan*, 376 US 254, 266 (1964).

[260] Id at 337.

[261] *Lingens v Austria*, 8 EHRR 407, 408-409 (1986).

[262] Id at 419.

[263] *Bladet Tromso & Stensaas v Norway*, 29 EHRR 125, 158 ¶ 90 (1999).

[264] *Derbyshire County Council v Times Newspapers Ltd.*, 1 All ER 1011, 1019 (HL 1993).

[265] *Reynolds v Times Newspapers*, 4 All ER 609, 630 (HL 1999).

[266] Id at 640.

[267] Id at 650.

[268] *New York Times*, 376 US at 256.

[269] Id at 268, quoting *Beauharnais v Illinois*, 343 US 250, 263-264 and n 18 (1952); Similar safeguards apply to criticism and discussion of government and public institutions. As Justices Black and Douglas noted in their *New York Times* concurring opinion, "If the rule that libel on government has no place in our constitution is to have real meaning, then libel on the official conduct of governors likewise can have no place in our constitution" (*New York Times*, 376 US at 299).

[270] *Gertz*, 418 US at 345, 351-352

[271] Id at 353; According to the Court, "private individuals are not only more vulnerable to injury than public officials and public figures; they are also more deserving of recovery" (Id at 345).

[272] See id at 337.

[273] *Lingens*, 8 EHRR at 419, for example, the ECHR reasoned: The limits of acceptable criticism are accordingly wider as regards a politician as such than as regards a private individual. Unlike the latter, the former inevitably and knowingly lays himself open to close scrutiny of his every word and deed by

both journalists and the public at large, and he must consequently display a greater degree of tolerance.

274 *Castells v Spain*, 14 EHRR 445, ¶ 46 (1992).

275 *Derbyshire*, 1 All ER at 1017, quoting Lord Bridge of Harwich in *Hector v A-G of Antigua and Barbuda*, 2 All ER 103, 106 (1990).

276 *Reynolds v Times Newspapers*, 3 All ER 961, 996 (CA 1998)(Lord Bingham, CJ), quoting Supreme Court Procedure Committee Report on Practice and Procedure in Defamation (1991).

277 *Theophanous v Herald & Weekly Times Ltd.*, 182 CLR 104, 160 (1994)(Brennan, J).

278 *New York Times*, 376 US at 269.

279 Id, citing *Roth v United States*, 354 US 476, 484 (1957).

280 *New York Times*, 376 US at 299 (Goldberg, J., concurring).

281 *Gertz*, 418 US at 345-346; see also *Dun & Bradstreet v Greenmoss*, 472 US 749, 763-764 (1985).

282 *Lingens*, 8 EHRR at 418 ¶ 41, citing *Sunday Times v United Kingdom*, 2 EHRR 245, 280 ¶ 65 (1979); see also *Castells*, 14 EHRR ¶ 43.

283 *Bladet*, 29 EHRR at 172 ¶ 73.

284 *Derbyshire*, 1 All ER at 1017.

285 *Reynolds* [CA], 3 All ER at 993, citing Diplock J. in *Silken v Beaverbrook Newspapers Ltd.* [1958] 2 All ER 516 at 517, 1 WLR 743 at 746.

286 *Reynolds* [CA], 3 All ER at 1005.

287 *Reynolds* [HL], 4 All ER at 614.

288 Id.

289 Id at 629.

290 See *Reynolds* [HL], 4 All ER at 623.

291 *Nationwide News Pty Ltd v Wills*, 177 CLR 1, 32 (1992)(Mason CJ), citing *Ex parte Williams*, 53 CLR 434, 442 (1935).

292 *Nationwide News*, 177 CLR at 33.

293 Id at 34.

294 *Theophanous*, 182 CLR at 121 (Mason CJ, Toohey J, and Gaudron J), quoting *Australian Capital Television v the Commonwealth*, 177 CLR 106 at 138, 142 (1992), *per* Mason CJ; id at 169, *per* Deane and Toohey JJ; id at 214, *per* Gaudron J; id at 227, *per* McHugh J; *Nationwide News*, 177 CLR at 50, *per* Brennan J.

295 *Theophanous*, 182 CLR at 123, citing *Nationwide News*, 177 CLR at 72 *per* Deane and Toohey JJ.

296 *Theophanous*, 182 CLR at 133; see also *Lange v Australian Broadcasting Corporation* (1997) 189 CLR 520, 569-570.

297 *Theophanous*, 182 CLR at 136.

298 *New York Times*, 376 US at 269.

299 Id at 270, quoting Judge Learned Hand in *United States v Associated Press*, 52 F Supp 362, 372 (D C S D NY 1943).

300 *Gertz*, 418 US at 339.

301 *Dun & Bradstreet*, 472 US at 767.

[302] *New York Times*, 376 US at 296 (Black and Douglas, JJ., concurring).

[303] Id at 296-297.

[304] Id at 301 (Goldberg J., concurring).

[305] *Dun & Bradstreet*, 472 US at 783 (Brennan, J., dissenting).

[306] *Lingens*, 8 EHRR at 418 ¶ 41.

[307] *Castells*, 14 EHRR at ¶ 43, citing *Lingens*, 8 EHRR at 418-419 ¶ 42.

[308] *Lingens*, 8 EHRR at 418-419 ¶ 42.

[309] *Reynolds* [CA], 3 All ER at 1004.

[310] *Reynolds* [HL], 4 All ER at 621.

[311] Id at 638, quoting Holmes J., in *Abrams v United States*, 250 US 616, 630 (1919).

[312] *Reynolds* [HL], 4 All ER at 657.

[313] *Nationwide News*, 177 CLR at 47 *per* Brennan J.

[314] Id, citing *The Observer and the Guardian v United Kingdom*, 14 EHRR 153, 178 (1991).

[315] See id at 50, 123.

[316] *Theophanous*, 182 CLR at 122, *per* Mason CJ, Toohey J, and Gaudron J.

[317] *New York Times*, 376 US at 269.

[318] Id at 270, citing *Terminiello v Chicago*, 337 US 1, 4 (1949); *De Jonge v Oregon*, 299 US 353, 365 (1937).

[319] *New York Times*, 376 US at 278.

[320] Id at 279-280.

[321] See id at 293. Justices Black and Douglas' concurring opinion claimed an absolute immunity for criticism of the official conduct of public officials, holding that the press and people who criticize officials and discuss public affairs must do so with impunity.

[322] See id at 298. Justice Goldberg argued in his concurring opinion that the press and citizens have absolute and unconditional privilege to criticize official conduct despite excesses and abuses that may happen. He concluded that public officials have greater access to the communication media to defend themselves if wrongfully criticized. See also id at 304.

[323] *Gertz*, 418 US at 343.

[324] Id.

[325] Id at 354; See also *Dun & Bradstreet*, 472 US at 770 (White, J., concurring) as Justice White said: "If the press could be faced with possibly sizable damages for every mistaken publication injurious to reputation, the result would be an unacceptable degree of self-censorship, but would also often prevent the timely flow of information that is thought to be true but cannot be readily verified."

[326] *New York Times*, 376 US at 272.

[327] *Bladet Tromso*, 29 EHRR at 166-167 ¶ 58, citing *Sunday Times v United Kingdom*, 2 EHRR ¶ 62.

[328] *Castells*, 14 EHRR at ¶ 42; see also id at ¶ 46.
[329] *Bladet Tromso*, 29 EHRR at 175.
[330] Id at 176.
[331] *Reynolds* [CA], 3 All ER at 991.
[332] Id at 994.
[333] *Reynolds* [HL], 4 All ER at 625-626.
[334] Id at 630, Lord Steyn commented: "[Qualified privilege] is to be contrasted with each case being considered in the light of its own particular circumstances, that is, in an ad hoc manner, in the light of the concrete facts of the case, and balancing in each case the gravity of the damage to the plaintiff's reputation against the value of publication on the particular occasion."
[335] *Lange*, 189 CLR at 571.
[336] *Theophanous*, 182 CLR at 124.
[337] *Lange*, 189 CLR at 573-574, citing *Stephens*, 182 CLR 211, 252-253.

CHAPTER FIVE

[1] The design of multiple methods for this study involved linking the data to general theoretical constructs. It related the legal regimes to free speech theory. Further, the multiple methods facilitated analysis and validity checks (Thomas R. Lindlof, *Qualitative Communication Research Methods* 238-239 [Sage, 1995]; see also Catherine Marshall and Gretchen B. Rossman, *Designing Qualitative Research* 134 [Sage, 3d ed 1999]). Like any systematic inquiry, this research considered the "truth value" of the study, its applicability, consistency, and neutrality (or validity, reliability and objectivity)(Y. Lincoln and E. Guba, *Naturalistic Inquiry* 290 [Sage, 1985]). Though changes in legal philosophy over time could affect this study's external validity, the multiple procedures used enhance reliable interpretation. The study worked within the prevailing jurisprudential contexts, and the inquiry could still establish credibility because the choice of cases considered development of precedent in each jurisprudence and its application in other important cases. So this study's credibility rested with identifiable cases that represent the authoritative case law in each regime. As a result, similar questions of practice about the four regimes could yield findings comparable to those of this study. In addition, following the theoretical concepts used for the data collection and analysis, legal researchers and policy-makers who design research studies within the same parameters should find this study relevant. Moreover, the court decisions studied are permanent artifacts and retrievable. They represent accurate measurement of current jurisprudence in the four regimes under study, so by following this design researchers can reanalyze the data, demonstrate the connection between those data and interpretations of this study, and either confirm or disconfirm the general findings. Still further, the study noted that the interpretive nature of the analysis could cast doubt on the internal validity of the inquiry. To subject the findings from the case analysis to scrutiny and enhance the study's generalizability, the technique of multiple methods of

gathering and analyzing data (historical analysis, case-law analysis and qualitative content analysis of cases) was built into the research design to inspire confidence that the study achieved right interpretations.

[2] *New York Times v Sullivan*, 376 US 254, 270 (1964).

[3] Rodrigo J. Bustos Sierra, *The Accommodation of Interests in Freedom of the Press and Protection of Reputation in the Constitutional Doctrine of the United States and Spain* (Ph.D. diss., Stanford University, 1998), abstract *in Dissertation Abstracts International* 59 (1999): 3946A.

[4] Rodney Smolla, *Free Speech in an Open Society* 14-15 (Alfred A. Knopf, Inc., 1992).

[5] Id at 5. For similar ideas about multiple rationales, see Steven Shiffrin, *Liberalism, Radicalism, and Legal Scholarship*, 30 UCLA L Rev 1103, 1197-1198 (1983); see also Kent Greenawalt, *Speech, Crime, and the Uses of Language* 9-34 (Oxford University Press, 1989); and see Thomas Emerson, *Freedom of Expression* 6-9 (Random House, 1970).

[6] See generally Joshua Cohen, *Freedom of Expression*, in David Heyd, ed, *Toleration* 173-225 (Princeton University Press, 1996).

Bibliography

CASES AND LEGISLATIVE MATERIALS

Abrams v United States, 250 US 616 (1919).
Accompanying Government White Paper, 1997, Cmnd 3782.
Adam v. Ward, 31 T L R 299 (1915), aff'd AC 309 (HL 1917).
American Communications Ass'n v Douds, 339 US 382 (1950).
Associated Newspapers Group v Wade, 1 WLR 697 (1979).
Attorney General v British Broadcasting Corporation, 3 All ER 161 (1980).
Attorney General v Guardian Newspapers Ltd., 1 WLR 1248 (1987).
Attorney General v John Peter Zenger, in Thomas B. Howell, Vol 17 A Complete Collection of State Trials and Proceedings for High Treason and Other Crimes 675 (1735)("State Trials").
Austl Const Acts, 63-64 Vict ch 12 (1900).
Australian Capital Television Pty. Ltd. v Commonwealth of Australia, 177 CLR 106 (1992).
Australian Law Reform Commission, Unfair Publication: Defamation and Privacy, Report No 11 (1979).
Australian National Airways Pty. Ltd. v The Commonwealth, 71 CLR 29 (1945).
Babbitt v United Farms Workers, 442 US 289 (1979).
Barr v Matteo, 360 US 564 (1959).
Barthold v Germany, 7 EHRR 383 (1985).
Beauharnais v Illinois, 343 US 250 (1952).
Bjelke-Petersen v Burns, 2 QR 129 (1988).
Blackshaw v Lord, 2 All ER 311 (1983).
Bladet Tromso and Stensaas v Norway, 29 EHRR 125 (1999).
Bognor Regis Urban District Council v Campion, 2 All ER 6, 2 QB 169 (1972).
Bose Corp v Consumers Union, 466 US 485 (1984).
Branzburg v Hayes, 408 US 665 (1972).
Bridges v California, 314 US 252 (1941).
Brown v Board of Education, 347 US 483 (1955).
Buckley v Valeo, 424 US 1 (1976).
Cal Civ Code §§ 45-46.
Carey v Brown, 447 US 455 (1980).
Cassidy v Merin, 582 A2d 1039 (NJ Super Ct App Div 1990).
Castells v Spain, 14 EHRR 445 (1992).

Central Hudson Gas & Elec. Corp v Public Service Comm'n of New York, 447 US 557 (1980).

Chief Constable of the North Wales Police v Evans, 3 All ER 141 (1982).

City of Chicago v Tribune Co., 307 Ill 595, 139 NE 86 (1923).

City of Houston, Texas v Hill, 482 US 451 (1987).

Cohen v California, 403 US 15 (1971).

Coleman v MacLennan, 78 Kan 711, 98 P 281 (1908).

Columbia Broadcasting Sys., Inc. v Democratic Nat'l Comm'n, 412 US 94 (1973).

Commonwealth v Child, 30 Mass 198 (1832).

Commonwealth v Snelling, 32 Mass 321 (1834).

Connick v Myers, 461 US 138 (1983).

Consolidated Edison Co. v Public Serv Comm'n, 447 US 530 (1980).

Crosswell v People, Vol 3 Reports of Cases Adjudged in the Supreme Court of Judicature of the State of New York 337 (William Johnson, ed, E. F. Backus 1834-1836), quoting the Act of April 6, 1805, Sess 28 ch 90.

Cunliffe v The Commonwealth, 182 CLR 272 (1994).

Curtis Publishing Co. v Butts, 388 US 130 (1967).

De Haes and Gijsels v Belgium, 25 EHRR 1 (1998).

De Jonge v Oregon, 299 US 353 (1937).

De Libellis Famosis, 77 Eng Rep 250 [Star Chamber], 5 Coke 125A (1605).

Derbyshire County Council v Times Newspapers Ltd., 1 All ER 1011 (1993).

Dun & Bradstreet, Inc. v Greenmoss Builders, Inc., 472 US 749 (1985).

Electric Furnace Corp. v Deering Milliken Research Corp., 352 F2d 761 (6th Cir 1963).

Ex parte Williams, 53 CLR 434 (1935).

Feldbrugge v Netherlands, 99 Eur Ct HR (Series A) ¶ 24 (29 May 1986).

First Amendment Act, 1 Stat Art I at 21 (1798).

First Nat'l Bank of Boston v Bellotti, 435 US 765 (1978).

Fox Libel Act 1792, 32 Geo 3 ch 60, 37 Statutes at Large at 627-628 (Archdeacon, n.d.).

Garrison v Louisiana, 379 U.S. 64 (1964).

Gertz v Robert Welch, Inc., 418 US 323 (1974).

Gitlow v New York, 268 US 652 (1925).

Gleaves v Deakin, AC 477 (1980); 2 All ER 497 (HL 1979).

Goodwin v United Kingdom, 22 EHRR 123 (1996).

Gorton v Australian Broadcasting Commission, 22 FLR 181 (1974).

Great Britain, Defamation Act 1952 § 17(2).

Great Britain, Libel Act 1843 § 6;

Greenmoss v Dun & Bradstreet, 143 Vt 66, 146 A 2d 414 (1983).

Grigoriades v Greece, 27 EHRR 464 (1997).

Guccione v Hustler Magazine, Inc., 632 F Supp 313 (SDNY 1986), rev'd, 800 F2d 298 (2d Cir 1986), cert denied, 479 US 1091 (1987).

Handyside v United Kingdom, 1 EHRR 737 (1976).

Hector v Attorney General of Antigua and Barbuda, 2 All ER 103, 2 AC 312 (1990).
Herbert v Lando, 441 US 153 (1979).
Hill v Church of Scientology of Toronto, 126 DLR (4th) 129 (1995).
HL Deb, 18 Nov 1997, cols 514, 515.
HL Deb, 19 Jan 1998, cols 1270, 1271.
Horrocks v Lowe [1974] 1 All ER 662, [1975] AC 135.
Hotchkiss v Porter, 30 Conn 414 (1862).
Howell, T. B., comp. *A Complete Collection of State Trials and Proceedings for High Treason and Other Crimes and Misdemeanors* ("State Trials"). London: Hansard, 1812.
Human Rights Act 1998, 9 Nov 1998.
Human Rights Bill, Original Bill and Explanatory Memorandum (HL 1997-1998).
Hutchinson v Proxmire, 443 US 111 (1979).
James v Commonwealth, 55 CLR 1 (1936).
James v United Kingdom, 8 EHRR 123 (1986).
Jersild v Denmark, 19 EHRR 1 (1995).
Judiciary Act 1903.
Jumbunna Coal Mine NL v Victorian Coal Miners Association, 6 CLR 309 (1908).
King v John Wilkes, 19 State Trials 982 (1763).
Konigsberg v State Bar of California, 366 US 36 (1961).
Lange v Australian Broadcasting Corp., 189 CLR 520 (1997).
Law Commission [Great Britain], Report on Criminal Libel, 1985, Cmnd 9618, L Com No 149.
Law Reform Commission of Australia, Unfair Publication 19-22 (1979).
Levy v Victoria, 189 CLR 579 (1997).
Libel Act 1792, 13 Halsbury's Statutes of England 1120 (1949).
Libel Act 1843.
Libel and Slander, 28 Halsbury's Laws of England (London: Butterworths, 4th ed 1997).
Lingens v Austria, 8 EHRR 407 (1986).
Madison, James. Vol 4 Annals of Congress 934 (1794).
---. *Report on the Virginia Resolutions, Vol. 4 The Debates in Several State Conventions on the Adoption of the Federal Constitution ... and Other Illustrations of the Constitution.* Edited by Jonathan Eliot. Philadelphia: Lippincott, 2d ed 1937.
Manchester Corporation v Williams, 1 QB 94, 63 LT 805 (1891).
Marbury v Madison, 5 US 137 (1803).
Medico v Time, Inc., 643 F2d 134 (3d Cir 1981).
Milkovich v Lorain Journal Co., 497 US 1 (1990).
Mills v Alabama, 384 US 214 (1966).

Ming Pao, AC 957 (1994).
NAACP v Claiborne Hardware Co., 458 US 886 (1982).
Nationwide News Pty. Ltd. v Wills, 177 CLR 1 (1992).
Near v Minnesota, 283 US 697 (1931).
Nebraska Press Ass'n v Stuart, 427 US 539 (1976).
Negley v Farrow, 60 Md 158 (1882).
New York [State]. Journal of the Senate of the State of New York [1804] 27th sess (Albany, 1805).
New York Times Co. v Sullivan, 273 Ala 656, 144 So 2d 25 (1962).
New York Times Co. v Sullivan, 376 US 254 (1964).
Oberschlick v Austria, 19 EHRR 389 (1991).
Observer and Guardian v United Kingdom, 14 EHRR 153 (1991).
Philadelphia Newspapers, Inc. v Hepps, 475 US 767 (1986).
Porter v Mercury Newspaper, Tas St R 279, 283-286 (1964).
Proceedings against Mr. Baxter, 11 State Trials at 502 (1685).
Procunier v Martinez, 416 US 396, 427 (1974).
Public Acts Passed by the General Assembly of the State of Connecticut, May Sess at 99 (Hartford, 1855).
Queen v Tutchin, 90 Eng Rep 1133 (1704).
Quincy, Josiah, Jr., ed. *Reports of Cases Argued and Adjudged in the Superior Court of Judicature of the Province of Massachusetts Bay between 1761 and 1772*. Boston: Little, Brown & Co., 1865.
R v Central Independent TV plc, 3 All ER 641 (1994).
R v Perryman (1892) in 115 Cent Crim Ct Sess Papers 358, 378.
R v Wicks, 1 All ER 384 (1936).
Rajagopal v State of Tamil Nadu, 6 SCC 632 (1994).
Regan v Time, Inc., 468 US 641 (1984).
Reno v American Civil Liberties Union, 521 US 844 (1997).
Renouf v Federal Capital Press, 16 ACTR 35 (ACT S Ct 1977).
Restatement of Torts §§ 568, 606 (1938).
Restatement (Second) of Torts §§ 566, 558, 606-611 (1977).
Reynolds v Times Newspapers, 3 All ER 961 (CA 1998).
Reynolds v Times Newspapers, 4 All ER 609 (HL 1999).
Richmond Newspapers, Inc. v Virginia, 448 US 555 (1980).
Roth v United States, 354 US 476 (1957).
Rowe v Metz, 195 Colo 424, 579 P 2d 83 (1978).
Royal Commission on the Press, Final Report, 1977.
Schenck v United States, 249 US 47 (1919).
Seattle Times Co. v Rhinehart, 467 US 20 (1984).
Sedition Act 1798, 1 Stat 596.
Sedition Act 1918, 40 Stat ch 75 at 553.
Seven Bishops' Trial, 12 State Trials at 183 (1688).
Silken v Beaverbrook Newspapers Ltd., 2 All ER 516, 1 WLR 743 (1958).
St. Amant v Thompson, 390 US 727 (1968).
State v Burnham, 31 Am Dec [NH] 217 (1838).

Statutes of the Realm, 2 Rich II, ch 5 (1378).
Statutes of the Realm, 3 Edw I, ch 34 (1275).
Stephens v West Australian Newspapers Ltd., 182 CLR 211 (1994).
Stromberg v California, 283 US 359 (1931).
Sunday Times v United Kingdom, 2 EHRR 245 (1979).
Sunday Times v United Kingdom [No 2], 14 EHRR 229 (1991).
Supreme Court Procedure Committee Report on Practice and Procedure in
    Defamation (1991).
Terminiello v Chicago, 337 US 1 (1949).
Theophanous v The Herald and Weekly Times Ltd., 182 CLR 104 (1994).
Thorgeir Thorgeirson v Iceland, 14 EHRR 843 (1992).
Thornhill v Alabama, 310 US 88 (1940).
Time, Inc. v Hill, 385 US 374 (1967).
Toogood v Spyring, 1 CM & R 18. 149 ER 1044 (1834).
Trial of Dover, Brewster and Brooks, 6 State Trials 558 (1663).
Trial of John Tutchin, 14 State Trials 1095 (1704).
Trial of Sir Samuel Barnardiston, 9 State Trials at 1334-1335 (1684).
United Communist Party of Turkey and Others v Turkey, 26 EHRR 121 (1998).
United States v Associated Press, 52 F Supp 362 (D C S D NY 1943).
United States v Hudson and Goodwin, 7 Cr. [U.S.] 32 (1812).
Uren v John Fairfax & Sons Ltd., 117 CLR 118 (1966).
Virginia Pharmacy Bd. v Virginia Citizens Consumer Council, Inc., 425 US
    748 (1976).
Vogt v Germany, 21 EHRR 202 (1996).
Webb v Times Publ'g Co., 2 Q B 535 (1960).
Whitney v California, 274 US 357 (1927).
Wood v Georgia, 370 US 375 (1962).

BOOKS & ARTICLES

Abrams, Floyd. *Why We Should Change the Libel Law*, NY Times Mag 34
    (Sept 29, 1985).
Addison, Alexander. *Liberty of Speech and Press: A Charge to the Grand
    Juries of the County Courts of the Fifth Circuit of the State of
    Pennsylvania*. Washington, Pa., 1798.
Adler, Renata. *Reckless Disregard: Westmoreland v CBS et al; Sharon v Time*.
    New York: Alfred A. Knopf, Inc., 1986.
Amar, Akhil Reed. *The Bill of Rights: Creation and Reconstruction*. New
    Haven: Yale University Press, 1998.
Applbaum, Arthur Isak. *Democratic Legitimacy and Official Discretion*, 21 (3)
    Phil & Pub Aff 240 (Summer 1992).
Armstrong, Mark, Michael Blakeney, and Ray Watterson. *Media Law in
    Australia*. Melbourne: Oxford University Press, 1983.

Baker, C. Edwin. *Human Liberty and Freedom of Speech*. New York: Oxford
    University Press, 1989.
---. *Scope of First Amendment Freedom of Speech*, 25 UCLA L Rev 964
    (1978).
Barendt, Eric. *Freedom of Speech*. Oxford: Clarendon Press, 1987.
Barendt, Eric et al. *Libel and the Media: The Chilling Effect*. Oxford:
    Clarendon Press, 1997.
Bauer, Gary L. *Our Hopes, Our Dreams: A Vision for America*. Colorado
    Springs, Colo.: Focus on the Family Publishing, 1996.
Beloff, Michael. *What does It All Mean? Interpreting the Human Rights Act
    1998*, in Lammy Betten, ed, The Human Rights Act 1998 What It means
    11-56. Hague, Netherlands: Kluwer Law International, 1999.
Benditt, Theodore M. *The Public Interest*, 2 (3) Phil & Pub Aff 291 (Spring
    1973).
Bentham, Jeremy. *An Introduction to the Principles of Morals and Legislation*.
    Edited by J. H. Burns and H. L. A. Hart. Oxford: Clarendon Press, 1996.
Bernhardt, R. *The Convention and Domestic Law*, in R. St. J. Macdonald, F.
    Matscher, and H. Petzold, eds, *The European System for the Protection of
    Human Rights* 25-40. Boston: Martinus Nijhoff, 1993.
Betten, Lammy, ed. *The Human Rights Act 1998 What It Means: The
    Incorporation of the European Convention on Human Rights into the
    Legal Order of the United Kingdom*. Hague, Netherlands: Kluwer Law
    International, 1999.
Beveridge, Albert Jeremiah. *The Life of John Marshall* vol 3. Boston, Mass.:
    Houghton Mifflin, 1919.
Bezanson, Randall P. *Libel Law and the Realities of Litigation: Setting the
    Record Straight*, 71 Iowa L Rev 226 (1985).
Bezanson, Randall, Gilbert Cranberg, and John Soloski. *Libel Law and the
    Press: Myth and Reality*. New York: Free Press, 1987.
Blackburn, Robert. *Towards a Constitutional Bill of Rights for the United
    Kingdom*. London: Pinter, 1999.
Blackstone, William. *Commentaries on the Laws of England* vol 2. London,
    1765-1769; Chicago 1873.
Blasi, Vincent. *The Checking Value in First Amendment Theory*, ABF Res J
    523 (1977).
Bogart, Leo. *Media and Democracy*, in E. F. Dennis and R. W. Snyder, eds,
    Media and Democracy 3-11. New Brunswick, N.J.: Transaction
    Publishers, 1998.
Bohman, James and William Rehg, eds. *Deliberative Democracy: Essays on
    Reason and Politics*. Cambridge, Mass: The MIT Press, 1997.
Bollinger, Lee C. *The Tolerant Society: Freedom of Speech and Extremist
    Speech in America*. New York: Oxford University Press, 1986.
Bork, Robert H. *Neutral Principles and some First Amendment Problems*, 47
    Ind L J 1 (1971).

---. *Slouching toward Gomorrah: Modern Liberalism and American Decline.* New York: ReganBooks, 1996.

Boston, Robert. *Why the Religious Right Is Wrong about Separation of Church and State.* Buffalo, New York: Prometheus Books, 1993.

Brant, I. *Seditious Libel: Myth and Reality*, 39 NYUL Rev 1 (1964).

Buergenthal, Thomas. *International Human Rights in a Nutshell.* St. Paul, Minn.: West Publishing Co., 1988.

Bunker, Matthew D. *Critiquing Free Speech: First Amendment Theory and the Challenge of Interdisciplinarity.* Mahwah, NJ: Lawrence Erlbaum Associates, 2001.

Bustos Sierra, Rodrigo J. *The Accommodation of Interests in Freedom of the Press and Protection of Reputation in the Constitutional Doctrine of the United States and Spain.* Ph.D. diss., Stanford University, 1998. Abstract in *Dissertation Abstracts International* 59 (1999): 3946A.

Bybee, Carl. *Can Democracy Survive in the Post-Factual Age?: A Return to the Lippmann-Dewey Debate about the Politics of News*, 1 Journalism and Mass Communication Monograph 1 (1999).

Carnegie, Les P. *Privacy and the Press: The Impact of Incorporating the European Convention on Human Rights in the United Kingdom*, 9 Duke J Comp & Intl L 311 (1998).

Carr, Frank. *The English Law of Defamation*, 18 (pts 1-2) L Q Rev 255, 388 (1902).

Carter, T. Barton et al. *Mass Communication Law in a Nutshell.* St. Paul, Minn.: West Publishing Co., 4th ed 1994.

Cavell, Stanley. *Conditions Handsome and Unhandsome: The Constitution of Emersonian Perfectionism.* Chicago University Press, 1990.

Chafee, Zechariah, Jr. *Free Speech in the United States.* Cambridge, Mass.: Harvard University Press, 1941.

Chesterman, Michael R. *Freedom of Speech in Australian Law: A Delicate Plant?* (Aldershot: Ashgate, 2000).

Chevigny, Paul. *More Speech: Dialogue Rights and Modern Liberty.* Philadelphia: Temple University Press, 1988.

Christiano, Thomas. *Freedom, Consensus and Equality in Collective Decision Making*, 101 Ethics 151 (1990).

---. *The Rule of the Many: Fundamental Issues in Democratic Theory.* Boulder, Colo.: Westview Press, 1996.

---. *The Significance of Public Deliberation*, in James Bohman and William Rehg, eds, *Deliberative Democracy: Essays on Reason and Politics* 243-278. Cambridge, Mass.: The MIT Press, 1997.

Cohen, Jeremy, and Timothy Gleason. *Social Research in Communication and Law.* Newbury Park, Calif.: Sage Publications, 1990.

Cohen, Joshua. *Deliberation and Democratic Legitimacy*, in Alan P. Hamlin and Philip Pettit, eds, *The Good Polity* 17-34. Oxford: Blackwell, 1991.

---. *Freedom of Expression*, in David Heyd, ed, *Toleration: An Elusive Virtue* 173-225. Princeton, N.J.: Princeton University Press, 1996.

Coliver, Sandra. *Defamation Jurisprudence of the European Court of Human Rights*, 13 J Media L & Prac 250 (1992).

Cooley, Thomas M. *A Treatise on the Constitutional Limitations* vol 2. Boston: Little, Brown and Co., 8th ed 1927.

Cranberg, Gilbert. *Fanning the Fire: The Media's Role in Libel Litigation*, 71 Iowa L Rev 221 (1985).

Critical Notice: A Treatise on the Law of Slander and Libel, 2 Am L Mag 247 (1843-1844).

Cumper, Peter. *A Path to a Bill of Rights*, New L J 100 (1991).

Curtis, Michael Kent. *Free Speech, "the People's Darling Privilege": Struggles for Freedom of Expression in American History*. Durham, N.C.: Duke University Press, 2000.

Davis, Kenneth C. *Discretionary Justice: A Preliminary Inquiry*. Urbana: University of Illinois Press, 1971.

Dewey, John. *Practical Democracy*, New Republic 52 (Dec 2, 1925).

---. *Democracy and Education*. Edited by J. A. Boydston, Vol 9 the Middle Works 1916. Carbondale: Southern Illinois University, 1980.

---. *Human Nature and Conduct*. Edited by J. A. Boydston, Vol 14 the Middle Works 1922. Carbondale: Southern Illinois University, 1983.

---. *The Public and Its Problems*. Edited by J. A. Boydston, Vol 2 the Later Works 1916. Carbondale: Southern Illinois University, 1984.

---. *Individualism Old and New 1929-1930*. Edited by J. A. Boydston, Vol 5 the Later Works. Carbondale: Southern Illinois University, 1984.

---. *Liberalism and Social Action*. Edited by J. A. Boydston, Vol 11 the Later Works 1935-1937. Carbondale: Southern Illinois University, 1987.

Doctrine of the Margin of Appreciation under the European Convention on Human Rights: Its Legitimacy in Theory and Application in Practice, 19 HR L J 1-36 (April 30, 1998).

Douglas, William O. *The Right of the People*. Garden City, N.Y.: Doubleday & Co. Inc., 1958.

Duniway, Clyde Augustus. *The Development of Freedom of the Press in Massachusetts*. New York: Longmans, Green & Co., 1906.

DuVal, Benjamin S, Jr. *Free Communication of Ideas and the Quest for Truth: Toward a Teleological Approach to First Amendment Adjudication*, 41 Geo Wash L Rev 161 (1972).

Eaton, Joel D. *The American Law of Defamation through Gertz v Robert Welch, Inc. and Beyond: An Analytical Primer*, 61(7) Va L Rev 1349 (1975).

Edelstein, Alex S. *Comparative Communication Research*. Beverly Hills, Calif.: Sage Publications, 1982.

Editorial, Eur HR L Rev 1 (Launch Issue 1995).

Elder, David A. *The Fair Report Privilege*. Stoneham, Mass., 1987.

Eldridge, Larry D. *A Distant Heritage: The Growth of Free Speech in Early America.* New York: New York University Press, 1994.

Emerson, Thomas Irwin. *Toward a General Theory of the First Amendment.* New York: Random House, 1966.

---. *The System of Freedom of Expression.* New York: Random House, 1970.

---. *First Amendment Doctrine and the Burger Court,* 68 Cal L Rev 422 (1980).

Esthund, David. *Beyond Fairness and Deliberation: The Epistemic Dimension of Democratic Authority,* in James Bohman and William Rehg, eds, *Deliberative Democracy: Essays on Reason and Politics* 173-204. Cambridge, Mass.: The MIT Press, 1997.

Etzioni, Amitai. *The Spirit of Community, Rights, Responsibilities of the Communist Agenda.* New York: Touchstone, 1993.

---. *The New Golden Rule: Community and Monthly in a Democratic Society.* New York: Basic Books, 1996.

Fleming, John G. *The Law of Torts.* Sydney: The Law Book Co., 8th Austl ed 1992.

Franklin, Marc A. *Winners and Losers and Why: A Study of Defamation Litigation,* 1980 Am B Found Res J 455-500.

---. *Suing Media for Libel: A Litigation Study,* 1981 Am B Found Res J 795-831.

Fricke, Graham. *Libel, Lampoons and Litigants.* Hawthorne, Vic.: Hutchinson Publishing Group, 1984.

Gardner, John. *Freedom of Expression,* in C. McCrudden and G. Chambers, eds, *Individual Rights and the Law in Britain* 209. Oxford: Clarendon Press, 1994.

Gaus, Gerald F. *Reason, Justification, and Consensus,* in James Bohman and William Rehg, eds, *Deliberative Democracy: Essays on Reason and Politics* 205-242. Cambridge, Mass.: The MIT Press, 1997.

Gauthier, David P. *The Logic of Leviathan: The Moral and Political Theory of Thomas Hobbes.* Oxford: Clarendon Press, 1969.

---. *Taming Leviathan,* 16 (3) Phil & Pub Aff 280 (Summer 1987).

Gibson, Michael T. *The Supreme Court and Freedom of Expression from 1791 to 1917,* 55 (3) Fordham L Rev 263 (1986).

Greenawalt, Kent. *Speech and Crime,* ABF Res J 647 (1980).

---. *Speech, Crime, and the Uses of Language.* New York: Oxford University Press, 1989.

Gutmann, Amy. *How Liberal Is Democracy?* in Douglas MacLean and Claudia Hills, eds, *Liberalism Reconsidered* 25-50. Totowa, N.J.: Rowman & Allanheld, 1983.

Hale, Dennis. *The Impact of State Prohibitions of Punitive Damages on Libel Litigation: An Empirical Analysis,* 5 Vand J Ent L&Prac 96 (2003).

Hale, William G. *The Law of the Press.* St. Paul, Minn.: West Publishing Co., 1923.

Hall, Kermit L. *Cultural History and the First Amendment: New York Times v Sullivan and Its Times*, in Sandra F. VanBurkleo, Kermit L. Hall and Robert J. Kaczorowski, eds, *Constitutionalism and American Culture: Writing the New Constitutional History* 267. Lawrence, Kans.: University Press of Kansas, 2002.

Hamburger, Philip. *The Development of the Law of Seditious Libel and the Control of the Press*, 37 Stan L Rev 661 (Feb 1985).

Handford, Peter. *Defamation and the Conflict of Laws in Australia*, 32 (2) Intl & Comp L Q 452 (April 1983).

Harel, Alon. *The Boundaries of Justifiable Tolerance*, in David Heyd, ed, *Toleration* 114-126. Princeton, N.J.: Princeton University Press, 1996.

Hargreaves, Robert. *The First Freedom: A History of Free Speech*. Stroud: Sutton, 2002.

Harris, D. J., M. O'Boyle, and C. Warbrick. *Laws of The European Convention on Human Rights*. London: Butterworths, 1995.

Haworth, Alan. *Free Speech*. New York: Routledge, 1998.

Hay, George. *An Essay on the Liberty of the Press*. Philadelphia, 1799.

Held, David. *Models of Democracy*. Stanford, Calif.: Stanford University Press, 2d ed 1996.

Helle, Steven. *Judging Public Interest in Libel: The Gertz Decision's Contribution*, 61 Journalism Q 117 (Spring 1984).

Heyd, David, ed. *Toleration: An Elusive Virtue*. Princeton, N.J.: Princeton University Press, 1996.

Hill, Alfred. *Defamation and Privacy under the First Amendment*, 76 Colum L Rev 1205 (Dec 1976).

Hobbes, Thomas. *Leviathan*. Edited by Richard Tuck. Cambridge University Press, 1991.

Holdsworth, W. S. *Defamation in the Sixteenth and Seventeenth Centuries* (pts 1-3), 40 L Q Rev 302 (1924), 41 L Q Rev 13 (1925).

Holmes, Oliver Wendell. *The Path of the Law*, 10 Harv L Rev 447 (1918).

Hunt, David. *Why No First Amendment? The Role of the Press in Relationship to Justice*, 54 (8) AL J 458 (August 1980).

Ingber, Stanley. *The Marketplace of Ideas: Legitimizing Myth*, 1984 Duke L J 1 (Feb 1984).

Jackson, D. and N. Tate, eds. *Comparative Judicial Review and Public Policy*. Westport, Conn.: Greenwood Press, 1992.

Jackson, Donald W. *The United Kingdom Confronts the European Convention on Human Rights*. Gainesville: University Press of Florida, 1997.

Janis, Mark W., Richard S. Kay, and Anthony W. Bradley. *European Human Rights Law: Text and Materials*. Oxford: Clarendon Press, 1995.

Junius Wilkes [pseud]. *Independent Gazetteer* (Oct 19, 1782).

Kagan, Donald. *Pericles of Athens and the Birth of Democracy*. New York: The Free Press, 1991.

Kalven, Harry, Jr. *The New York Times Case: A Note on "The Central Meaning of the First Amendment,"* 1964 S Ct Rev 191.

---. *A Worthy Tradition: Freedom of Speech in America.* New York: Harper and Row, 1988.

Kamensky, Jane. *Governing the Tongue: The Politics of Speech in Early New England.* New York: Oxford University Press, 1997.

Kavka, Gregory S. *Hobbesian Moral and Political Theory.* Princeton, N.J.: Princeton University Press, 1986.

Kentridge, S. *Freedom of Speech: Is it the Primary Right?* 45 Intl & Comp L Q 253 (April 1996).

Koffler, Judith Schenck and Bennett L. Gershman. *The New Seditious Libel,* 69(4) Cornell L Rev 816 (1984).

Labunski, Richard E. *Libel and the First Amendment: Legal History and Practice in Print and Broadcasting.* New Brunswick, N.J.: Transaction Books, 1987.

Lawhorne, Clifton O. *Newspapermen v Public Officials: The Evolving Law of Libel.* Ph.D. diss., Southern Illinois University at Carbondale, 1968.

---. *Defamation and Public Officials: The Evolving Law of Libel.* Carbondale: Southern Illinois University Press, 1971.

---. *The Supreme Court and Libel.* Carbondale: Southern Illinois University Press, 1981.

Levy, Leonard W. *Freedom of Speech and Press in Early American History: Legacy of Suppression.* New York: Harper & Row, 1963.

---. *Emergence of a Free Press.* New York: Oxford University Press, 1985.

Lewis, Anthony. *New York Times v Sullivan Reconsidered: Time to Return to "The Central Meaning of the First Amendment,"* 83 Colum L Rev 603 (1983).

---. *Make No Law: The Sullivan Case and the First Amendment.* New York: Random House, 1991.

Libel Defense Resource Center, *Public Official Libel Action: A Comparison of Reported Cases 1976-1979 and 1979-1984,* LDRC Bull, No 16 (Winter 1986).

Lincoln, Y. S. and E. G. Guba. *Naturalistic Inquiry.* Beverly Hills, Calif.: Sage Publications, 1985.

Lindlof, Thomas R. *Qualitative Communication Research Methods.* Thousand Oaks, Calif.: Sage Publications, 1995.

Locke, John. *A Letter Concerning Toleration.* Edited by Mario Montuori. Hague, Netherlands: Martinus Nijhoff, 1963; original work 1689.

---. *The Second Treatise of Government.* Edited by J. W. Gough. New York: Macmillan Co., 1956; original work 1690.

Loveland, Ian. *Taking the Constitution out of the Common Law: Political Libels and Freedom of Communication in Australia,* 21 Liverpool L Rev 17 (1999).

Lovell, Colin Rhys. *The "Reception" of Defamation by the Common Law,* 15 Vand L Rev 1051 (1962).

Lynch, Judy D. *Public Officials, the Press, and the Libel Remedy: Toward a Theory of Absolute Immunity*, 67 Or L Rev 611 (1988).

Macdonald, R. St. J., F. Matscher, and H. Petzold, eds. *The European System for the Protection of Human Rights*. Hague, Netherlands: Martinus Nijhoff, 1993.

Mahoney, Paul. *Universality versus Subsidiarity in Free Speech Cases*, 1997 Eur HR L Rep 364.

---. *Marvelous Richness of Diversity or Invidious Cultural Relativism*, 19 HR L J 1 (April 30, 1998).

---. *Principles of Judicial Review As developed by the European Court of Human Rights: Their Relevance in a National Context*, in Lammy Betten, ed, *The Human Rights Act 1998 What it means: The Incorporation of the European Convention on Human Rights into the Legal Order of the United Kingdom*, 65-86 (Hague, Netherlands: Kluwer Law International, 1999).

Marshall, Catherine, and Gretchen B. Rossman. *Designing Qualitative Research*. Longwood Oaks, Calif.: Sage Publications, 3d ed 1999.

Marshall, Geoffrey. *Press Freedom and Free Speech Theory*, Pub L 40 (1983).

Matscher, F. *Methods of Interpretation of the Convention*, in R. St. J. Macdonald, F. Matscher, and H. Petzold, eds, *The European System for the Protection of Human Rights* 63-68 (Hague, Netherlands: Martinus Nijhoff, 1993).

McKewen, Robert and Philip Lewis. Gatley on Libel and Slander (7th ed 1977).

Meiklejohn, Alexander. *Free Speech and Its Relation to Self-Government*. New York: Harper, 1948.

---. *The First Amendment Is an Absolute*, 1961 S Ct Rev 245.

---. *Political Freedom: The Constitutional Powers of the People*. New York: Oxford University Press, 1965.

Merin, Jerome Lawrence. *Libel and the Supreme Court*, 11 Wm & Mary L Rev 371 (1969).

Merrills, J. G. *The Development of International Law by the European Court of Human Rights*. Manchester University Press: 1988.

Mill, John Stuart. *On Liberty*. Edited by David Spitz. New York: W. W. Norton and Company, Inc. 1975; original work 1859.

Milton, John. *Aeropagitica: A Speech for the Liberty of Unlicensed Printing to the Parliament of England*. Edited by Israel Gollancz. Boston: Beacon Press, 1951; original work 1644.

Miner, Ward L. *William Goddard: Newspaperman*. Durham, N.C.: Duke University Press, 1962.

Mitchell, James C. *The Accidental Purist: Reclaiming the Gertz All-Purpose Public Figure Doctrine in the Age of "Celebrity Journalism,"* 22 Loy L A Ent L Rev 559 (2002).

Mitchell, Paul. *Malice in Defamation*, 114 L Q Rev 639 (1998).

Nelson, Harold L. *Seditious Libel in Colonial America*, 3 Am J Legal Hist 160 (1959).

New York Times 25 (March 29, 1960).

Newcity, Michael. *The Sociology of Defamation in Australia and the United States*, 26 Tex Intl L J 1 (1991).

Nickel, James W. *Free Speech, Democratic Deliberation, and Valuing Types of Speech*, in Simone Chambers and Anne Costain, eds, *Deliberation, Democracy and the Media* 3-11. Lanham, Md.: Rowman & Littlefield Publishers, 2000.

Nordenstreng, Kaarle. *The Citizen Moves from the Audience to the Arena*, 18 (2) Nordicom Rev 13 (Nov 1997).

Note. *Developments in the Law -- Defamation*, 69 Harv L Rev 875 (1956).

Ogg, E. Jerald, Jr. *The European Convention and Freedom of Information: The Domestic Impact of a Human Rights Regime*. Ph.D. diss., Southern Illinois University at Carbondale, 1993.

Paine, Thomas. *Rights of Man* [Collected Writings]. New York: Library of America, 1995.

Palmer, Geoffrey. *Defamation and Privacy Down Under*, 64 Iowa L Rev 1209 (1979).

Parkinson, Patrick. *Tradition and Change in Australian Law*. Sydney: The Law Book Co. Ltd., 1994.

Paterson, James. *Liberty of the Press, Speech and Public Worship*. London: Macmillan, 1880.

Plucknett, Theodore F.T. *A Concise History of the Common Law*. Boston: Little, Brown and Co., 5th ed 1956).

Plumb, John H. *The Origins of Political Stability England, 1675-1725*. Boston: Houghton Mifflin, 1967.

Prosser, William Lloyd. *Handbook of Law of Torts*. St. Paul, Minn.: West Publishing Co., 4th ed 1971.

Pullan, Robert. *Guilty Secrets: Free Speech in Australia*. North Ryde: Methuen Australia, 1984.

Putman, Hilary. *Renewing Philosophy*. Cambridge, Mass.: Harvard University Press, 1992.

---. *Words and Life*. Edited by James Conant. Cambridge, Mass.: Harvard University Press, 1994.

Rabban, David M. *Free Speech in Its Forgotten Years*. Cambridge University Press, 1997.

Rawls, John. *A Theory of Justice*. Cambridge, Mass.: Harvard University Press, 1971.

Redish, Martin. *The Value of Free Speech*, 130 U Pa L Rev 591 (1982).

Reid, Loren. *Charles James Fox: A Man for the People*. Columbia: University of Missouri Press, 1969.

Richards, David A. J. *Free Speech and the Politics of Identity*. New York: Oxford University Press, 1999.

Rives, W and P. Fendall, eds. *Vol 3 Letters and Writings of James Madison, Fourth President of the United States*. Lippincott, 1865.

Robert, Eugene L., Jr. *Free Speech, Free Press, Free Society*, in Peggie J. Hollingsworth, ed, *Unfettered Expression: Freedom in American Intellectual Life* 151-160. Ann Arbor: University of Michigan Press, 2000.

Robertson, A. H. *Human Rights in Europe*. Manchester, U.K.: Manchester University Press, 1977.

Robertson, Geoffrey. *The Law Commission on Criminal Libel*, Pub L 208 (Summer 1983).

Romantz, David S. and Kathleen Elliott Vinson. *Legal Analysis: the Fundamental Skills*. Durham, N.C.: Carolina Academic Press, 1998.

Rosenberg, Norman L. *Protecting the Best Men: An Interpretive History of the Law of Libel*. Chapel Hill: University of North Carolina Press, 1985.

Rousseau, Jean-Jacques. *The Social Contract and Discourse on the Origin of Inequality*. Edited by Lester G. Crocker. New York: Pocket Books 1967.

---. *The Social Contract*. Translated by G. D. H. Cole. London: J. M. Dent, 1993.

Rudé, George. *Hanoverian London: 1714-1808*. Berkeley: University of California, 1971.

Sack, Robert D. *Libel, Slander, and Related Problems*. New York: Practicing Law Institute, 1980.

Scanlon, Thomas, Jr. *A Theory of Free Expression*, 1 (2) Phil & Pub Aff 204 (1972).

---. *Freedom of Expression and Categories of Expression*, 40 U Pitt L Rev 519 (1979).

Schauer, Frederick. *Free Speech: A Philosophical Enquiry*. Cambridge University Press, 1982.

---. *The Cost of Communicative Tolerance*, in Raphael Cohen-Almagor, ed, *Liberal Democracy and the Limits of Tolerance* 28-42. Ann Arbor: University of Michigan Press, 2000.

Schlag, Pierre. *An Attack on Categorical Approaches to Freedom of Speech*, 30 UCLA L Rev 671 (1983).

Schneiderman, David, ed. *Freedom of Expression and the Charter*. Calgary, Alta.: Thomson Professional Publications, 1991.

Schultz, Julianne. *Reviving the Fourth Estate: Democracy, Accountability and the Media*. Cambridge University Press, 1998.

Schumpeter, Joseph A. *Capitalism, Socialism, and Democracy*. Allen & Unwin, 1976.

Seigfried, Charlene Haddock. *Socializing Democracy: Jane Addams and John Dewey*, 20 (2) Phil Soc Sci 207 (June 1999).

Shiffrin, Steven. *Liberalism, Radicalism, and Legal Scholarship*, 30 UCLA L Rev 1103 (1983).

---. *The First Amendment and Economic Regulation: Away from a General Theory of the First Amendment*, 78 Nw U L Rev 1212 (1983).

Shurtleff, Nathaniel B., ed. Vol 1 *Records of the Governor and Company of the Massachusetts*. Boston: William White Co., 1853-1854.

Shusterman, Richard. *Putman and Cavell on the Ethics of Democracy*, 25 (2) Pol. Theory 193 (April 1997).

Siebert, Fredrick S. *Freedom of the Press in England*. Urbana: University of Illinois Press, 1965.

Smith, Anthony. *Publish and Be Damned*, 61 L Inst J 914 (1987).

Smith, James Morton. *Freedom's Fetters: The Alien and Sedition Laws and American Civil Liberties*. Ithaca, N.Y.: Cornell University Press, 1956.

Smolla, Rodney A. *Law of Defamation*. New York: Clark Boardman Co., 1986.

---. *Suing the Press: Libel, the Media and Power*. New York: Oxford University Press: 1986.

---. *Balancing Freedom of Expression and Protection of Reputation under the Charter*, in David Schneiderman, ed, *Freedom of Expression and the Charter*. Calgary, Alta.: Thomson Professional Publications, 1991.

---. *Free Speech in an Open Society*. New York: Alfred A. Knopf, Inc., 1992.

---. *Smolla and Nimmer on Freedom of Speech* vols 2. Deerfield, Ill.: Clark Boardman Callaghan, 1996.

Soloski, John. *The Study of the Libel Plaintiff: Who Sues for Libel*, 71 Iowa L Rev 217 (1985).

Speech by the Secretary General at the Commemorative Ceremony for the 50th Anniversary of the European Convention on Human Rights. Rome: 4 November 2000.

Spencer, J. R. *Criminal Libel: A Skeleton in the Cupboard*, Crim L Rev 383 (1977).

---. *Criminal Libel: The Law Commission's Working Paper*, Crim L Rev 525 (1983).

Starkie, Thomas. A Treatise on the Law of Slander, Libel, Scandalum Magnatum and False Rumors. London: Printed for W. Clarke, 1813.

Stephen James Fitzjames. *Liberty, Equality, Fraternity*. London: Smith and Elder, 1874.

---. *A History of the Criminal Law of England*. London, 1883.

Stevens, John D. et al. *Criminal Libel as Seditious Libel 1916-65*, 45 Journalism Q 110 (1966).

Stoler, Peter. *The War against the Press: Politics, Pressure and Intimidation in the '80s*. New York: Mead Dodd, 1986.

Storck, Thomas. *A Case for Censorship*, New Oxford Rev 23 (May 1996).

Strauss, David A. *Freedom of Speech and the Common Law Constitution*, in Lee C. Bollinger and Geoffrey R. Stone, *Eternally Vigilant: Free Speech in the Modern Era*. Chicago: University of Chicago Press, 2002.

Stroman, Carolyn A. and Kenneth E. Jones. *The Analysis of Television Content*, in Joy Keiko Asamen and Gordon L. Berry, eds, *Research Paradigms; Television, and Social Behavior* 271. Thousand Oaks, Calif.: Sage Publications, Inc. 1998.

Sunken, Maurice. *The Incidence and Effect of Judicial Review Procedures against Central Government in the United Kingdom*, in D. Jackson and N. Tate, eds, *Comparative Judicial Review and Public Policy*. Westport, Conn.: Greenwood Press, 1992.

Sunstein, Cass R. *Democracy and the Problem of Free Speech*. New York: The Free Press, 1993.

---. *The Partial Constitution*. Cambridge, Mass.: Harvard University Press, 1993.

Sykes, Edward I. *Some Aspects of Queensland Defamation Law*, 1951 U Q L J 19.

Tedford, Thomas L. *Freedom of Speech in the United States*. New York: McGraw-Hill, Inc., 1993.

Teitgen, P.-H. *Introduction to the European Convention on Human Rights*, in R. St. J. Macdonald, F. Matscher and H. Petzold, eds, *The European System for the Protection of Human Rights* 3-14 (Hague, Netherlands: Martinus Nijhoff, 1993).

The Republic and the States Papers Delivered at a TC Beirne Law School Symposium Held at the Heritage Hotel, Brisbane on 11 June 1998, 20 [2] U Q L J 54 (1999).

Thomas, Donald, ed. *State Trials: Treason and Libel*. London: Routledge and K. Paul, 1972.

Thompson, John B. *The Media and Modernity: A Social Theory of the Media*. Cambridge, U.K.: Polity Press, 1995.

Thompson, Mel. *Ethics*. Lincolnwood, Ill.: NTC Publishing Group, 1994.

Tocqueville, Alexis de. *Democracy in America*. London, 1835; New York: A.A. Knopf., 1994.

Trager, Robert, and Donna L. Dickerson. *Freedom of Expression in the 21st Century*. Thousand Oaks, Calif.: Pine Forge Press, 1999.

Trevor, Parry-Giles. *Parliament, Puritans, and Protestors: The Ideological Development of the British Commitment to "Free Speech*," 31 Free Speech Yearbook 16 (1993).

Tribe, Laurence H. *American Constitutional Law*. Mineola, N.Y.: Foundation Press, 2d ed 1988.

Trindade, F. A. *Defamation in the Course of Political Discussion -- The New Common Law Defense*, 114 L Q Rev 1 (January 1998).

Tucker, St. George. *Blackstone's Commentaries: With Notes and References*. Philadelphia, 1803.

Veeder, Van Vechter. *The History and Theory of the Law of Defamation* (pts 1-2), 3 Colum L Rev 546 (1903), 4 Colum L Rev 33 (1904).

Vom Baur, F. Trowbridge. *The License to Defame Government Officials: New York Times Co. v Sullivan Should be Overruled*, 30 Fed B News & J 501 (Dec 1983).

Voorhoof, Dirk. *Defamation and Libel Law in Europe -- The Framework of Article 10 of the European Convention on Human Rights*, 13 J Media L & Prac 254 (1992).

Waldron, Jeremy. *Liberal Rights*. Cambridge University Press, 1993.

Walker, Jeffrey K. A. *Poisen in ye Commonwealthe: Seditious Libel in Hanoverian London*, 25 (3) Anglo-Am L Rev 341 (1996).

Walker, Sally. *The Law of Journalism in Australia*. North Ryde, N.S.W.: Law Book Co., 1989.

---. *Lange v ABC: The High Court Rethinks the "Constitutionalization" of Defamation Law*, 6 Torts L J 9 (1998).

Walzer, Michael. *Philosophy and Democracy*, 9 Pol Theory 379 (1981).

Weithman, Paul J. *Contractualist Liberalism and Deliberative Democracy*, 24 (2) Phil & Pub Aff 315 (Fall 1995).

Wellington, Harry H. *On Freedom of Expression*, 88(6) Yale L J 1105 (1979).

Wheeler, Joseph Towne. *The Maryland Press 1777-1790*. Baltimore: Maryland Historical Society, 1938.

Wilkes [pseud]. *Independent Gazetteer* (Nov 9, 1782).

Wolff, Robert Paul. *A Critique of Pure Tolerance [by] Robert Paul Wolff, Barrington Moore, Jr. [and] Herbert Marcuse*. Boston: Beacon Press, 1969.

Wootton, David, ed. *Political Writings of John Locke*. New York: Mentor, 1993.

Wortman, Tunis. *A Treatise concerning Political Inquiry and the Liberty of the Press*. 1800; New York: DaCapo Press, 1970.

Index

x

l